MODELS OF START-UP THINKING AND ACTION: THEORETICAL, EMPIRICAL AND PEDAGOGICAL APPROACHES

ADVANCES IN ENTREPRENEURSHIP, FIRM EMERGENCE AND GROWTH

Series Editors: Jerome A. Katz and
Andrew C. Corbett

Recent Volumes:

ADVANCES IN ENTREPRENEURSHIP, FIRM EMERGENCE
AND GROWTH   VOLUME 18

MODELS OF START-UP THINKING AND ACTION: THEORETICAL, EMPIRICAL AND PEDAGOGICAL APPROACHES

EDITED BY

JEROME A. KATZ
*Cook School of Business, Saint Louis University,
Saint Louis, MO, USA*

ANDREW C. CORBETT
Babson College, Babson Park, MA, USA

United Kingdom – North America – Japan
India – Malaysia – China

Emerald Group Publishing Limited
Howard House, Wagon Lane, Bingley BD16 1WA, UK

First edition 2016

Reprints and permissions service
Contact: permissions@emeraldinsight.com

British Library Cataloguing in Publication Data
A catalogue record for this book is available from the British Library

ISBN: 978-1-78635-486-0
ISSN: 1074-7540 (Series)

Printed and bound by CPI Group (UK) Ltd, Croydon, CR0 4YY

ISOQAR certified
Management System,
awarded to Emerald
for adherence to
Environmental
standard
ISO 14001:2004.

Certificate Number 1985
ISO 14001

INVESTOR IN PEOPLE

CONTENTS

LIST OF CONTRIBUTORS

Andrew C. Corbett	Babson College, Babson Park, MA, USA
Per Davidsson	Queensland University of Technology, Brisbane, Australia; Jönköping International Business School, Jönköping, Sweden
Dimo Dimov	University of Bath, Claverton Down, Bath, UK
Christophe Garonne	IESEG School of Management, Lille, France; CERGAM, Aix-en-Provence, France
Charles Hofer	University System of Georgia, Atlanta, GA, USA
Benson Honig	McMaster University, Hamilton, ON, Canada
Christian Hopp	RWTH Aachen University, Aachen, Germany
Aparna Katre	University of Minnesota Duluth, Duluth, MN, USA
Reed E. Nelson	Graduate School of Management, UNINOVE, Sao Paulo, Brazil
Anderson Santana	Fundacao Dom Cabral, Nova Lima, MG, Brazil
Matthew S. Wood	Baylor University, Waco, TX, USA
Zhaocheng (Elly) Zeng	McMaster University, Hamilton, ON, Canada

INTRODUCTION

The technology for improving the start-up process has a relatively long history in entrepreneurship, but has arguably entered a period of explosive growth in the past five years or so. Capturing the historic and nascent approaches has been the goal of this volume in the *Advances in Entrepreneurship, Firm Emergence and Growth* series.

Realize that in the past 5–10 years we have seen the emergence of multiple new technologies focused on the startup process — customer development methodologies, lean startup techniques, online pilot testing, bricolage and effectuation approaches, design-based approaches, business model canvases as well as a plethora of new business models themselves, pitch decks, data rooms, co-working spaces, and accelerators, to name a few. It is safe to say there have never been so many ways to help people think about and go about starting new businesses.

The new approaches have also injected a renewed vibrancy in entrepreneurship, driven in part by the promise of the new technologies, and by the admonitions of the proponents of these new approaches. There is tremendous promise in so many of the new approaches, but as new approaches, technique is far in advance of efficacy data about these approaches. This is an inherent truth of education — technique and face validity checks of effect always come first, with painstaking assessment taking years to formulate, implement, and evaluate. Rigorous evaluations of business plans are a phenomenon of the past 15 years, although as we'll see, it has been around a lot longer.

The call for this volume was intended as an effort to get individuals and institutions who saw themselves as proponents of established and emerging startup technologies to bring their theoretical and empirical works to a broader audience. We believe the entrepreneurship education and research community wants to think about what techniques work best, and when and where and why they do so. We expressly wrote the call to capture both traditional and new startup technologies, because we see the value of all, and recognize the impact of history and institutionalization on traditional technologies, and see how they will likely have an impact on today's newest ideas, as they too become the new institutional standards.

HISTORY AND INSTITUTIONALIZATION

Despite the ubiquity of the business plan, and the impression it has been around forever, it came into its own on the eve of the entrepreneurial revolution initiated by Ronald Reagan in the United States and Margaret Thatcher in the United Kingdom in 1981. At that point Bangs and Osgood's (1976) how-to book on business planning was only five years old, and textbooks of the period were only beginning their coverage of the business plan as a start-up device.

The 1980s saw business plans become a strong element of entrepreneurship and small business texts, and presumably in courses of the period also. Insofar as this was also a period of rapid growth of the venture capital industry, the creation of business plans, especially in entrepreneurship classes, received strong external validation. As Hofer notes in his contribution to this volume, the first competitions started during this period, often in concert with local venture capitalists.

The 1990s saw a period of explosive growth in the nature of start-up technologies. Business plans became a centerpiece of entrepreneurship programs, with this decade showing the tremendous growth in business plan competitions, as described in the Hofer article. Meanwhile, training in business planning became mainstream, a fixture of Small Business Development Centers, and new training programs. Arguably the watershed program occurred in 1986 with the introduction of the FastTrac programs developed by Richard Buskirk, Courtney Price, and Mack Davis (Buskirk, Price & Davis, 1987). Building on their long experience in collegiate entrepreneurship education (as faculty at USC, which had started their MBA in entrepreneurship in 1972 and their undergrad program in 1981). The lock-step approach they used in their academic program became the basis for the FastTrac programs.

The word programs is important. FastTrac actually introduced the feasibility analysis as a necessary precursor for doing a business plan for a start-up business. The FastTrac programs of today reflect this. FastTrac I is a feasibility analysis. FastTrac II is a business plan. What is worth noting is that the FastTrac I program was intended as a multi-month effort, giving prospective entrepreneurs time to conduct research, including potential customer interviews, surveys and focus groups (Entrepreneurial Education Foundation, 1992/1996). It is worth taking a moment to note that when the feasibility study was a new idea, the goal was to explore the potential of an idea, and do so in as realistic a way as possible, getting into the market, the industry and the community in person to explore the possibilities and challenges. Reading the original FastTrac I books, it is clearly reminiscent of today's clarion call "get out of the building!" (Blank & Dorf, 2012). Concurrent with this, Small Business Development Centers developed a myriad of techniques for evaluating early stage ideas, which were again new to entrepreneurs of the time. The successors to the SBDC approaches are still evident today (Missouri Small Business & Technology Development Centers, 2005), but in general the SBDC's internal approaches were designed and implemented to make fewer requirements on entrepreneurs to go out and interact with potential customers.

FastTrac had a second watershed moment when it was adopted by the Kauffman Foundation as it bellwether program to promote entrepreneurship nationally in 1993. Ewing Marion Kauffman himself presided over the launch in January, signaling the importance of the program in the eyes of the Foundation. The importance no doubt grew because it was one of the last initiatives Mr. Kauffman personally presided over, given his death in August, 1993. FastTrac continues to this day as a major initiative of the Foundation (FastTrac.org), and has continued to develop its basic versions (FastTrac I is now called FastTrac NewVenture) grown to include academic (Planning the Entrepreneurial Venture) and technology (FastTrac TechVenture) versions as well as specialized programs for boomer, female, and veteran entrepreneurs.

FastTrac was designed to be a methodical way to evaluate early stage ideas among peers (fellow aspiring entrepreneurs), expert trainers, and customers, and then take the best of those ideas and build business plans to translate ideas into viable businesses. As that model was increasingly adopted in academia, it was done in piecemeal fashions. Texts that had a full chapter on a business plan might have little or no material on feasibility analysis. This process reflects the classic problem of the diffusion of innovation (Rogers, 1962) where individuals adapt the innovation eclectically. Similarly, faculty through overwork or a lack of belief in the FastTrac model, began to let students do fewer actual customer interviews, and in time let archival research take the place of in-person research with prospective customers.

This trend applied over a long time to a solid model from 20 years in the past, produced an environment at a long remove from what Buskirk, Price and Davis (or their contemporaries) envisioned, wrote and taught. It was that later-date environment that arguably made today's proponents of the new wave of startup technologies so passionate about what had become problematic in startup processes, and what needed to be done to improve the techniques for creating high-quality startups.

That said, the very energy of the new proponents has made many traditionalists look at how the older approaches are practiced, and how they can be improved — many times by better embracing the founding ideas behind the established techniques. Together, those thoughtful reflections on traditional approaches to startup processes and those passionate proponents of contemporary approaches working to establish their first generation of analysis and consideration are represented in the chapters in this volume.

CHAPTERS IN THIS VOLUME

In our thought provoking first chapter outlining a design-science perspective for entrepreneurship, Dimo Dimov examines how the opposing forces of a need for academic legitimacy and practitioner relevance can be better balanced in order to provide more fruitful outputs for scholars and practitioners. He begins by outlining a conundrum of sorts that is based upon the temporal mismatch of starting a venture versus the researcher's study of the process. We as scholars will study the entrepreneur and her start up process but most often do so by looking backward while the entrepreneur herself is forward looking and already blazing a new trail. At a time with widespread use of tools and approaches such as the business model canvas, lean start-up methodology, design thinking, and others, the question arises of how researchers can contribute to a startup process that appears so idiosyncratic and beyond its natural occurrence.

Dimov's work here focuses on the enactment of entrepreneurial purpose, that is, on the reasoning, action, and reflection of the next step. As such, he blends a perspective of action as both a mode of experimentation and a generator of new information with the nature of design as the creation of artifacts towards a purpose. In deriving its focus, the chapter draws together a variety of perspectives that can shed new light on the startup process. Entrepreneurship involves solving multi-faceted problems, but most entrepreneurship scholarship is driven by researcher-centered curiosity that often times does not meet the needs of practicing entrepreneur. Dimov's chapter addresses this concern directly by revisiting the fundamental premises of scholarly inquiry in entrepreneurship and identifying roads not taken. It then sketches out a new logic of inquiry, grounded in design science, and articulates new types of research activities that can help us better understand the startup process.

Our second chapter exemplifies a new type of research activity albeit in a bit different way than Dimov envisions. Reed E. Nelson, Anderson Santana and Matthew S. Wood use insightful theorizing and a unique research setting to investigate how startup thinking, action thinking, and action can effect the more traditional measures of revenue growth, employment growth, GDP, and other financial and economic metrics. Relying upon sociocultural theorizing and the recognition that entrepreneurship evolves from a complex interaction of individuals and their environment, these authors examine how entrepreneurs' startup actions influence culture change and other factors in the local community. They set their study in an exclusive tourist destination (Tiradentes, Brazil) with a unique architectural, cultural, and economic heritage that is undergoing a somewhat stressful reimagination due to differing aspirations from locals and non-natives who have settled there.

The investigation of Nelson and his colleagues reveals that entrepreneurs' backgrounds (native vs. non-native) and social identities come together with the sociocultural fabric of the community in a way that moved each individual toward one of two distinct mindsets. These mindsets had implications for entrepreneurs' conceptualizations of start-up models possible while also influencing the geographic location chosen for their business and different business practices they used. The authors find that entrepreneurs favoring one orientation over another tended to occupy predictable physical and social positions in the community while also espousing similar values and perspectives. Nelson and his co-authors dissect their results to theorize about the link between the external and internal explanations for entrepreneurial thinking and action. The chapter uncovers complex sociocultural interactions between the entrepreneur and the environment that heretofore have gone understudied. As such this chapter brings new understanding to understanding 'entrepreneurs in context' while also providing scholars new research avenues for thinking about how different models of startup thinking and action can be investigated. Our next chapter builds upon this theme by also revealing the importance of context, learning, and other institutional factors upon startup action.

What path should nascent entrepreneurs follow as they attempt to develop their new venture? What actions and activities should they take? Does predictive based strategies work or should would-be entrepreneurs follow a more experiential path? In this chapter, Benson Honig and Christian Hopp analyze the comparative performance of several commonly recommended approaches – from talking to customer and researching the competition, to writing and reworking a business plan. What is perhaps most telling in Honig and Hopp's research is that which actions and activities that a nascent entrepreneur undertakes appears to matter little. This is because the pre-venture activities undertaken by nearly all entrepreneurs are the same; thus, the activities themselves do not robustly link with successful new venture foundation. Instead, the research provided in this chapter shows us that pre-start-up experiences, venture characteristics, and the institutional environment are more important in explaining successful performance than any recommended activities.

The authors show that some entrepreneurs were likely to be attracted to research and planning, as well as experimentation, however, they were not necessarily more effective and efficient at carrying out these routines. Another group of entrepreneurs, in comparison, were more successful when they modified their business model. Honig and Hopp conclude that the ability of an entrepreneurs to learn from his environment, is an important, and perhaps the most critical element of the entrepreneurial journey. They tell us that it is not likely to be the venture organizing activities that entrepreneurs engage in that lead to success, but rather *who* engages in them (skills and other endowments) and perhaps most importantly how they learn.

The implications of this chapter are many but perhaps most importantly that we need to understand when predictive or experimental activities are needed. Grasping these differences is critical in empirically disentangling performance impacts for scholars but also for providing practical advice. In sum, Honig and Hopp' research suggests that developing an adaptive consultative approach that considers personal and cultural characteristics with other circumstances could well increase the chances of helping entrepreneurs through the startup process and toward stability and growth.

The next chapter is a bit orthogonal to Honig and Hopp in that Aparna Katre does seek out specific activities but she does so in a very particular context: solving wicked problems! In her chapter, Katre uses a cognitive foundation to examine the effectiveness of various design thinking-based practices for social value creation. Building from the cognitive tradition, Katre uses a sense-making approach of knowing, thinking, and doing together with structural equation modeling to understand how entrepreneurs attack the 'wicked problems' of today's world. Specifically, she analyzes how nascent social entrepreneurs take action while also investigating what specific activities they undertake to address society's large, complex, interconnected and ambiguous problems.

Katre's work advances our understanding of the applicability of design-based approaches to start up actions by providing measurement for various components while also providing empirical validation of Weick's classic sense-making manager model. Beyond these contributions for scholars, this chapter also has implications for practitioners by highlighting the need for cross-sector partnerships and specific actions necessary to gain micro-commitments from various stakeholders. Katre's work provides an excellent foundation for others scholars to investigate the growing number of wicked problems that today's social entrepreneurs are trying to solve.

A research collection that examines the startup process for entrepreneurs would be remis if it did not speak to the issue of business plans. Today, after four decades of research the community of entrepreneurship researchers, scholar and educators are still divided on the need and usefulness of this, the most archetypal of all entrepreneurship documents. The next two chapters address the issue of business plans and combined bring a new perspective by looking both backward and looking forward.

First, Charles Hofer, one of the pioneers in the field of entrepreneurship and a key contributor to the canon of venture capital research, examines the history and evolution of the business plan and collegiate business plan competitions. His chapter describes how these competitions have evolved over time due to the strong influence of venture capitalists. While Hofer concludes that while the basic purpose of the business plan today is essentially the same, he explores why certain parts of the structure, content, and critical parameters have changed.

Hofer's chapter provides more than just a rich history, however, as he also distills what VCs looks for and how they analyze plans. Specifically, he explores the investment criteria that VCs use and provides the "Seven P's of Venture Capital Funding." From his historical analysis he provides the rubrics and broad rules that most VCs tend to follow as well as information on terms sheets and other decision making processes used by VCs. The chapter also provides a "future look" as Hofer speculates, based on his 25 years of data and experience, what the future business plan will look like. The chapter concludes with details on the structure and content of the business plan of the future. Overall, Hofer's chapter provides practitioners with a keener sense of how business plans have been and will be used. At the same time he gives scholars a solid foundation for future work.

Taking this cue from Hofer, in our next chapter provides insight into the scholarly debate on the use of business plans. Christophe Garonne and Per Davidsson note that most prior work on business plans examined various outcomes against the dichotomous variable of whether someone had developed a business plan or not. For instance, researchers have most often examined whether or not the development and use of a business plan had any discernable impact on growth, sales, or survival rates. However, examining the use of business plans at this level has left us with confounding results. Garonne and Davidsson argue that we need a more finely grained view of business planning and as such, they go down a deeper level and investigate the *degree of formalization* of plans, the *revision* processes of plans, and *types of use* of planning.

From their descriptive analysis, Garrone and Davidsson bring forward a number of stylized facts about business plans including that roughly half of entrepreneurs use them while the other half does not. They also find that plans are constantly revised, that planning wanes over time, but those who do use one use it seriously and find great value in it. Interestingly, the chapter notes that entrepreneurs did not use the business plan as a tool for obtaining funding but saw its greatest value as a tool to help them analyze their business and think through options and opportunities. Beyond these enlightening, stylized facts, Garonne and Davidsson highlight the need for a more accurate operationalization of business planning and finer granularity in the operationalization. In sum, the depth of analysis provided in this chapter gives a portrayal of business planning in nascent and young firms and also serves as an important input to future theory-development and theory testing.

The emphasis in our volume so far has been mostly focused on the needs of researchers and practitioners, but this final chapter by Zhaocheng (Elly) Zeng and Benson Honig turns our attention to the classroom. Their chapter focuses on pedagogy and provides novel insights with regard to how entrepreneurship programs should be designed for students with different levels of entrepreneurship experience. The authors build experiential education models that can be used by educators' depending upon whether they are teaching (1) students without any entrepreneurship experience, (2) students with previous entrepreneurship experience, and (3) students who are currently running their start-ups.

Crafted from Dewey's theories of education together with other pedagogical, human capital, and role theories, Zeng and Honig tease out a systematic set of conceptual models for designing entrepreneurship education. Their findings provide current educators with more options in order to develop better pedagogical foundations. For scholars, the models give a baseline for future investigations across a number of important entrepreneurship education issues.

CONCLUDING THOUGHTS

Entrepreneurship researchers and academics know better than most the passion that drives founders, and this passion is as true for founders of new techniques as it is for founders of new businesses. So it is easy to see parallels between the founders of business plan approaches in the 1970s and 1980s with those of the new approaches of the new millennium. But it is important to note that despite the passion of the founders, those who adopted and adapted the techniques over the years let important parts of the original thinking drift away or become lost. This type of institutionalization is a sad, but common, event. In reality, it is likely that similar processes will begin to nibble away at techniques like lean startups or accelerators, even as both become increasingly popular. The inevitability of such institutionalization processes does not have to portend a steady erosion of all that was right about the new thinking. But what it does remind us all to think about is occasionally sparing time to look back at what the founders said and intended, recognize how our adaptations may have diluted important elements of the original thinking, and ask ourselves and our colleagues what we might do to reinvigorate and reinvent that which was worthy, for that which is tomorrow.

Jerome A. Katz
Andrew C. Corbett
Editors

REFERENCES

Bangs, D. H., & Osgood, W. R. (1976). *Business planning guide: A handbook to help you design, write, and use a business plan tailored to your specific business needs: Includes worksheets for financial data.* Boston, MA: Federal Reserve Bank of Boston.

Blank, S. G., & Dorf, B. (2012). *The startup owner's manual: The step-by-step guide for building a great company* (1st ed.). Pescadero, CA: K&S Ranch Press.

Buskirk, R. H., Price, C. H., & Davis, R. M. (1987). *The entrepreneur's planning handbook.* Denver, CO: Creative Management.

Missouri Small Business & Technology Development Centers. (2005). Evaluating your business idea. Columbia, MO: Curators of the University of Missouri. http://www.missouri business.net/docs/evalbus.pdf. Accessed July 23, 2016.

Rogers, E. M. (1962). *Diffusion of innovations* (1st ed.). New York, NY: The Free Press.

CHAPTER 1

TOWARD A DESIGN SCIENCE OF ENTREPRENEURSHIP

Dimo Dimov

ABSTRACT

This chapter outlines a design-science perspective of entrepreneurship. It zooms in on the junction between present and future to distinguish entrepreneurship as a natural and as an artificial phenomenon. While the current study of entrepreneurship speaks to the former, it has been silent on the latter. The chapter discusses design as a distinct mode of research, opportunity as a design artifact, and the generative power of recursive action to make the case for problematizing entrepreneurial action as a focus of research. It then defines its research questions, discusses the logic and process for addressing them, and outlines the nature of research outputs.

Keywords: Entrepreneurial action; design-science; logic; research

INTRODUCTION

Entrepreneurs feature prominently in theories of entrepreneurship. Their defining feature is acting in the face of uncertainty in pursuit of opportunities (McMullen & Shepherd, 2006). But an encounter with a real-life

Models of Start-up Thinking and Action: Theoretical, Empirical and Pedagogical Approaches
Advances in Entrepreneurship, Firm Emergence and Growth, Volume 18, 1–31
Copyright © 2016 by Emerald Group Publishing Limited
All rights of reproduction in any form reserved
ISSN: 1074-7540/doi:10.1108/S1074-754020160000018001

entrepreneur – someone who is acting in the face of uncertainty and appears to be pursuing an "opportunity" – can be an enervating experience. On the one hand, the person is too "rugged" to fit neatly in our theoretical conceptions. S/he invites a complex interplay of multiple theoretical perspectives, each of which can provide a partial understanding of her situation. But perhaps most importantly, the person is not really interesting to us as scholars ... unless she completes an action or some outcome transpires, so that we can then focus on explaining what has occurred. In other words, we have to follow a step behind and look backwards rather than forwards in her entrepreneurial journey. Before the entrepreneur acts there is not really a phenomenon to explain.

On the other hand, s/he can seek to engage our research prowess to answer the question "what shall I do?." The appeal of this research question depends on implicit norms about the nature and purpose of research. To the extent that research aims to produce propositional knowledge in the form of general theory, whereby the researcher stands independent of the research context, the question has limited appeal. Indeed, to offer an answer would be to "contaminate" the entrepreneur's journey as a potential research setting. And even if an answer were provided, it would be seen as mere deductive application of prior research knowledge, based on the closest match between the current context and the theoretical domains and a *ceteris paribus* proviso. In our encounter, the entrepreneur's practical activity is subsumed by our academic conception, to be represented and not lived (Nicolini, 2012). In the process, we retreat to the "high ground" of well defined problems that lend themselves to technical solutions, while leaving the entrepreneur in the "swampy lowland" of confusing problems that defy technical solutions (Schon, 1987).

We can of course stay in the "swamps" and use our expertise honed in many years of research and teaching to help the entrepreneur understand the situation s/he is facing and consider courses of action. While this can be dismissed as a form of consulting and thus not *bona fide* research activity (i.e. that would lead to publication in a prominent outlet), deliberate, and reflective engagement of this sort can constitute a powerful endeavor that blends the principles of action science (Argyris, Putnam, & Smith, 1985) with the creative, purposeful power of design (Simon, 1969/1996).

In the meantime, the entrepreneur may look for answers elsewhere, in the experience and stories of those who have gone and succeeded before them, or in the advice of their trusted friends, colleagues, or professional advisors. Regardless of the sources, the entrepreneur does something ... and leaves a trail of sorts. And the trail attracts the scientist who can describe it and explain it. But while the scientist looks backwards, the entrepreneur keeps looking forward, blazing the trail. Now, the trail exists once made but there is nothing natural or pre-existing about it — it represents a journey of worldmaking (Sarasvathy, 2012), reflecting the idiosyncratic nature of the problems defined, actions taken, advice received and the complexity of the situation in which the action occurred, triggering reactions from other market actors.

In the context of the popularity and widespread use of tools and approaches such as the business model canvas, lean start-up methodology, customer discovery methodology, and design thinking, the question arises of how academic scholars can engage in and contribute to these conversations. This is a crucial question because the formalized toolbox of entrepreneurial practice raises doubts about whether entrepreneurial phenomena are natural in the sense of unfolding out of some universal, law-like necessity, to be studied by detached, impartial observers. To the extent that this is not the case, a new logic of inquiry arises that offers an opportunity for a better alignment between academic scholarship and entrepreneurial practice.

This chapter addresses these questions by revisiting the fundamental premises of scholarly inquiry in entrepreneurship and identifying roads not taken. It then sketches out a new logic of inquiry, grounded in design science, and articulates the new types of research activities that comprise it.

NATURAL VERSUS ARTIFICIAL PHENOMENA

The main starting point for discussion is Simon's (1969/1996) distinction between natural and artificial phenomena, the former defined by "necessity" and the latter by "contingency," molded by goals and purposes. This distinction poses a problem of artificiality related to how to make empirical propositions about contingent phenomena, that is, those that could turn out differently under different circumstances. The term "natural" is used here in the sense of *existing*, that is, what already is, rather than as limited to the realm of the natural sciences (i.e. biology, chemistry, physics). Thus, phenomena such as an airplane or a new firm can be treated as both natural and artificial. As the former, they are taken for granted and analyzed through the methods of description, modeling and explanation. As the latter, the focus is on how they are designed or constructed, which falls into the realm of the design disciplines (e.g., arts, architecture, engineering).

Entrepreneurial phenomena lend themselves to both natural and design science approaches. Their processes unfold over time and one inevitably has to choose a time reference point in studying them (McMullen & Dimov, 2013). This reference point creates an arbitrary separation between what has already happened and what is yet to happen, both of which can serve as objects of research. A definite outcome, such as an established new venture or a failed effort to do so, is something that can be described and explained retrospectively, as an object of theory grounded in natural science. In contrast, the open-ended process lying ahead offers hardly anything that can be taken for granted, to be described or explained. Thus, scholars operating in the natural-science paradigm only become interested in the acting entrepreneur when something happens that can then become the focus of description and explanation. Until then, s/he is empirically irrelevant.

In the current study of entrepreneurship, the dominant conception is of a natural phenomenon, that is, one to be described and explained retrospectively. This conception represents a paradigm within which the very nature of the phenomenon under study is taken for granted and rarely questioned. As a result, attempts to articulate entrepreneurship as a science of the artificial (Sarasvathy, 2003; Selden & Fletcher, 2015; Venkataraman, Sarasvathy, Dew, & Forster, 2012) have remained disparate and gathered little traction. What is more, their output can become an easy target of criticism within the existing paradigm. A case in point is the difficulty of understanding the nature and purpose of effectuation as a theoretical perspective (Sarasvathy, 2001). In a recent critical assessment, Arend, Sarooghi, and Burkemper (2015) conclude that effectuation is an underdeveloped, not yet solid theory, falling short on most criteria for a scientific theory. That this criticism asks the wrong question is not immediately evident.

Nevertheless, there is a strong momentum toward developing a perspective of entrepreneurship as a design activity. One thrust has come from embracing the open-ended, worldmaking nature of entrepreneurial action based on the logic of non-predictive control (Sarasvathy, 2012). Another has come from the importance of design thinking in teaching entrepreneurship (Neck & Greene, 2011). As they stand, both of these lines of thought are limited to articulating a generic sense of unbounded possibilities, that is, entrepreneurial action for its own sake. What they lack is the sense of purpose that defines individual entrepreneurs and gives some focus and meaning to their efforts. Indeed, artificial phenomena are to be understood through the goals and purposes molding them (Simon, 1969/1996).

By making purpose front and central, we can position the intellectual effort away from non-committal speculation, as a focused, deliberate, qualitatively different branch of inquiry. Contextualizing the "artificial" aspect of entrepreneurship can preempt its treatment as an offshoot of the existing paradigm, and thus its rendering as a misfit on the basis of the fundamental logic that defines the paradigm. The next section attempts to provide such contextualization.

DESIGN AS A DISTINCT MODE OF RESEARCH

Romme (2003) outlines three ideal-typical modes of engaging in research. The first two, science and humanities, are well familiar and present in entrepreneurship research. The science mode is oriented toward explaining phenomena through uncovering general patterns, while the humanities mode is oriented toward describing the human experience. The third, design mode is distinct in that it studies systems that do not yet exist. Its orienting question is "will it work?" rather than "is it valid or true?." Its view of knowledge is pragmatic, driven by whether knowledge is useful for action toward a particular purpose. As such, it fits with design and engineering disciplines as well as the creative arts.

Among the business-related disciplines, design has been a dominant mode of inquiry in information technology and information systems research, based on the recognition that it studies artificial phenomena, must be grounded in real-world problems, and thus must create artifacts that serve human purposes (March & Smith, 1995). As March and Smith (1995) argue, design and science are interrelated in three ways: (1) the artifacts created through design can become the subject of scientific inquiry; (2) artifacts are created with understanding of natural laws; (3) the effectiveness of artifacts can provide substantive tests for (natural) science research.

In a similar manner, Vincenti (1993) draws a distinction between engineering and scientific knowledge. The former is developed for practical utility, to solve particular problems, while the latter is developed for the sake of understanding. In turn, engineers use knowledge to design artifacts, while scientists use it to derive new knowledge. Although there is great overlap between the two in terms of the knowledge-generation activities carried out (i.e. methods), the epistemological distinction between the two categories is derived from priority and purpose. In the context of entrepreneurship, this distinction raises the simple question of whether scholars of entrepreneurship should be seen as scientists or engineers. There is clearly room for both roles, even though over time the quest for academic standing and legitimacy has led to a dominant identity as scientists.

Given the distinct nature of design knowledge, it is useful to understand the nature of activities associated with its generation. March and Smith (1995) provide a research framework that distinguishes research activities and research outputs and, further, maps these to the domains of natural and design science. Research activities include build, evaluate, theorize, and justify. The first two belong to the design science, pertaining respectively to the construction of specific artifacts and demonstrating that they meet the desired goals or performance criteria. The latter two belong to natural science, pertaining to developing theoretical explanation of how something works and validating that explanation with empirical data. This framework is presented in Table 1.

Research outputs include constructs, models, methods, and instantiations. These apply to the full range of research activities, but can play slightly different role depending on whether the research efforts are grounded in natural or design science. *Constructs* represent the basic vocabulary of the domain in thinking about and describing the phenomenon at hand. Examples in the entrepreneurship space include customers, value proposition, business model, business plan, etc. *Models* capture relationships among constructs as a way of representing the situation at hand. Natural scientists use models as a synonym for theory to inform their empirical research, while design scientists use models to define the problem at hand and thus inform its solution. Thus, while in the former conception, a model constitutes a rigid representation that needs to be verified, in the latter conception it is a fluid marker of emergent possibilities. In the context of entrepreneurship, an example of the former are the relationships of

Table 1. Research Activities and Outputs.

	Constructs	Model	Method	Instantiation
Build		Design science		
Evaluate				
Theorize		Natural science		
Justify				

Source: Adapted from March and Smith (1995).

human capital and business planning with venture development or performance; examples of the latter are sketches of how a venture is to operate or of the customer journey in engaging with a product.

Methods refer to the set of steps necessary to carry out a task. Natural scientists are primarily users of methods, whereas design scientist produce as well as use them. For instance, the former may look at methods for data collection and analysis, while the latter may consider ways of visualizing data or gathering novel data that, although not suitable for testing hypotheses, facilitates decisions. Finally, *instantiations* refer to the realization of artifacts, such as the creation of product prototypes, eliciting reactions or parameters for commitment by customers, partners or investors or simply getting a yes/no closure on such commitments. These represent the forging of a path of history, whereby multiple possibilities at a given junction are subsumed under what actually happens. These are carried out primarily by design scientists although, once introduced, studying them can advance both natural and design science.

In his discussion of the "anatomy" of engineering knowledge, Vincenti (1993) identifies different categories of knowledge as well as different forms of knowledge-generation activities. The knowledge categories include: (1) fundamental design concepts; (2) criteria and specifications; (3) theoretical tools; (4) quantitative data; (5) practical considerations; and (6) design instrumentalities. *Fundamental design concepts* refer to operational principles and configurations. In the entrepreneurship context these are reflected, for example, in the notions of profitability and firm, and are well articulated in the business model canvas as an operational model of a business with all the inter-relationships among its activities.

Criteria and specifications refer to the goals at hand. In entrepreneurship, these can pertain to the economic, social, or environmental impact of the venture as well as the specific psychic income that the entrepreneur may derive from these activities (Gimeno, Folta, Cooper, & Woo, 1997). *Theoretical tools* facilitate thinking about design and the making of relevant design calculations. Relevant examples include the fundamental constructs through which we describe entrepreneurship (e.g., opportunity, customer, value), theories from marketing and operations that inform the design of the venture as well as financial tools such as capital planning and discounted cash flow that inform financing and valuation. *Quantitative data* refer to accumulated evidence about the effectiveness of various venture parameters.

Practical considerations pertain to the tacit understanding that originates from practice and is often codified in rules of thumb used by practitioners.

For example, the VC method of valuation has arisen from the difficulty of valuing early-stage companies in the face of uncertainty and lack of operating history. Other examples include specific milestones such as incorporation, IP protection, 2-year survival, reaching revenue stage, cashflow positive, certain revenue stages ($100k, $1m) or opening a second location. *Design instrumentalities* pertain to procedural knowledge or the way of doing things. These comprise procedures, ways of thinking, and judgment skills. Examples include building a minimum viable product and gathering customer feedback, running small product trials, building a financial model, resource planning for expansion, assessing total market size, thinking about how easy it is for competitors to replicate or retaliate, or staying true to one's passion.

In regard to knowledge-generation activities, Vincenti (1993) discusses the following categories: (1) transfer from science; (2) invention; (3) theoretical research; (4) experimental research; (5) design practice; (6) production; and (7) direct trial. *Transfer from science* refers to theories and empirical findings from scientific studies that can inform problem definition and solving in the context of design practice. Although perhaps not directly translatable, in its classic form, to entrepreneurship, *invention* refers to the creation or serendipitous discovery of fundamental concepts. This may resonate with entrepreneurial efforts with serendipitous beginnings where market validation is provided for concepts previously not considered probable or viable. In a broader sense, we can also consider the invention of different uses for a given product or technology. *Theoretical* and *experimental research* correspond to familiar activities in scientific practice, except that their focus is more explicitly on application rather than understanding. *Design practice* refers to day to day practice that can hone judgment and develop rules of thumb that can motivate further research. Classic examples are the abilities of angel and VC investors to screen out investment proposals and of experienced mentors to identify gaps in reasoning or potential hurdles. *Production* can codify experience into various kinds of quantitative data such as customer acquisition costs or gross margin. *Direct trial* pertains to the testing of products with potential users to reveal if their performance is as intended. It is a fundamental part of contemporary entrepreneurial practice as exemplified by the lean start-up or customer discovery methodologies.

Vincenti maps research activities onto the various forms of knowledge that they can generate, as shown in Table 2.

Clearly, there are sets of activities and outputs that, while important for entrepreneurial practice, currently do not represent legitimate forms of

Table 2. Knowledge-Generation Activities and Knowledge Categories.

	Fundamental Design Concepts	Criteria and Specifications	Theoretical Tools	Quantitative Data	Practical Considerations	Design Instrumentalities
Transfer from science			X	X		
Invention	X					
Theoretical research	X	X	X	X		X
Experimental research	X	X	X	X		X
Design practice		X			X	X
Production				X	X	X
Direct trial	X	X	X	X	X	X

Source: Adapted from Vincenti (1993).

entrepreneurship research. In other words, the core issues here are the meaning of the term "research," the relative standing and interrelationship of basic and applied research, and whether an academic engaging in such activities can be deemed to be research active. These activities fall within the realm of design science and are represented as the shaded areas in Tables 1 and 2. Although ostensibly of applied nature, they provide context for reflection that can make a contribution as basic research.

In Table 1, the activities of building and evaluation stand out as a blind-spots for entrepreneurship research. Whereas an arts academic can deliver a piece of composed music as research output, can an entrepreneurship academic's contribution to start-up efforts be seen in the same light? In Table 2, the activities of design practice, production, and direct trial are of similar nature. But there are also two knowledge categories – practical considerations and design instrumentalities – that do not live up to their full potential in current research. While the examples of these categories, as specified above (milestones, planning, etc.) certainly do show up as constructs or variables in current research, they do so in categorical rather than qualitative sense. Thus, the research questions around them have been poised in terms of whether these factors make a difference without consideration of how they are used or if they can be used better. A good example relates to the theoretical question of whether having a business plan (regardless of the nature of the plan) matters of performance as opposed to the practical question of what makes a good business plan, ascertained through its use. Before discussing how these outputs can be implemented in entrepreneurship research, it is necessary to define the context in which they will arise.

OPPORTUNITY AS DESIGN ARTIFACT

In its natural-science mode, entrepreneurship research seeks to connect the present and the future by explaining the link between the present and the past. Compared to the past, the present always contains novel elements: new goods, new services, new raw materials or new organizing methods (Casson, 1982) as well as various artifacts of failed efforts. Their presence now suggests that they have been possibilities of a past future, a set of lucrative opportunities (Venkataraman, 1997), whether perceived or mis-perceived, exploited or blundered. The aim of entrepreneurship theory has been to explain how, starting from the past, such opportunities come to be realized; and then use this knowledge to project the process forward. This question has proven elusive to conceptual assimilation, despite being tackled from different directions.

One line of analytical attack has been to define the nature of opportu-nities as endpoints of a process and then portray entrepreneurial activity accordingly. The ideas of Austrian economists – and particularly the notion that entrepreneurs are alert to and discover profit opportunities (Kirzner, 1979) – have been seminal in the field. Although this notion had been put forward as a metaphor for the micro drivers of the economic sys-tem (Kirzner, 2009), as the field moved from economics to management, this metaphor has been reified and its literal interpretation has made oppor-tunities an exogenous endpoint: "objective phenomena that are not known to all parties at all times" (Shane & Venkataraman, 2000, p. 220). In this sense, they are deemed to be discovered, evaluated, and exploited by enter-prising individuals (Venkataraman, 1997).

In contrast, opportunities can also be seen as endogenous endpoints, defined while pursued, within the worldview of individual entrepreneurs. In this sense, opportunities lie at the tail end of a stream of continuously developed and modified ideas (Davidsson, 2003; Dimov, 2007). Until realized, they exist in the imagination of entrepreneurs (Klein, 2008; Shackle, 1955) and thus cannot be separated from them (Companys & McMullen, 2007; Sarason, Dean, & Dillard, 2006). In the way that they ultimately become known to external observers, they are subject to path-dependent formation from the actions of entrepreneurs (Alvarez, Barney, & Anderson, 2013).

Although each view highlights important aspects of the individual-opportunity link — objective boundaries and subjective process — neither view provides empirical content, that is, to enable the entrepreneurial process to be specified or observed, let alone applied. Whether opportunities are found or formed is but a semantic link between process and outcome in the sense that the process is defined only in terms of what it is supposed to achieve (Drazin & Sandelands, 1992). Thus, when opportunities are seen as fixed endpoints, they are associated with a process of discovery; when they are seen as path-dependent creations, they are associated with a process of formation, development or design. Because these semantic descriptions are cast in a generic sense — of the process as a whole — they do not offer a substantive account of what is actually happening or achieved (Dimov, 2011), that is, what does opportunity discovery or opportunity creation really mean? How does one know that s/he has discovered/created an opportunity? As such, they do not offer any tangible markers for acting toward a future not yet known; they are inherently retrospective.

In response to this, recent work has sought to identify empirical premises for the entrepreneurial process. It is triggered by venture ideas, driven by actions from these ideas, and instituted in market exchange relationships that become the tangible markers of an opportunity (Dimov, 2011). Similarly, opportunities can be portrayed as artifacts arising from the actions and interactions of entrepreneurs (Venkataraman et al., 2012). What is missing from this line of thought, however, is a sense of defining boundary, a purpose or driving logic to the actions and interactions that would enable a set of discrete, seemingly idiosyncratic actions and events to be strung together in a coherent entrepreneurial process. In other words, what can we learn from one realization of the process to another? What actions or interactions are relevant or useful?

So, what is an opportunity? Let us answer this question by attempting to construct one. We need two sets of elements, agents and artifacts. Some of the agents act as consumers and what they consume is an artifact, that is, product or service. Other agents act as providers of labor or other artifacts to help produce the artifact to be consumed. The entrepreneur(s) is yet another agent who controls the focal product or service and thus brings together the production and consumption sides. The opportunity is not the simple collection of such agents and artifacts. Its essence lies in the set of particular relationships created among them. Each relationship denotes a pattern of interaction between actors. It represents an ongoing exchange activity such as employment, supply, production, distribution, and consumption and is an indelible part of the realization of the opportunity.

Described in such concrete terms, an opportunity is a social structure. It is a meso-level, macroscopic structure, above the individual agents but below the economic system as a whole. Except for some novel artifacts, its elements can be largely deemed to exist. It is their weaving into the particular relationship pattern that constitutes the construction of the opportunity. In this sense, an opportunity is an emergent entity — more than the collection of its individual parts and arising from the interactions among them. Similar to other social structures such as organizations, an opportunity is both objective and subjective: it cannot exist without its elements; but, equally, it cannot be seen without "drawing" the relationships among them (Drazin & Sandelands, 1992).

In between the unconnected elements and their connected structure operates an evolving entrepreneurial intent (McMullen & Dimov, 2013) as well as an organizing process (Weick, 1979) marked, aside from its intentionality, by the combination and control of resources, establishment and maintenance of boundaries, and engagement in exchange relationships (Katz & Gartner, 1988). The entrepreneur is effectively a progenitor of this social structure in the sense that s/he "sees" possible relationships among currently unconnected actors and artifacts and works on establishing them. Sometimes they arise as envisioned, other time they do not and are possibly replaced by other, more workable relationships. Thus, the ultimate social structure may bear little resemblance to the one envisioned at the start. In this sense, opportunity as social structure is a design artifact that arises at the intersection of entrepreneurial intent with the constraints of the economic, social, and technical context.

The current difficulty for entrepreneurship theory in taming the opportunity construct lies in its grounding in natural science, that is, in the need to take opportunity for granted, as something that is, as something to be described and explained through some inevitable, law-like tendency. The first part, taking opportunity for granted, works as long as an opportunity is already realized. Indeed, opportunities are retrospectively clear but prospectively opaque (Dimov, 2011). The second part, however, remains elusive in the sense that retracing the history of an opportunity readily reveals the contingent nature of its path, that is, that it could have turned out differently if different decisions had been taken at various junctions (Sarasvathy, Dew, Read, & Wiltbank, 2008). Precisely because the developmental path of an opportunity is marked not by a single decision but by a series of decisions, each contingent upon the previous (Dimov, 2007) in a constantly extending "corridor" (Ronstadt, 1988), the idea of an over-arching law as a relationship between inputs and outputs may be the problem itself. The next section develops the notion of recursivity as a different generative source.

RECURSIVE ACTION AS GENERATIVE MECHANISM

Drazin and Sandelands (1992), synthesizing a vast array of prior work in both natural and social science disciplines, distinguish three levels of social structure: observed, elemental, and deep. The *observed* level is the one at which an observer can make out a social fact such as an organization or an opportunity. This is the level at which the opportunity is perceived in a holistic sense, as a single entity, and at which the arguments about the nature of opportunities reside. At the *elemental* level, one observes the states and interactions of the actors that compose the observable structure. The elemental structure thus consists of what entrepreneurs do and with whom they interact. Empirical studies of the nascent entrepreneurial process as a series of actions and milestones (e.g., Carter, Gartner, & Reynolds, 1996; Davidsson & Honig, 2003) effectively map out the elemental structure of opportunities.

The *deep* structure is not observable. It pertains to the (tacit) rules and positional information that drive the actions and interactions of the actors that create the elemental structure and, over time, give rise to the observed structure. As actors have bounded rationality and only partial, limited information, these rules are simple but recursive in nature, that is, they are applied repeatedly to the changing circumstances of the actor. Another key feature of deep structure is the actor's positional information, that is, the knowledge and information available to the actor at a given point in time. It reflects the actor's personal knowledge, experience, and social network. In this sense, deep structure pertains to how actors decide what to do based on the information they have at that moment, as repeated enactment of simple rules.

To specify the deep structure of opportunity requires an elaboration of the considerations or rules that different actors – for example, entrepreneurs and prospective customers – follow in their actions and interactions. These rules are applied to their positional information to determine their response. In turn, their responses as well as exogenous developments, change their positional information and thus give rise to new responses when the rules are applied recursively, that is, when the output of one action becomes the input to the next. The power of recursivity lies in its ability to open non-linear paths and generate complex structures.

The idea of recursivity is linked to the broader notion of iterated functions as simple dynamical systems. Under the logic of a covering law as a linear relationship between inputs and outputs (nomothetic explanation), explaining a complex phenomenon necessarily triggers a search for a complex set of causes. The study of simple dynamical systems, however, suggests that simple, deterministic rules, when applied recursively can lead to non-predictable outcomes that are highly sensitive to initial conditions (May, 1976). Indeed, May's concluding statement has become seminal:

> The fact that a simple and deterministic equation can possess dynamical trajectories which look like some sort of random noise has disturbing practical implications. It means, for example, that apparently erratic fluctuations in the census data for an animal population need not necessarily betoken either the vagaries of an unpredictable environment or sampling error: they may simply derive from a rigorously deterministic population growth relationship. (1976, p. 8)

A core issue with nomothetic explanation is the search for a deterministic relationship between inputs and outputs. However, they belong to different sets — expanded both in space and time. That is, outcomes reflect factors from outside the factor space and from the way this space has changed over time. In addition, theoretically, the relationship works as a one-time shot. What is missing is the recursive nature of the expansion of the space-time domain. In contrast to a nomothetic explanation based on causal regularities, generative explanation is based on specifying the mechanisms that give rise to a macroscopic regularity (Cederman, 2005). One core mechanism is the recursive nature of entrepreneurial problem solving, that is, the idea that entrepreneurs repeatedly seek to solve the problems that arise from their actions. It is therefore essential to understand how problems and actions are intertwined in an entrepreneurial setting.

PROBLEMATIZING ENTREPRENEURIAL ACTION

Tracing the development of an entrepreneurial endeavor is likely to reveal a winding path. The path in between is marked by actions and interactions driven by some underlying, evolving purpose (Venkataraman et al., 2012). In other words, each stage of the path represents a snapshot of the entrepreneur "doing" something. But a sequence of behaviors can appear meaningless to an external observer without accounting for their underlying purpose. Rather than simply enlist the nature and sequence of actions, we need to account for the evolving symbolic blueprint behind them, that is, how the entrepreneur defines them and deliberates them at each step of the way. To use the metaphor of driving a vehicle off road, in addition to simply describing the twists and turns of its path, it is also useful to try to capture the forging of the path through the eyes of the driver. That path is an artifact of sort and, as such, lies at the intersection of inner and outer environments: the former reflects the purpose behind the effort and the latter the molding effect of the terrain (Selden & Fletcher, 2015; Simon, 1969/1996). In this sense, the path is jointly created by two forces, one pushing forward (purpose) and the other backward (constraints, obstacles, or lack thereof). In other words, each action can be seen as purposeful, forward pushing against constraints ... just like the flow of water.

A flow of water seeks to retain its circular shape against the shape of the vessel in which it flows, thereby creating various forms of turbulence (Schwenk, 1996). In a similar fashion, the entrepreneurial process can be portrayed as flow working against constraints. The impetus for the flow is the entrepreneur's quest to complete a sense of wholeness via new relationships. This quest represents, more broadly, an adaptive tension as an energy differential (McKelvey, 2004) or, more specifically, an opportunity tension as an internal drive (Lichtenstein, 2009). It can arise from a variety of factors such as desire for financial wealth, need for recognition, sense of role fulfillment, or social values (Carter, Gartner, Shaver, & Gatewood, 2003), which create the forward flow. The sense of purpose is expressed in a symbolic blueprint of what the ultimate relationships would look like (Dimov, 2011). The inertial force of the status quo acts to constrain the flow in the sense that the envisioned relationships are unlikely to arise unless proactively instituted. The flow is ultimately realized in the creation of new artifacts that complete these relationships and the exchanges inherent to them (Venkataraman et al., 2012). The process is open ended in the sense that the set of directions and outcomes is unbounded, generated from the constant interaction of emerging constraints and the evolving momentum of the flow.

Collectively, the process is described by all its twists and turns. Each of these, in turn, represents a momentary realization of the flow-constraint interaction, akin to the notion of a derivative of a function at a particular point (i.e. it represents the slope of the function or the "direction" of its travel at that point). Therefore, the recursive nature of the process lies in the repeated interaction between flow and constraints. At each point, this interaction is represented by what the entrepreneur is trying to do or achieve and by the degree to which the outer environment yields. The move by the entrepreneur is a key focal point as it not only elicits a response by the outer environment but also reflects the way the entrepreneurs views the situation at hand and defines what problem to tackle. Indeed, while the overarching purpose to the journey may be clear, what to do in each particular situation (i.e. which of several possible paths to take) may not be.

Problem setting or framing is a key aspect of action (Argyris et al., 1985) and problem solving (Newell & Simon, 1972). There are different ways to make sense of a situation, to define the problem to be solved, and to enlist possible actions. This is consistent with the chaotic nature of the early stages of the entrepreneurial process (Cheng & Van de Ven, 1996). The idiographic nature of the entrepreneur's positional information and his or her sense for what to do in the particular situation interplay at full force, reflecting a wealth (or lack thereof) of life experience. In this regard, constructs such as prior knowledge, intuition, and judgment are simply collective descriptions of the unbounded nature of the sets of prior experience and actions undertaken. Thus, the generalized statements that entrepreneurs make sense of the situation, define a problem they wish to solve, and act according to their intuition or judgment are simply placeholders for a closer and more elaborate description of their deliberation.

The above arguments suggest that to understand why an entrepreneur engages in a particular action, we need to account for the problem that the entrepreneur is trying to solve, that is, for the way s/he is framing the situation at hand. For instance, while the fact that one entrepreneur looks for a premise and another files a patent application poses the issue of unfathomable heterogeneity among entrepreneurs, both activities can be represented as solutions to problems that the entrepreneurs face. Thus, when we seek to draw inferences from observed action, we need to be conscious of the fact that the problem toward which the action is directed − as defined by the entrepreneur − most often remains hidden.

Fig. 1 represents the interplay between entrepreneur, situational framing/problem definition, and action. The top part shows the situation as we currently experience in empirical research, whereby we observe entrepreneurs and their actions but the problems for the sake of which actions are undertaken are entirely subsumed in the entrepreneur and thus unobservable to us. Thus, to use the earlier terminology, while we observe the elemental structure of the entrepreneurial effort (i.e. the actions undertaken), we cannot observe its deep structure, that is, how the entrepreneur links positional information to action through the framing of the situation and definition of a problem.

It is therefore essential to bring the underlying framing/problem definition to the fore, by examining it separately from the entrepreneur, as shown in the bottom part of Fig. 1. The figure recognizes not only that the given problem (Framing 1) is solved by the particular entrepreneur through the given action (Action_0), but also that it is possible to undertake other actions to solve the particular problem (Action_1) as well as to pose different problems in the given situation (Framing 2) which in turn would lead to different actions (Action_2). Indeed, if other entrepreneurs were put in the same situation, they are likely to act differently, whether because they choose different actions for the same type of problem or see different problems in the same situation.

The underlying questions therefore relate to examining the merits of (1) an action given a particular framing of the situation and (2) a framing of the situation given an overarching purpose. In terms of theory of action, the first question represents single-loop learning, while the second double-loop learning (Argyris & Schon, 1978). In current research, these questions do not arise as we take the entrepreneur's actions for granted, regardless of their "quality." In other words, we do not take into account what the entrepreneurs are trying to do in undertaking the particular actions. This suggests that, within a conception of an individual-opportunity nexus in which we look to identify the characteristics of lucrative opportunities on

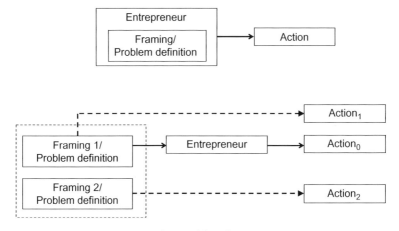

Fig. 1. Separating Problem from Entrepreneur.

the one hand and enterprising individuals on the other (Venkataraman, 1997), significant variability can arise from an examination of the actions that comprise an entrepreneurial effort (cf. Ramoglou & Tsang, 2016).

The separation of the problem from the entrepreneur addresses a blind-spot in current research. More importantly, the definition of the problem and the way to solve it can be turned into an object of research. As an endeavor motivated by pragmatic use, it belongs to the domain of design science in the sense that it deals with the creation of artifacts and builds upon the foundations laid by action science in the sense that it requires knowledge in the service of action (Argyris et al., 1985). It is therefore pos-sible to define a research program by elaborating the distinct nature of its knowledge-generating activities and outputs.

TOWARD A DESIGN SCIENCE OF ENTREPRENEURSHIP

The primary mission of design-oriented disciplines, such as medicine and engineering, is the creation of preferred futures, driven by search for solu-tions to real-world problems (Van Aken & Romme, 2012). In a similar vein, a design-science approach to entrepreneurship would focus on the effort to envision and generate products, services, ventures, firms and other artifacts that do not yet exist, oriented toward the fulfillment of specific purposes. The consideration of purpose is key since the question of how things ought to be can be raised only in reference to that purpose (Simon, 1969/1996). In this sense, the design-science approach described here is situ-ated in a broader realm of "worldmaking" (Sarasvathy, 2012) but is anchored by purpose that makes some futures preferred to others and oriented toward informing and being informed by specific actions. Thus, while goals do emerge in the worldmaking process as enacted through the principles of effectuation (Sarasvathy, 2001), these principles leave signifi-cant leeway for the formulation of specific actions and there is no feedback loop whereby they can be questioned or modified in the light of the conse-quences of the action.

Therefore, the starting point to a design-science inquiry would be some initial or preliminary business idea that contains a sense of product or ser-vice and a reason for its use (e.g., a need). The business idea represents a concrete path toward the fulfillment of a broader purpose such as the solu-tion of a social or other real-world problem, desire for autonomy or desire for financial gain. In view of this, there are two relevant questions that can be asked:

1. Does the realization of the particular business idea fulfill the broader purpose?
2. Given the business idea, what shall one do to realize it?

Although this section focuses largely on the second question, the first question itself can also be the basis of a design inquiry, albeit of a different nature. It relates to how to identify possible entrepreneurial solutions to real-world aspirations or challenges. It also acknowledges that solutions need not be necessarily entrepreneurial and that entrepreneurial solutions need not necessarily be possible. Thus, it helps contextualize the second question as representing a developmental loop embedded within a broader solution loop. In other words, it represents an important place for retreat and reflection when current entrepreneurial efforts reach an impasse or a dead end.

It is important to reiterate here that the design science perspective developed here is intended to complement rather replace the natural science perspective. The distinction between the two lies in the choice by the researcher to study entrepreneurship "as it is" or "as it could be." The choice of direction brings with it a distinct purpose for the research efforts, distinct role of the researcher in the research process, and distinct research outputs. These can be seen in the inter-relationships between the community of inquiry, that is, those undertaking the research efforts, and community of practice, that is, the entrepreneurs. A choice to study entrepreneurship-as-it-is presupposes a defined object, an end point or a stable state toward which the explanation needs to converge. It allows for the two communities to be kept separate, whereby the community of inquiry can focus exclusively on precision in causal explanation, by isolating factors and thereby downplaying practical considerations (Argyris et al., 1985).

But if one studies the world-as-it-could-be, it is not possible to specify a steady state, since the focus is on intended, not yet existing changes that may or may not materialize, subject to both intended and unintended dynamics. In this setting, the two communities cannot be separated and the aim is to form a community of inquiry within the community of practice and thus generate knowledge in the service of action (Argyris et al., 1985). The relevant focus here is on learning about the situation by exploring it through different framings and different actions, while being aware of the implicit assumptions (tacit knowledge) behind each framing and action and reflecting on the consequences to generate new frames and new actions.

Research Questions

In focusing on how to realize a particular business idea, given the earlier discussion of the generative power of recursive action, the unit of analysis is the momentary problem or task that an entrepreneur faces in pushing forward. The definition of the problem arises from the way the entrepreneur frames the situation at hand, thereby making some features of the situation salient. This corresponds to dealing with the issue of isotropy (i.e. what is relevant?) as a fundamental element of the entrepreneur's design space (Sarasvathy et al., 2008). I propose three general framings or meta-categories of design problems as pertaining to the entrepreneurial space: market desirability, operational or technical feasibility, and financial viability. These reflect the basic definition of opportunity as profitable introduction of new products or services (Casson, 1982), prior discussions on the conditions for the existence of entrepreneurial opportunities (Eckhardt & Shane, 2012) and the earlier notion of (realized) opportunity as social structure and capture the different relationships in that structure. In other words, there needs to be actual demand for the product or service in the market (someone needs to buy it), the product or service need to be made of a requisite quality and price to meet that demand (someone needs to make it), and the economics of the effort need to work out over time (the effort needs to be profitable). Successful entrepreneurial efforts lie at the intersection of these challenges, as represented in Fig. 2.

In view of this, the following specific research questions emerge in the context of the broader question of what to do in order to realize a business idea:

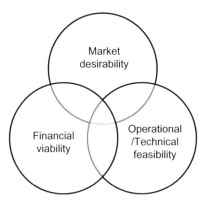

Fig. 2.   Archetypal Design Problem in Entrepreneurship.

1. What shall one do to establish market desirability?
2. What shall one do to establish operational/technical feasibility?
3. What shall one do to establish financial viability?
4. How (in what order) should the above design sub-problems be tackled?

Logic of Inquiry

The previous discussion of the research questions underpinning a design-science perspective highlights the interplay between problem framing and action, whereby different actions can be considered within a particular framing and different framings can be considered within the broader purpose (each giving rise to a new set of actions). The same logic of inquiry arises from the design literature, albeit operating at a different level of abstraction and with different terminology. This section thus represents an opportunity to bring the two together.

Dorst (2011) describes the core design challenge as one of applying abductive reasoning, that is creating value through identifying relevant means and working principles, neither of which are given at the start. He uses a simple framework – the equation WHAT + HOW = OUTCOME – to contrast different formal logics of reasoning. WHAT pertains to people and things, representing different means or elements that can be put together to achieve an outcome. HOW pertains to the interactions and relationships between these elements. OUTCOME pertains to the result of the ensuing process.

In deductive reasoning, knowing the WHAT and HOW enables one to predict the result. In inductive reasoning, by knowing the WHAT and the OUTCOME one can propose a set of working principles (HOW) that links the two. These two approaches largely reflect the dominant logics within a natural science paradigm. In abductive reasoning, one aims for a particular result and looks to identify appropriate WHAT and HOW. In its closed form, designers operate within a given set of working principles (HOW) and aim to identify a set of means that can achieve the outcome. In an open-form abductive reasoning, however, the working principles are not known or chosen and thus have to be identified in conjunction with the means. This view is well captured by Schon (1987):

> In contrast to analysts or critics, designers put things together and bring new things into being, dealing in the process with many variables and constraints, some initially known and some discovered through designing. (p. 42)

Dorst refers to the combination of HOW and OUTCOME as a "frame," a particular way of looking at the problem situation and acting within it, building on earlier ideas by Schon (1983) that the ability to frame problem situations represents is a core skill of designers. It is notable that the concept of frame is a point of convergence. Dorst (2011) describes frame as a hypothesis that a particular set of relationships (working principles) can create a desired outcome. Schon (1983) discusses frame as the naming of a problem situation, which creates implications for how it should be approached. Argyris et al. (1985) discuss framing as the tacit assumptions that underlie one's approach to the situation at hand.

The identification of a frame thus represents a major milestone of design enquiry. Indeed, design problems are unstructured or wicked problems (Martin, 2009). In their seminal discussion of wicked problems, Rittel and Webber (1973) identify several key features that define them. Such problems have no definitive formulation and are thus both susceptible to multiple framings (based on the viewpoint of the observer) and not understood until a solution is formulated. They have no stopping rule, that is, there is no clear sense of when the problem is solved. As a consequence, their solutions cannot be judged as right or wrong but as good or bad, depending on the results achieved. The set of potential solutions is not enumerable which makes it impossible to derive an "optimum" solution. Every problem is novel and unique and attempted solutions work as "one-shot operations." That is, an attempted solution can give rise to new problems and these have to be handled; it is impossible to re-set the process, to return to the original point and thus avoid experiencing the new problem.

The conception of wicked problem readily applies to entrepreneurial situations. Indeed, Sarasvathy et al. (2008) point out that such situations are characterized by uncertainty, goal ambiguity, and isotropy (no clear sense of what information is relevant). Framing the situation, the imposition of a structure on it, is thus an essential component of the entrepreneurial process. It allows specific problems to be formulated and triggers search for solutions. This aligns with Dewey's definition of inquiry as "the controlled or directed transformation of an indeterminate situation into one that is so determinate in its constituent distinctions and relations as to convert the elements of the original situation into a unified whole" (1938 [1991], p. 108).

But crucially, frames should be seen as working hypotheses, to be tested and refined, discarded or replaced. Action or intervention represents the means for doing so, akin to experimentation in the natural-science domain (Argyris et al., 1985). In the spirit of Lewin, this represents a quest to understand something by attempting to change it. The design enquiry rests on awareness of and reflection on the tripartite role of such action: (1) to test a hypothesis, (2) to explore the situation, and (3) to change the situation (Schon, 1983).

Role of Researcher

A design perspective requires a fundamental shift of role for the researcher, from independent observer to active and engaged stakeholder, leading the scholarly enquiry from within (rather than without) the domain of entrepreneurial practice. It is clear from the nature of the research questions and the (open) abductive logic of inquiry that the exercise of judgment is fundamental to the design approach. Thus, the researcher needs to be as close to the formation and evolution of judgment as possible, in order to capture and reflect on the tripartite role of the action it informs. Aside from acting as an entrepreneur herself, the researcher can work closely with entrepreneurs, whether in a standalone collaborative effort or as part of the experiential activities in an entrepreneurship class. The latter represents a fusion of research and teaching. It links to recent work on a practice-based approach to teaching entrepreneurship that emphasizes the practices of play, empathy, creation, experimentation, and reflection (Neck, Greene, & Brush, 2014).

Fundamental to understanding the judgment behind each entrepreneurial action is what Schon (1987) describes as reflection-in-action, that is, thinking what one is doing while doing it. This entails continuous consideration of current choices and the tree of further choices they open up. The evaluation of possible moves focuses on the desirability of their consequences, conformity to implications set by earlier moves, and potential for opening new problems and moves. The tangible marker in this process becomes the decision that forges a particular path forward. Schon (1987) provides a vivid description of its nature:

> At some point, he must move from a "what if?" to a decision, which then becomes a design note with binding implications for further moves. Thus, there is a continually evolving system of implications within which the designer reflects-in-action. (p. 100)

In addition, the researcher needs to maintain a reflective stance − reflection-on-action (Schon, 1987) − that enables her to inform the next moves of the entrepreneur. The consequences of action generate information about (1) the situation, (2) suitability of the framing, and

(3) suitability of the action, as inferred from whether its consequences are "good" and "bad" (Argyris et al., 1985). Reflecting on these can help formulate tentative action principles for future situations. As these principles become field-tested over time, their (pragmatic) validity increases (Van Aken & Romme, 2012). Therefore, the role for the researcher in a design enquiry can be seen as one of facilitating reflection and mindful selection of frames and actions to apply in given situations as well as of reflecting on their usefulness and retaining/modifying them for future use.

Research Outputs

The outputs to design inquiry reflect the type of the knowledge that arises from it. Synthesizing the frameworks by March and Smith (1995) and Vincenti (1993) there are three categories of knowledge that can arise from design inquiry. They build upon the foundations laid by the worldmaking perspective (Sarasvathy, 2012) and the principles of effectuation (Sarasvathy, 2001) by articulating a more precise role for their service of action toward a given purpose.

Constructs
These represent some basic vocabulary for representing the phenomenon at hand (March & Smith, 1995). This also captures Vincenti's (1993) notions of *fundamental design concepts*. Constructs allow diverse phenomena or experiences to be seen in the same way. Examples of such constructs include value proposition, business plan, pivot (Ries, 2011) or affordable loss (Sarasvathy, 2001). Although constructs are also essential to a theory-driven, natural-science inquiry, they need to have pragmatic utility in a design mode. In other words, they have to be tangible and meaningful to a prospective entrepreneur, and this is where the opportunity lies to expand the design enquiry.

The articulation of new constructs arises from close interaction with the entrepreneurial practice community and entails capturing and synthesizing the various terms used by them. For instance, in providing feedback to aspiring entrepreneurs, experienced entrepreneurs or investor would probe them on customer acquisition costs, the customer pain they are solving, the size of the opportunity or an exit multiple. Another investor would refer to a framework of angle, opportunity, timing, and people. With such diversity and overlap of constructs, the academic community can play an important role in developing shared understanding.

Models
These capture relationships among constructs as a way of representing the situation at hand (March & Smith, 1995). They also reflect what Vincenti (1993) refers to as *practical considerations*, that is, rules of thumb that arise from practice. Again, the formulation of a model allows meaning to be transferred from one design situation to another. A prominent example of a model is the business model canvas developed by Osterwalder and Pigneur (2009) and informed by Osterwalder's (2004) doctoral dissertation on business modeling. Curiously, this dissertation was developed within the domain of information systems and focused on developing a business model ontology as a basis for a programming effort. The notion of a model is used in a relatively loose sense here and thus includes any type of framework for making sense of a situation at hand and thus informs action. Thus, the primary function of a model is to help structure the decision space to highlight the relative importance of its different aspects and the inter-relationships among them.

Another example of a model is the 7-domains framework for opportunity assessment (Mullins, 2003), which arose from synthesizing the approaches by investors in evaluating opportunities. The framework brings together market (demand), industry (competition), and team considerations as well as distinguished macro and micro levels of assessment, each posing distinct questions. More broadly, new models can arise from a design enquiry as a means to make sense of and direct attention to various factors at various junctions of the entrepreneurial process, for example, when articulating and sifting through ideas or when looking to grow a business that has been proven on a smaller scale.

Methods
These refer to the set of steps necessary to carry out a task (March & Smith, 1995). They also comprise what Vincenti (1993) refers to as *design instrumentalities*, which also include ways of thinking and judgment. Methods can be proposed in the form of design propositions or principles on the basis of review and synthesis of prior research findings (e.g., Van Burg & Romme, 2014). An example of this is the set of design principles for university spinoff creation initially developed by Van Burg, Romme, Gilsing, and Reymen (2008). Methods can also be proposed based on extrapolation from entrepreneurial practice, such as synthesizing the expertise of serial entrepreneurs in the principles of effectuation (Sarasvathy, 2001) or the formulation of the lean start-up methodology (Ries, 2011).

As these knowledge outputs become applied, the researcher aims to answer the questions "Does it work?" and "Is it helpful?." Because these questions are posed in the context of a specific framing/action hypothesis, by reflecting on what has worked and what has not, the researcher can then suggest ways to refine, extend or otherwise improve these models as well as to specify the contextual conditions in which they work. An important question here is drawing the distinction between failure (deficiency) of the model/method itself and failure in its application. This in turn can lead to new constructs, models or methods. In addition, observed regularities can give rise to new research questions from a natural-science perspective in search of the theoretical explanation of the mechanism generating them. Once developed, these explanations can become incorporated in new design propositions.

It is clear that the outputs discussed above need different forms of dissemination. They do not readily fit the criteria set by top academic journals, which typically emphasize theoretical contribution based on seeing theory as an end in itself. While books and practice-oriented journals represent viable dissemination outlets, the question of their perceived value in assessing academic performance looms large. Although citation counts may represent a useful proxy for dissemination, much of the pragmatic value may be associated not with a bibliographic reference but with direct application. In addition, while evidence-based approaches to entrepreneurship research can also facilitate the systematic accumulation of knowledge (Frese, Bausch, Schmidt, Rauch, & Kabst, 2012), the constructs, methods, and models they evaluate are largely limited to those articulated within a mainstream science perspective. To the extent that they focus on design-related knowledge, this may be in terms of categorical rather than substantive use. These considerations call for different metrics.

CONCLUSION

From the position of the present, at the interface between past and future, one can look in two directions: toward the past, to make sense of what has happened, or toward the future, to enact a purpose. Mainstream scholarship in entrepreneurship delineates the former as a domain of inquiry and the latter as a domain of practice. Thus, while an entrepreneur is interested in facing and acting toward the future, an empirically minded academic may be drawn by prevailing norms toward explaining the past, waiting for the entrepreneur to create a new "past" and thus maintaining a stance of impartial observer. This chapter seeks to close the separation between entrepreneur and academic, blending the domains of inquiry and practice, by orienting inquiry toward the future and positioning the academic as an active and engaged stakeholder in the entrepreneurial process.

The chapter scopes a design science of entrepreneurship, focused on the enactment of entrepreneurial purpose, that is, on the reasoning, action, and reflection of the next step. It blends a perspective of action as both a mode of experimentation and a generator of new information with the nature of design as the creation of artifacts toward a purpose. To derive its focus, the chapter draws together a variety of perspective that can help put entrepreneurial phenomena in a new light.

First, it outlines the distinction between natural and artificial phenomena, the former taken for granted and the latter contingent on purposes and the process of enacting them. Second, it discusses design as distinct mode of research, driven by pragmatic considerations in the name of a given purpose and associated with specific knowledge outputs and knowledge-generation activities. Third, it portrays a realized entrepreneurial opportunity as a design artifact, a social structure arising in behalf of an entrepreneurial purpose. Fourth, it offers a generative explanation for social structures based on recursive action. Fifth, it articulates the recursive, generative mechanism of an entrepreneurial process as the problem solving activity of the entrepreneur, operating as a flowing interplay between forward (purpose) and backward (inertial constraints) forces. The core of a design science approach to entrepreneurship lies in separating the problem from the entrepreneur, thereby turning the action deliberation into an object of systematic inquiry and putting knowledge in the service of action.

The ultimate benefits of the adoption of a design science approach to entrepreneurship lie in reducing or even closing the gap between theory and practice, as currently evident in discussions of rigor versus relevance. The more specific benefits along the way include (1) turning real-world problems into questions for entrepreneurship research via the design of entrepreneurial solutions; and (2) developing new theories and methods and thus a richer, more collaborative research ecosystem in which researchers with different philosophical orientations can come together to define problems, enact solutions, and reflect on their consequences.

In closing, the academic study of entrepreneurship is pulled apart on the one hand by striving for academic legitimacy within the University and, on the other hand, by needing to demonstrate practical relevance outside it. Acknowledging that these forces cannot be contained within a single

paradigm is an important step toward balancing them. To the extent that
they represent competing conceptions of entrepreneurial scholarship, there
are winners and losers. Instead, they should be seen as complementary,
symbiotic activities, enabling one another toward greater fulfillment:
natural-science scholars can ask more meaningful research questions, while
design-science scholars can follow a more rigorous process and develop
better outputs.

There is a broader institutional challenge around recognizing the design-
science perspective on equal footing with a natural-science perspective.
This is essential for the long-term future of universities, as recently captured in a Financial Times special report: "The world is in the business of
finding solutions to multi-faceted problems and yet universities are still in
the business of finding applications for curiosity-driven research ... The
threat is not recognizing this and becoming less and less relevant as time
goes on" (Financial Times, 2014, p. 9).

REFERENCES

Alvarez, S. A., Barney, J. B., & Anderson, P. (2013). Forming and exploiting opportunities:
The implications of discovery and creation processes for entrepreneurial and organizational research. *Organization Science*, *24*(1), 301–317.

Arend, R. J., Sarooghi, H., & Burkemper, A. (2015). Effectuation as ineffectual? Applying the
3E theory-assessment framework to a proposed new theory of entrepreneurship.
Academy of Management Review, *40*(4), 630–651.

Argyris, C., Putnam, R., & Smith, D. M. (1985). *Action science*. San Francisco, CA:
Jossey-Bass.

Argyris, C., & Schon, D. A. (1978). *Organizational learning*. Reading, MA: Addison-Wesley.

Carter, N. M., Gartner, W. B., & Reynolds, P. D. (1996). Exploring start-up event sequences.
Journal of Business Venturing, *11*(3), 151–166.

Carter, N. M., Gartner, W. B., Shaver, K. G., & Gatewood, E. J. (2003). The career reasons
of nascent entrepreneurs. *Journal of Business Venturing*, *18*, 13–39.

Casson, M. (1982). *The entrepreneur: An economic theory*. Totowa, NJ: Barnes & Noble Books.

Cederman, L. E. (2005). Computational models of social forms: Advancing generative process
theory. *American Journal of Sociology*, *110*(4), 864–893.

Cheng, Y. T., & Van de Ven, A. H. (1996). Learning the innovation journey: Order out of
Chaos? *Organization Science*, *7*(6), 593–614.

Companys, Y. E., & McMullen, J. S. (2007). Strategic entrepreneurs at work: The nature, discovery, and exploitation of entrepreneurial opportunities. *Small Business Economics*,
28, 301–322.

Davidsson, P. (2003). The domain of entrepreneurship research: Some suggestions. In J. A.
Katz & D. A. Shepherd (Eds.), *Advances in entrepreneurship, firm emergence and growth*
(Vol. 6, pp. 315–372). Oxford: Elsevier/JAI Press.

Davidsson, P., & Honig, B. (2003). The role of social and human capital among nascent entrepreneurs. *Journal Business Venturing, 18*(3), 301–331.

Dewey, J. (1938 [1991]). Logic: Theory of inquiry. In J. A. Boydston (Ed.), *Later works* (Vol. 12). Carbondale, IL: Southern Illinois University Press.

Dimov, D. (2007). Beyond the single-person, single-insight attribution in understanding entrepreneurial opportunities. *Entrepreneurship: Theory and Practice, 31*(5), 713–731.

Dimov, D. (2011). Grappling with the unbearable elusiveness of entrepreneurial opportunities. *Entrepreneurship Theory and Practice, 35*, 57–81.

Dorst, K. (2011). The core of 'design thinking' and its application. *Design Studies, 32*, 521–532.

Drazin, R., & Sandelands, L. (1992). Autogenesis: A perspective on the process of organizing. *Organization Science, 3*(2), 231–249.

Eckhardt, J. T., & Shane, S. A. (2013). Response to the commentaries: The individual-opportunity (IO) nexus integrates objective and subjective aspects of entrepreneurship. *Academy of Management Review, 38*(1), 160–163.

Financial Times. (2014). The future of the university. *Financial Times*, October 7.

Frese, M., Bausch, A., Schmidt, P., Rauch, A., & Kabst, R. (2012). Evidence-based entrepreneurship: Cumulative science, action principles, and bridging the gap between science and practice. *Foundations and Trends in Entrepreneurship, 8*(1), 1–62.

Gimeno, J., Folta, T. B., Cooper, A. C., & Woo, C. Y. (1997). Survival of the fittest? Entrepreneurial human capital and the persistence of underperforming firms. *Administrative Science Quarterly, 42*(4), 750–783.

Katz, J., & Gartner, W. B. (1988). Properties of emerging organizations. *Academy of Management Review, 13*(3), 429–441.

Kirzner, I. M. (1979). *Perception, opportunity, and profit: Studies in the theory of entrepreneurship*. Chicago, IL: Chicago University Press.

Kirzner, I. M. (2009). The alert and creative entrepreneur: A clarification. *Small Business Economics, 32*, 145–152.

Klein, P. G. (2008). Opportunity discovery, entrepreneurial action, and economic organization. *Strategic Entrepreneurship Journal, 2*(3), 175–190.

Lichtenstein, B. B. (2009). Moving far from far-from-equilibrium: Opportunity tension as the catalyst of emergence. *Emergence: Complexity and Organization, 11*(4), 15–25.

March, S. T., & Smith, G. F. (1995). Design and natural science research on information technology. *Decision Support Systems, 15*, 251–266.

Martin, R. (2009). *The design of business*. Cambridge, MA: Harvard Business School Press.

May, R. M. (1976). Simple mathematical models with very complicated dynamics. *Nature, 261*, 459–467.

McKelvey, B. (2004). Toward a complexity science of entrepreneurship. *Journal of Business Venturing, 19*, 313–341.

McMullen, J. S., & Dimov, D. (2013). Time and the entrepreneurial journey: The problems and promise of studying entrepreneurship as a process. *Journal of Management Studies, 50*, 1481–1512.

McMullen, J. S., & Shepherd, D. A. (2006). Entrepreneurial action and the role of uncertainty in the theory of the entrepreneur. *Academy of Management Review, 31*, 132–152.

Mullins, J. W. (2003). *The new business road test*. London: FT Prentice Hall.

Neck, H. M., & Greene, P. G. (2011). Entrepreneurship education: Known worlds and new frontiers. *Journal of Small Business Management, 49*(1), 55–70.

Neck, H. M., Greene, P. G., & Brush, C. G. (2014). *Teaching entrepreneurship: A practice-based approach*. Cheltenham: Edward Elgar.

Newell, A., & Simon, H. A. (1972). *Human problem solving.* Englewood Cliffs, NJ: Prentice-Hall.

Nicolini, D. (2012). *Practice theory, work, and organization.* Oxford: Oxford University Press.

Osterwalder, A. (2004). *The business model ontology: A proposition in a design science approach.* Doctoral dissertation. Lausanne, Switzerland: University of Lausanne.

Osterwalder, A., & Pigneur, Y. (2009). *Business model generation.* Hoboken, NJ: Wiley.

Ramoglou, S., & Tsang, E. W. K. (2016). A realist perspective of entrepreneurship: Opportunities as propensities. *Academy of Management Review, 41*(3), 410–434.

Ries, E. (2011). *The lean startup.* New York, NY: Crown Publishing Group.

Rittel, H. W. J., & Webber, M. M. (1973). Dilemmas in a general theory of planning. *Policy Sciences, 4,* 155–169.

Romme, A. G. L. (2003). Making a difference: Organization as design. *Organization Science, 14,* 558–573.

Rondstadt, R. (1988). The corridor principle. *Journal of Business Venturing, 3*(1), 31–40.

Sarason, Y., Dean, T., & Dillard, J. F. (2006). Entrepreneurship as the nexus of individual and opportunity: A structuration view. *Journal of Business Venturing, 21,* 286–305.

Sarasvathy, S. D. (2001). Causation and effectuation: Toward a theoretical shift from economic inevitability to entrepreneurial contingency. *Academy of Management Review, 26,* 243–263.

Sarasvathy, S. D. (2003). Entrepreneurship as a science of the artificial. *Journal of Economic Psychology, 24,* 203–220.

Sarasvathy, S. D. (2012). Worldmaking. In A. C. Corbett & J. A. Katz (Eds.), *Entrepreneurial action* (Vol. 14, pp. 1–24). Advances in Entrepreneurship, Firm Emergence and Growth. Bingley, UK: Emerald Group Publishing Limited.

Sarasvathy, S. D., Dew, N., Read, S., & Wiltbank, R. (2008). Designing organizations that design environments: Lessons from entrepreneurial expertise. *Organization Studies, 29,* 331–350.

Schon, D. A. (1983). *The reflective practitioner.* New York, NY: Basic Books.

Schon, D. A. (1987). *Educating the reflective practitioner.* San Francisco, CA: Jossey-Bass.

Schwenk, T. (1996). *Sensitive* chaos. Forest Row: Sophia Books.

Selden, P. D., & Fletcher, D. E. (2015). The entrepreneurial journey as an emergent hierarchical system of artifact-creating processes. *Journal of Business Venturing, 30*(4), 603–615.

Shackle, G. L. S. (1955). *Uncertainty in economics and other reflections.* Cambridge: Cambridge University Press.

Shane, S., & Venkataraman, S. (2000). The promise of entrepreneurship as a field of research. *Academy of Management Review, 25,* 217–226.

Simon, H. A. (1969/1996). *The sciences of the artificial.* Cambridge, MA: MIT Press. (First edition published in 1969; third edition in 1996).

Van Aken, J. E., & Romme, A. G. L. (2012). A design-science approach to evidence-based management. In D. M. Rousseau (Ed.), *The Oxford handbook of evidence-based management.* New York, NY: Oxford University Press.

Van Burg, E., Romme, A. G. L., Gilsing, V. A., & Reymen, I. M. M. J. (2008). Creating university spin-offs: A science-based design perspective. *Journal of Product Innovation Management, 25,* 114–128.

Van Burg, J. C., & Romme, A. G. L. (2014). Creating the future together: Toward a framework for research synthesis in entrepreneurship. *Entrepreneurship Theory and Practice, 38,* 369–397.

Venkataraman, S. (1997). The distinctive domain of entrepreneurship research. In J. A. Katz (Ed.), *Advances in entrepreneurship, firm emergence, and growth* (Vol. 3, pp. 119–138). Greenwich, CT: JAI Press.

Venkataraman, S., Sarasvathy, S., Dew, N., & Forster, W. R. (2012). Whither the promise? Moving forward with entrepreneurship as a science of the artificial. *Academy of Management Review, 37*(1), 21–33.

Vincenti, W. (1993). *What engineers know and how they know it.* Baltimore, MD: The Johns Hopkins University Press.

Weick, K. E. (1979). *The social psychology of organizing.* Reading, MA: Addison-Wesley.

CHAPTER 2

SOCIOCULTURAL CONTEXT, ENTREPRENEUR TYPES, MINDSETS AND ENTREPRENEURIAL ACTION IN TIRADENTES, BRAZIL

Reed E. Nelson, Anderson Santana and Matthew S. Wood

ABSTRACT

Entrepreneurship involves complex interactions between individuals and environments but there is little research on these dynamics. We address this gap by conducting an inductive qualitative study of entrepreneurs in the exclusive tourist destination of Tiradentes, Brazil. Tiradentes has a unique architectural, cultural, and economic heritage that serves as a unique sociocultural backdrop that influences entrepreneurs' models of start-up thinking and action. Specifically, our investigation revealed that entrepreneurs' backgrounds (native vs. nonnative) and social identities come together with the sociocultural fabric of the community in a way that moved them towards a "Joia" or "Bijuteria" orientation, each

Models of Start-up Thinking and Action: Theoretical, Empirical and Pedagogical Approaches
Advances in Entrepreneurship, Firm Emergence and Growth, Volume 18, 33–74
ISSN: 1074-7540/doi:10.1108/S1074-754020160000018002

of which were associated with a distinct mindset. This diversity had implications for entrepreneurs' conceptualizations of start-up models possible within the backdrop of Tiradentes sociocultural fabric and this influenced the actions entrepreneurs took such as the geographic location chosen for the business and the business practices used. We discovered that entrepreneurs favoring one orientation over another tended to occupy predictable physical and social positions in the community while also espousing similar values and perspectives. These results are used to elaborate the theory on the link between the external and internal explanation for entrepreneurial thinking and action. The net effect is new understanding regarding ways models of start-up thinking and action can be investigated.

Keywords: Entrepreneurship; entrepreneurial action; entrepreneur types; entrepreneur mindsets; Brazil

INTRODUCTION

An entrepreneur is "someone who specializes in taking responsibility for and making judgmental decisions that affect the location, the form, and the use of goods, resources or institutions."

Hebert and Link (1988, p. 155)

Entrepreneurship involves individuals interacting with their environments to introduce new products or services to specific markets. In this regard, Herbert and Link's characterization of entrepreneurs is powerful because it is indicative of the central role entrepreneurs play as they think about business start-ups both as planning techniques and as patterns of structured action designed to effectively allocate resources while trying something new. It is also provocative because it highlights the varied impacts that models of start-up thinking and action can have as entrepreneurs allocate resources in ways that shape the evolution of their sociocultural environment. This means that thinking and action are central to the entrepreneurial process and this has resulted in a substantial body of research devoted to understanding the drivers of entrepreneurial thinking and action (Klein, 2008; McMullen & Shepherd, 2006; Sarasvathy, 2012). These efforts have generally favored one of two approaches. The first approach takes an *internal* focus where entrepreneurial thinking and action is seen largely as driven by idiosyncratic dispositions, knowledge, or experience. In this view the environment is typically held constant as variations between individuals are considered the source of action (Corbett, 2005; Dimov, 2010; Hull, Bosely, & Udell, 1980). The second approach is an *external* perspective that problematizes changes in the environment by suggesting that it is these changes that serve as the stimulus for entrepreneurs' actions (Holcombe, 2003; Shane, 2003). Adopting the external perspective requires holding the entrepreneur constant so that one can document how variations in environmental variables influence thinking and action.

Despite the pioneering insights these two perspectives provide, important limitations occur when either perspective is used by itself. The internal approach comes at the cost of assuming environments are equal, while the external approach comes at the expense of assuming that entrepreneurs are homogenous. Each approach rests on its own unique set of assumptions so that the two research streams are developing along parallel but separate paths. The fear, then, is that by keeping these perspectives largely separate, the limitations associated with each perspective may lead to the creation of a picture of entrepreneurial thinking and action that lacks explanatory power. Chiles, Meyer, and Hench (2004) reinforce this as they point out that an exclusive reliance on external perspectives, for example, is problematic because: "causes flow down from contexts rather than up from actors, such studies offer ... only an infinite regress of higher level contexts" (p. 500). Similar criticisms can be made of an exclusive reliance on internal perspectives. The point is that entrepreneurs operate in dynamic environments (McKelvie et al., 2011) and each individual brings their own idiosyncrasies to these environments as they decide on a course of action (Grégoire et al., 2011; Stinchfield et al., 2012; Wood, McKelvie, & Haynie, 2013). Hence, to develop more comprehensive models of start-up thinking and action we need to forge robust ties between the external and internal perspectives.

The purpose of our study is to build a tighter link between the internal and external approaches through *theory elaboration* (Lee, Mitchell, & Sabylinski, 1999) where we "contrast preexisting understanding with observed events" to expand theory in way that better explains the dynamics of start-up thinking and action models (Greenwood & Suddaby, 2006, p. 31). In that spirit, we inductively derive theoretical insights about the ways entrepreneurs conceptualize start-up techniques and discern patterns of structured action by studying entrepreneurs' thoughts, feelings, and actions within the environments where they live and work. To do so, we follow research that suggests the community is an important context within which entrepreneurial thinking and action takes place (e.g., Mezias & Kuperman, 2001) and using the community as a setting we ask: How do communities and individuals come together to spawn distinct types of entrepreneurs and what mindsets and actions (e.g., choices entrepreneurs make in setting up and managing their businesses) are associated with those distinctions? Investigating this question is paramount if we are to understand how the reciprocal relationship between entrepreneurs and their environments drive entrepreneurial thinking and action.

An investigation of this nature requires us to work across multiple units of analysis (i.e., entrepreneur, firm, community), but it also forces us to reconsider some of the assumptions that underpin mainline research on entrepreneurial action. The literature to date implicitly assumes that entrepreneurs have full discretion over the form, location, and timing of action (e.g., McMullen & Shepherd, 2006). However, if circumstances at least partially determine entrepreneurial action, as Grégoire et al. (2011) and others have argued, then this assumption is problematic. Entrepreneurs are likely faced with structural, social, and economic considerations that constrain what models of start-up thinking and action are acceptable and in turn this determines when, where, and how action unfolds. These constraints may be self-imposed by individual perceptions and inclinations (Stinchfield, Nelson, & Wood, 2012) or superimposed by institutional forces (Bradley, Shepherd, & Wiklund, 2011). In either case, it is clear that entrepreneurs have freedom to design their firms, but must do so within the confines of contextual constraints (Venkataraman et al., 2012). Because the literature to date has not thoroughly considered the constraints faced by entrepreneurs we must remain open to the possibility that there are complex considerations in play as the entrepreneur decides on the form, location, and timing of the start-up model.

By reconsidering entrepreneurial thinking and action in a way that simultaneously allows for variations in individuals *and* circumstances, gaps in current theory become apparent. Specifically, we suffer from an incompleteness problem (Locke & Golden Biddle, 1997) because we have yet to account for how one's background, experience, attitudes, and so on come together with the various aspects of sociocultural contexts that influence the thinking and actions of even the most individualistic entrepreneurs. Our research addresses this by elaborating existing theory through insights derived from an inductive qualitative study of entrepreneurs, their thinking and actions within the community of Tiradentes, Brazil. Because of its history and setting, Tiradentes offers a unique opportunity to study the entrepreneur-sociocultural context interaction. Tiradentes is a rather isolated community in the mountains of Brazil that went from a gold rush town in the 1700s, to partial abandonment in the 1800s, and was then "rediscovered" as a symbol of authentic Brazilian culture during the first part of the 20th century. Today, Tiradentes is one of the premier tourist destinations in Brazil and is being transformed by entrepreneurial activity. Given this history and the criticality of entrepreneurial activity within the community, Tiradentes is an appropriate venue for studying models of start-up thinking and action and allows us to do so from the vantage point of an emerging economy which is comparatively underrepresented in entrepreneurial studies (Bruton, Ahlstrom, & Obloj, 2008).

CONCEPTUAL GROUNDING

Differentiating Entrepreneurs as an Internal Approach

Since the early days of entrepreneurship research, scholars have recognized that entrepreneurs are unique. Early studies of entrepreneurship sought to distinguish between entrepreneurs as a special category and the rest of the population (Carland & Carland, 1992; Hornaday & Bunker, 1970). Many studies attempted to develop a profile of entrepreneurs by documenting traits and characteristics unique to the class. The hope was that differences in these profiles could be used to predict who is more or less likely to engage in entrepreneurial action. While many insights have been gleaned from this endeavor, empirical results have been mixed (see Rauch & Frese, 2007; Stewart & Roth, 2001; Zhao & Seibert, 2006, for reviews). Although entrepreneurs often exhibit comparatively high ratings on some trait dimensions, such as need for achievement (Brandstätter, 2011), these traits do not readily correlate with entrepreneurial action (Brockhaus, 1980; Koh, 1996). Hence it appears that researchers limited their analytical perspectives by classifying entrepreneurs under a single umbrella. To escape this, researchers have slowly shifted from looking at how entrepreneurs are different from the population at large to considerations of how they vary one from another. In 2004, Sarasvathy, for example, dedicated the better part of an influential article to the proposition that the assumption of homogeneity among entrepreneurs hampers efforts to more fully understand entrepreneurship as a phenomenon.

The field's early focus on distinguishing entrepreneurs as a distinct group, followed by contemporary work distinguishing entrepreneurs from one another, is at the core of the internal approach to entrepreneurial action. Specifically, the internal perspective assumes that characteristics unique to the individual facilitate or constrain the recognition of business opportunities and the actions taken to capitalize on them. In that spirit, it has been shown that characteristics such as alertness (Gaglio & Katz, 2001); knowledge (Baron & Ensley, 2006); and experience (Corbett, 2005) are all related to entrepreneurial action.

This line of research is nearly silent regarding what action entrepreneurs take and to what effect. There is, however, a small but growing body of literature that looks at the specific actions entrepreneurs take and why they take them. Baker and Nelson (2005), for example, discovered a class of entrepreneurs called "bricoleurs" who use non-conventional methods to meet the basic needs of cost conscious customers. Likewise, Stinchfield et al. (2012) document stark differences in identities, goals, and work practices between entrepreneurs in five categories. These differences influenced the types of actions entrepreneurs took (e.g., borrowing capital vs. bootstrapping) as some individuals sought to "get rich" while others looked to "get by." Similarly, Fauchart and Gruber (2011) reveal that entrepreneurs vary in their social identities and these variations influence strategic decisions about what customer needs are met, who is served, and what resources are used in the process.

Taken together, the studies outlined above reveal that entrepreneurs vary in goals, motivation, and identities. The entrepreneur's social identity, in particular, appears to be a salient factor. Navis and Glynn (2010) point out that identities are supported by narratives that give people a sense of "who we are" and "what we do." These identity-driven narratives, in turn, are thought influence the goals people set for themselves and their ventures and the actions taken (Hogg & Terry, 2000). It is important to note that identities are related to social relationships and membership in social categories (Fauchart & Gruber, 2011; Vignoles et al., 2000). This is where the internal approach to explaining entrepreneurial action begins to break down because it largely assumes away the idea that questions of "who are we" and "what do we do" are conditioned by circumstances. A member of an Amish community, for instance, would answer the "what do we do" question very differently than someone living in the suburbs of Seattle. Yes, the internal aspects of their identity are different, but so are the environments where they live and work. As such, we need to simultaneously consider the role sociocultural context plays.

Sociocultural Context as an External Approach

At the same time that mainline entrepreneurial studies have investigated the internal approach, there has been interest from diverse quarters in the context or environment where entrepreneurship plays out. If early thinking on entrepreneurship emphasized individual attributes and microeconomic individualism (Carland et al., 1996; Collins & Moore, 1964; Hornaday & Bunker, 1970; Schumpeter, 1942), it is now much more common to think of entrepreneurship as taking place within a social and cultural context. At the epistemological level, the tendency to see entrepreneurship as enactments rather than objective discoveries (Companys & McMullen, 2007) has provoked a greater interest in social contexts (Baker & Nelson, 2005; Dimov, 2010; Wood & McKinley, 2010). At a more practical level, scholars and practitioners from policy studies and community development have long recognized that the actions of local entrepreneurs drive regional development and this leads to initiatives designed to stimulate entrepreneurial activity (Hindle, 2010; Selsky & Smith, 1994). At the same time, it has been documented that certain geographical regions, such as Massachusetts Rt 128, Silicon Valley, or Branson Missouri generate disproportionate numbers of entrepreneurial events (Dana, 1995; Hagan, 1962; Hwang & Powell, 2009; Kenney, 2000; Lee et al., 2000).

The studies outlined above vary in theoretical orientation and unit of analysis, but nonetheless are indicative of the external explanation for entrepreneurial action, that is, that the environment in which entrepreneurship occurs plays a vital role in enabling, constraining, and imprinting the timing and type of action taken. Definitions and operationalizations of the environment or context vary (e.g., ethnic entity, industrial space, national or geographical entity), but the common idea is that the setting where entrepreneurs act influences their behaviors and outcomes and at the same time entrepreneurs themselves influence the environments in which they are embedded. This is consistent with the idea that members of a collective must translate actions and events into shared understanding (Daft & Weick, 1984) and that understanding constitutes the social structure (i.e., norms, rules, and conditions) that constrains action (Giddens, 1979). However, it is also well understood that actors have the ability to modify social structures in a way that allows them to move toward an envisioned future (Giddens, 1984; Shackle, 1979). As such, the recursive relationship between human agency and structure is an important part of entrepreneurship.

Community Context as a Link

As we argued in the introduction, a more powerful theory of models of start-up thinking and action is likely if closer ties between the external and internal perspectives can be established. It is clear that these two perspectives are complimentary, but they take very different approaches. One way to bring the perspectives together is to focus on entrepreneurs' local community (e.g., where they live and work) because of the immediacy and intimacy of the local environment. Studies that simultaneously work at the level of the community and that of individual entrepreneurs are rare, but there are precedents. Two exemplary studies are Mezias and Kuperman's (2001) study of the early U.S. film industry and Chiles, Meyer, and Hench's (2004) study of entrepreneurial dynamics in Branson, Missouri. The Mezias and Kupferman study identified the ways in which different actors in the early U.S. film industry influenced the evolution of a new business sector through their various actions that included competitive actions and cooperative behavior. Chiles et al.'s study of new enterprise creation in Branson documents how historical accidents, local culture and government, and outmigration of prominent musical acts from Nashville together created a "dissipative structure" which encouraged diversity and dynamism in start-up techniques and this resulted in channeling specific resources into the local community.

The value of both studies to our investigation is that they demonstrate the utility of conceptualizing exogenous institutional forces as drivers of start-up thinking and action at the same time they connect to the internal approach by showing how exogenous social structures are the result of a particular configuration of individuals, their dispositions, beliefs, interrelationships and resources. The lesson here is that the community is reciprocally intertwined with the individual and by including community level variables and the interactions between the sociocultural fabric of the community and the individual entrepreneur, a tighter link between the external and internal explanations for entrepreneurial thinking and action may be achieved.

The idea of using the community as a structural link to the individual agent brings to our mind what Giddens (1984) called *contextuality* — situated interactions in time and space (p. 373). Giddens proposed that human thinking and action flows from a set of interactions that occur in a specific time and context. By considering the community as a context for the thinking and actions of entrepreneurial agents, contextuality becomes a construct that may be a useful addition to entrepreneurship theory because it holds the potential to bridge between internal and external explanations. By investigating this bridge we can better understand how a given community would become populated by entrepreneurs who hold disparate views, as well as why the mix of entrepreneurs and start-up models utilized within a given community, might have important implications for the economic and social climate of that community. Despite the conceptual importance of such dynamics, we are unaware of research that explicitly tackles these questions, especially in emerging economies. It is with these ideas in mind we entered the field.

METHOD

Theory Elaboration via Inductive Study

In the absence of well-developed theory that concomitantly considers the influence of the circumstances where entrepreneurship is to take place alongside the idiosyncrasies of the entrepreneur and how these variations influence entrepreneurial action and community dynamics, our study relied on qualitative methods and theory elaboration techniques. Theory elaboration is a form of inductive research where scholars differ sharply in the degree to which they entertain the usage of preexisting constructs in guiding data collection and interpretation (Glaser, 1978; Glaser, 1992; Kelle, 2005; Strauss, 1987; Strauss & Corbin, 1998). Despite this dissensus, most qualitative methodologists would agree that the less that is known about a phenomenon, the less researchers should impose preconceived ideas on the data and the later in the research process they should do so (Denzin & Lincoln, 2000; Kelle, 2004, 2005). Given the comparative novelty of our topic and the fact that research on entrepreneurship and community in the emerging world generally, and in Brazil specifically, is in its infancy our research leans heavily toward the ethnographic approach.

Although this research is not ethnographic in the strict sense of the term, it does employ a number of ethnographic techniques. The ethnographic paradigm is well established in a variety of disciplines (Hammersley & Atkinson, 1983) and involves protracted contact in a field setting and immersing oneself in people's daily lives and activities in hopes of documenting phenomena and extrapolating meaning (Denzin & Lincoln, 2000; Emerson, Fretz, & Shaw, 1995). Ethnographic methods, then, involve participating in the daily life of the community through observation, conversation, and interactions and those experiences are recorded as field notes (Denzin, 1997). These notes are then used inductively to build mid-range theories as the researcher moves from data to theory construction. One clear advantage of inductive methods is they allow the researcher to elaborate theory by avoiding overly imposing existing thinking on the investigation (Glaser & Strauss, 1967; Glaser, 1978; Padgett, 2004). Researchers enter the field with knowledge of existing theory and initial expectations of how things might unfold, but once immersed in the context, they allow the data to guide them as opposed to honoring commitments to an initial plan (Lee, Mitchell, & Sablynski, 1999). In our case, a loose commitment to existing theory was required because extant theories of entrepreneurship have been developed using data collected almost entirely from developed economies and thus may not be applicable in developing countries such as the Brazilian community we studied.

Site Selection and Data Collection

Tiradentes, in the state of Minas Gerais, attracted us as a research venue for a number of reasons. The comparatively rapid transformation of the town from an isolated backwater to a premier tourist destination holds an inherent fascination in its own right, but it is especially attractive to those interested in entrepreneurship and economic development. In many ways, Tiradentes is a Latin American version of what Lessinger (1987) calls "Penturbia," a fifth wave of economic and social development which involves an exodus to small towns with strong local values and cultures, historical heritage, and a strong sense of community. It poses interesting questions about the role of small enterprises in the development of human communities. Moreover, with increasing affluence in Brazil and the emerging countries generally, internal tourism has grown rapidly and it can be expected that Tiradentes' model of economic development will become more common and more important in the future (Ministerio de Turismo, 2009).

Further, Tiradente's relative isolation from globalizing forces was advantageous for us. The town has, to our knowledge, received no direct foreign investment, and does not rely on multinational corporations for employment or technical assistance. As a result, we could be reasonably certain that the community dynamics and entrepreneurial behaviors we observed were expressive of local culture and institutions. The small size (population 6,000–9,000) of the town and the generally smaller size of its enterprises were also useful for our purposes. In the absence of a dominant employer, we could expect a somewhat level playing field for different community actors (i.e., entrepreneurs) to mobilize varied start-up techniques and hence discern what makes different start-up approaches attractive to particular types of entrepreneurs. Finally, because of the community's size, the number of social actors needed to study to get a working knowledge of models of thinking and action in the community and resultant community dynamics was much more manageable than it would have been in a larger setting.

Our data collection followed best practices in qualitative inductive methods (e.g., Denzin & Lincoln, 2000; Emerson, Fretz, & Shaw, 1995; Glaser & Strauss, 1967; Patton, 1990). We first gathered as much formal historical data about the town, its people, and its surroundings as possible. This served two objectives. First, it allowed us to construct a historical timeline and picture of the evolution of the community and the role entrepreneurs played in that evolution (reported below). Second, it allowed us to follow the recommendations of Benbasat et al. (1987) to scan newspapers and directories, as well as talking with community members, to identify potential research sites and participants. This resulted in the generation of a list of informants that could be interviewed because they had been present during different periods of the town's development and/or had some personal involvement or contact with persons who were identified as being personally involved in the economic development of Tiradentes. Our approach also allowed us to engage in purposive sampling (Glaser & Strauss, 1967) to identify and subsequently interview a cross-section of Tiradentes entrepreneurs who have founded and are currently involved in a variety of business enterprises throughout the town.

In all we made 9 trips to Tiradentes and interviewed 40 different individuals from 34 different institutions or businesses in over 110 hours of interviews. We interviewed the owners of 29 local businesses in addition to managers, representatives of local government, foundations, artistic cooperatives, and the Catholic parish. Interviews varied in length and structure, and became more selective as the study progressed, but included personal background and relation to the community, their account of changes to the community over time, the history, actions, and structure of business with which they were involved (or those others were involved for non-entrepreneur informants), and their view of the ideal future of the community and what needed to happen to realize that ideal. Our interview data was complemented by an additional 42 hours of field observation where we took detailed field notes related to the layout of the town, the location, approximate age, style, usage and distribution of its buildings, groupings of businesses and their clientele, size and character of neighborhoods, behavior and interactions of the townspeople, visitors, and prominent entrepreneurs. Included in these 42 hours were several walkabouts through the town, meals in local restaurants, use of both public and private

transportation and assessing the time it takes to move between neighborhoods and buildings, identifying flows of people and vehicles, describing
the architectural and decorative features of landmarks, neighborhoods, and
streets, observing how the types and numbers of visitors that moved
through different sectors of the town, attending public events, patronizing
local establishments, and generally analyzing the uses of physical spaces in
the community. With three exceptions all of the interviews were profession-
ally transcribed and yielded a total of 673 pages of text. As our data collection unfolded we surveyed pertinent literature on entrepreneurship,
community development, and work from related disciplines (e.g., sociology,
political science, etc.) and reoriented our last interviews based on the
insights gleaned from constant comparison between interviews and iterat-
ing between our data and the literature (Denzin & Lincoln, 2000). As part
of this process, we interpreted and reinterpreted our results several times by
writing working papers, discussing our study with interested colleagues,
and following-up emerging concepts in subsequent interviews and queries
at the research site. Table 1 contains an enumeration of our 40 informants,
their gender, approximate age, approximate size and nature of their business or institution, distance from the town's principal plaza, organizational
title, and distance of their birthplace from Tiradentes.

Data Interpretation Process

Using the information gleaned from the sources above, we first develop a
detailed composite history of the town and its economic and social trajectory from the 1700s on. We attempted to identify and characterize phases
in the community's evolution and the major socioeconomic actors and
forces at work during each phase. We also attempted to identify each of
our sources in relation to their role in the community and their personal
exposure to events in the development of the town. Next, we used open
coding to identify major native view (Gregory, 1983) categories that sur-
faced in the interviews. To do this, two authors carefully read the interview
transcriptions and generated a primary and secondary list of (1) categories
of entrepreneurs; (2) influence *by* sociocultural context/community; (3)
mindsets; (4) actions taken or advocated; and (5) influence *on* sociocultural
context/community.

Discussion between the authors reached consensus on the identification
of two general entrepreneurial postures or models among informants along
three dimensions which distinguished entrepreneurs in the community from

Table 1. Description of Informants, Establishments, Locations, and Classifications.

Informant	Demographics (Age, Mar. Status, Gender)	Birth Distance	Former Work	Current Position	Business Type	Size (# empl.)	Business Location	Joia–Bijuteria	Mindset
1	45,S,F	300	IT Prof.	Own	Restaurant	8	C	J	C
2	45,D,F	300	Homemaker	Own	Restaurant	8	C	J	C
3	45,S,M	250	Fashion	Own	Restaurant	12	C	J	C
4	35,F,S	15	–	Own	Retail	15	C	B	I
5	45,S,M	15	Public	Tec.	Agency	25	P	B	I
6	20,S,M	0	–	Manager	Band	25	P	B	I
7	45,D,F	0	Sales	Own	Lodging	115	P	B	I
8	25,S,F	0	–	Manager	Lodging	115	P	B	C
9	50,M,M	25	Physician	Own	Lodging	15	P	B	I
10	55,M,M	15	Attorney	Own	Lodging	25	P	J	C
11	25,M,S	15	–	Manager	Lodging	25	P	B	I
12	30,S,F	350	Attorney	Own	Lodging	7	C	J	C
13	30,S,F	0	Craft	Own	Lodging	2	C	J	C
14	30,M,M	0	–	Own	Transport	1	C	B	I
15	50,D,F	250	Dancer	Own	Restaurant	12	C	B	I
16	45,M,M	250	Auto Exec.	Own	Restaurant	3	P	J	C
17	30,M,F	0	Promoter	Own	Restaurant	6	C	J	C
18	M	0	–	Own	Restaurant	4	C	J	C
19	45,D,F	400	Psycholog.	Own	Lodging	10	C	J	I
20	65,M,M	4,000	Manufact.	Own	Lodging	45	C	B	I
21	65,M,F	250	Professional	Own	Lodging	45	C	B	I
22	45,M,M	0	–	Manager	Lodging	45	C	J	C
23	35,S,M	0	Public	Alderman	Government	100	C	N/A	C
24	45,M,M	350	Public	Own	Promotion	2	C	J	C
25	30,M,F	250	Public	Own	Lodging	25	C	J	C

Table 1. (*Continued*)

Informant	Demographics (Age, Mar. Status, Gender)	Birth Distance	Former Work	Current Position	Business Type	Size (# empl.)	Business Location	Joia–Bijuteria	Mindset
26	30,M,M	250	IT Prof.	Own	Lodging	25	C	J	C
27	60,S,M	0	–	Cleric	Church	25	C	N/A	C
28	30,S,F	250	Exec. Airline	Own	Lodging	35	C	J	C
29	30,S,F	250	–	Own	Lodging	35	C	J	I
30	50,M,M	450	Craft	Own	Lodging	20	C	J	C
31	30,S,F	0	–	Manager	Education	25	P	B	I
32	50,S,M	450	–	Own	Art Studio	1	C	J	C
33	50,M,M	0	Craft	Manager	Foundation	15	C	J	C
34	30,S,F	0	Craft	Manager	Association	25	C	B	I
35	65,W,M	250	Professor	Historian	–	1	C	N/A	C
36	30,M,M	5,000	IT	Own	Restaurant	8	C	J	C
37	30,M,F	0	–	Own	Restaurant	8	C	J	I
38	45,M,M	0	Craft	Own	Manufacture	15	P	B	C
39	65,S,F	6,000	–	Own	Art Studio	1	C	J	C
40	25,M,M	250	–	Own	Restaurant	5	C	J	C

Key: S = single; M = married; D = divorced.
C = Center; P = Periphery.
J = Joia; B = Bijuteria.
C = Collective Preservation; I = Individual Exploitation.
Notes: All distances are in kilometers. Age, distance from central plaza, and birth distance are approximations. If "Former Work" is blank, the informant's first paid job is with the current venture.

one another. Once this process was complete we conducted an N-Vivo analysis of the interview transcriptions using the computer software to corroborate the themes and subthemes identified in the interviews (Flick, 2009). N-Vivo 8 was used to generate mutually exclusive and exhaustive primary and secondary categories along the same dimensions used in our manual analysis (Bowen, 2006; Denzin & Lincoln, 2000; Dey, 2007; Giola & Thomas, 1996; Miles & Huberman, 1994).The computer-driven analysis varied little from our subjective reading of the transcriptions and thus there was a high degree of agreement between the two approaches. Both identified several clear oppositional themes or categories used by community members in describing the community and its members. We subsequently confronted the results of our inductively derived dimensions with existing literature on entrepreneurial types and entrepreneurship across nations and experimented with a number of finer grained classifications of local actors. However, we discovered that our data fit best with coarser and more robust native categories we initially identified in our analyses. None of these subsequent analyses compromised or contradicted our initial categories. Indeed, we reached theoretical saturation (Glaser and Strauss; Denzin and Lincoln) for the dimensions discussed below in our interviews and nothing in our computer-aided analyses or engagement with the scholarly literature cast doubt on the validity of the categories uncovered and thus we now report the collective outcome of our research efforts.

SOCIOCULTURAL FABRIC OF TIRADENTES

The Historical Evolution

In the early 1700s gold was discovered in the rugged and isolated mountains of central Brazil. The resulting gold rush brought over 600,000 settlers — many of them African slaves — to the region in a comparatively short period of time. The upstart of a substantial number of towns and cities followed across the 300 mile swath of territory where gold was found. Some of these towns, like Ouro Preto, grew to rival the population of the large European cities of the time. Throughout the region there was a flurry of construction, including palatial residences, churches, government and commercial buildings in the baroque and rococo styles. The isolation of the region and difficulty of transportation and communication led to the development of a distinct local style which is still valued today both nationally and internationally. This was true not only of architecture, but also of art, music, and cuisine.

Because the distribution of gold was uneven, the communities spawned by the gold rush were widely dispersed and varied in size. Tiradentes was of modest size — less than 20,000 in population at its height, and was located about seven kilometers from another, larger mining town called Sao Joao del Rei. By the early 1800s the major deposits had been exhausted and the region's economy collapsed. The remaining population reverted to subsistence farming mixed with a small volume of cash crops and livestock. Tiradentes' neighbor, Sao Joao de Rei, diminished but maintained some population because of its initially greater size and favorable location on an important trade route. Tiradentes, by contrast, was largely abandoned except for a few extended families that clung to the land and a handful of artisans who precariously carried on metal working trades. One unintended consequence of the abandonment of Tiradentes was the nearly complete preservation of the town's architectural and natural setting.

After a century of abandonment Tiradentes was "rediscovered" by members of the cultural elite — especially Brazilian artists and writers — during the first part of the 20th century. During this period there was a strong nativistic movement which attempted to redefine and celebrate Brazilian national identity, and it turned to the country's colonial past as part of this effort (Frota & Peterson, 1993). Because the towns' isolation favored the formation and preservation of a unique cultural identity, they attracted interest as a source and symbol of authentic Brazilian culture. Tiradentes' small size, coupled with relative ease of access, favored its emergence as an elite tourist enclave. This emergence was further favored when M. d. C. Nabuco, a wealthy woman from a regional dynasty, took an interest in the architecture of the town and established a foundation to catalogue and preserve local buildings, landmarks, and religious artifacts. This effort resulted in government decrees prohibiting demolition or substantial alteration of the town's historic buildings.

The small size, comparative ease of access, and preservation of the town made it an ideal location for the production of historical films and TV programs, and from the 1960s on the town was frequently used as a set by Brazil's major network, Rede Globo. Film production not only made the town more well known, it provoked frequent visits by Brazilian actors and producers, reinforcing elite exposure and stimulating demand for upscale accommodations and restaurants. Because the town was small and reasonably accessible, but not too accessible, and because visitors tended to belong to national elites, businesses tended to be small and focused on high-end products or services. Lodging and restaurants, for example, were concentrated in small, boutique "Pousadas" often situated in historical structures. However, changes were in the wind.

The frequent appearance of the town in media productions popularized Tiradentes as a tourist destination, and it began to receive regular tour bus traffic. All of this occurred in the absence of large hotels, restaurants, convention centers, or shopping malls as these larger scale commercial enterprises did not emerge until the 1990s and even today are comparatively rare. However, the increased number of visitors did have an important effect as they stimulated larger scale business and reduced purchases per capita, thereby triggering the emergence of street commerce, souvenir shops and convenience stores. The town also began to sponsor seasonal festivals of different types, which brought more varied publics to the town in large numbers during certain periods. No longer were Tiradentes businesses simply catering to the elite, but instead entrepreneurs had to at least consider accommodating a more diversified client base. Even with these considerations, the small boutique shop in historic buildings remains the dominate business model today as over 200 of these businesses currently dot the town.

Part of the reason that the boutique model seems to have endured is that as Brazil's economy matured and diversified, Tiradentes began to attract a wave of educated, middle-class "corporate refugees" who founded boutique style lodging, bars, shops, or restaurants. These migrants were educated and sophisticated, but possessed few entrepreneurial planning skills and only modest capital. They joined earlier migrants including numerous prominent artists who had formed a small corps of outsiders who had taken an interest in the town. At the same time, some natives of the region began to found businesses, often leveraging inherited real estate and family ties as resources. The beginning of the 21st century found the town full of small-scale entrepreneurial activity that had resulted in a prosperous community, with full employment, and robust growth, but collectively unsure of how to prosper in the future without diminishing the natural and cultural assets that led to its current prosperity. The city government appears to be of little help in discerning a viable economic path for the community because the small government has historically been in the hands of two rival family dynasties that have lived in the town for generations but had minimal involvement in local businesses. They often compete for the loyalty of townspeople by offering city jobs and public works projects to residents on a patronage basis. This creates a predictable, but ineffective regulatory environment for economic growth.

Developmental Trajectory

Our historical investigation, observations, and interviews revealed that the historical trajectory of the town stimulated a number of salient community issues and distinct groups formed around these issues. Our interviews, in particular, suggest that despite the very favorable current economic position of Tiradentes, and the small size of the community, the town is undergoing a process of economic and social transformation. Moreover, this process is marked by strong antitheses and contradictions which, among other things, impeded certain models of start-up thinking and action (McMullen & Shepherd, 2006) and serve as an especially significant barrier to concerted coordination and collective action by business owners as a class. We identified four major themes around which these tensions exits: (1) differences between geographic sectors in the town; (2) distinction between natives and nonnatives; (3) differences in identities and mindsets; (4) differences in the business practices; and (5) differences in visions for the future of the community. These themes were clearly associated with oppositional dichotomies that appeared frequently in our interviews and were easily identified both in our manual coding and were confirmed by N-Vivo word counts and nodes: Center-Periphery, Outsider-Native (ET-Minhoca in Portuguese), Original-Imitation (Joia-Bijuteria in Portuguese), and Individualism-Collectivism. Table 1 contains a summary of where we located each business owner or manager interviewed on these dimensions. We now discuss each of these dimensions in detail.

Geographic Sectors: Center versus Periphery

As the result of the notable increase in tourist traffic that occurred during the 1990s, the historic downtown district became distinguished from the rest of the town. The downtown district is dedicated primarily to commercial activity, despite the desires of some that the area entertain a greater proportion of cultural spaces and activity. Entrepreneurs covet downtown locations because most tourist traffic flows to that area. Because of this, most decisions which have implications for the cultural identity or quality of life of the town appear to focus on what is happening in the downtown area. Questions of vehicle and animal traffic, the location and routing of public transportation, the extent and intrusiveness of public works, and the nature and scheduling of seasonal events and festivals all take on comparatively greater significance when they involve the downtown historical district. Although lip service is paid to ensuring the quality of life for local residents, most would agree that investments in the historical district focus on economic considerations by making it tourist friendly rather than resident friendly. As a result, the interests, habits, and daily movement of the local residents are often a secondary concern.

Any space not belonging to the downtown district belongs to what is called the "periphery" (*periferia*), which in this setting can be translated as "neighborhoods" or "outlying" areas. Before the rebirth of the town as an upscale tourist destination, this area was sparsely settled with small farms and modest homesteads. The redevelopment of the town has changed this area so that it is now occupied in three contrasting ways. First, because the historical real estate in the downtown area has increased in value many fold, people who used to live downtown have sold or rented their properties to businesses and have built comfortable residences in the periphery neighborhoods. Second, because the periphery is not subject to the same restrictions as the historic district, in terms of size and style of buildings permitted, businesses which are larger in scale (e.g., larger hotels and shops, convention centers, and the like) are located there. Finally, residents who occupied modest housing before the tourist boom are still there, and these modest homes are mixed in with the businesses and more sumptuous housing. The difference between the use of space, the amount of time it takes to get from one place to another, the nature of buildings, population density, and degree of visible activity are palpable and was one of the things that we first noticed during our original contact with the field. Later, during the interviews, it became apparent that this geographical distinction interlocked with a host of social effects.

VARIANCE BETWEEN ENTREPRENEURS IN TIRADENTES

Native versus Nonnative

Another antinomy that emerged as the result of the community's unique historical path is that of "locals" and "outsiders." Much of the population growth in the town has come in the form of migrants who were attracted to Tiradentes' cultural atmosphere and natural setting. Entrepreneurs born in Tiradentes tended to employ different strategies and tactics in their business than from those outside, but the distinction goes beyond business practices or style to include worldview, mindset, and other factors. The distinction between native and nonnative was also the focus of considerable mistrust and tension, particularly on the part of the natives. The oppositional pair used in the town to identify natives and nonnatives is extratiradenter or "ETs" versus "worms" (*minhocas*). Although the flavor of these terms is somewhat difficult to render into English, it is possible to describe the symbolism. The ET, or extraterrestrial, implies something exotic and strange, with perhaps superior knowledge and capability but limited understanding of the local system and events. The "worm" by contrast comes from the ground and is more limited in its horizons, but also more "down to earth."

The terms express well the perceptions and frustrations of the natives vis-a-vis outsiders whose formal education, cosmopolitan experience, and external contacts make it apparently easier for these entrepreneurs to develop businesses that attract a similarly esoteric clientele that pays astronomical prices to sleep in old buildings and eat local specialties. The cultural differences between outsiders and natives create tension between business owners not only in the political realm but also in the relation between owners and employees, as we will see below. Despite these tensions, the ETs that remain in Tiradentes (there is a contingent of people who make the move to the town, but leave after a few years) appear to identify strongly with the community. They not only see Tiradentes as home, they tend to see themselves as change agents with a mission to improve the community socially, economically, and politically. The following passages from different informants are expressive of how this division is seen:

> There is a dichotomy in the local society separating people from outside and those that are already here—the originals, and the ETs. This makes alliances difficult and is of course a factor causing disharmony. Without fail, outsiders have more capital, more know-how, and more understanding of business. They end up getting established faster. They have outside contacts. The locals don't develop a network outside of the town. The outsiders come here with their network developed already, which is of course an advantage. This creates a climate of resentment and looks like exploitation, but it's not really the case. On the contrary, the outsiders don't come to exploit, they come to collaborate. But because the locals have a much harder time, it's difficult to collaborate. (Informant 19, Nonnative Female, Joia Owner)

> We have two opposites here, living side by side, and it causes a lot of division and friction because principally we who moved in from outside (the ETs) we brought the technique, the discipline, the good intentions, and the science, one might say to make something that's going to be sustainable. That conflicts with the local philosophy. It's not nice to say, but that's the way it is. (Informant 28, Nonnative Female, Joia Owner)

> We like to say that we are more "Tiradentinos" than they (the natives) are because they were born here and have never seen anything else. They've never been to Rio, never

> seen the ocean ....But we've been all over the world and we came here at our option. I wonder how many natives look at these mountains and say "Goodness, how beautiful." Every day I wake up and say, 'God, thanks for letting me live here'. (Informant 1, Nonnative Female, Joia Owner)

Native and nonnative and center versus periphery appear to constitute the most important and general oppositional dynamics in the town, but they are not the only ones. The last three oppositional pairs we discovered in our analyses covary and interrelate with the first two (center-periphery and native vs. nonnative), but they are expressed more within the social identities and mindsets of different entrepreneurs than they are at the general community level.

Social Identities and Entrepreneur Types

The unique sociocultural dynamics at work in Tiradentes appear to have both encouraged and constrained entrepreneurs in a variety ways. Specifically, entrepreneurs develop social identities and beliefs that are distinct but shared among others with similar views. Specifically, there is an important distinction between entrepreneurs who see their businesses as a reflection of their identity and mission and those for whom their business is seen in more utilitarian terms. The first category appears to be motivated by the opportunity to pursue a small town lifestyle. These entrepreneurs use start-up models that do not necessarily emphasize growth or profits. Their businesses are seen as extensions of their social identity and hence part of their role in a face to face, personalized community. The following quotes are typical of statements by the first category:

> We're not in this for profit. We make some money, but not big profits. We live modestly in a rural town. We don't see ourselves as businesspeople at all. (Informant 20, Male, Nonnative, Joia Owner)

> When I got here I said to myself 'I'm going to do something different from just working and making money all the time. I want to have .... social impact'. (Informant 28, Female, Nonnative, Joia Owner)

> You don't leave a job in the corporate world and move to a community like Tiradentes to make money. It's a life option. (Informant 16, Male, Nonnative, Joia Owner and former executive in the automotive industry)

The entrepreneurs who fall into this category often engage in thinking and actions that are congruent with the community's historic past and emphasis on cultural preservation. The local term used to describe these entrepreneurs is "joia" which can be roughly translated to "a jewel," "the original," or "the real thing." A "joia" in Portuguese, as in English, is something valuable and rare, which has aesthetic and status value. The symbolism contained in this term is descriptive of how informants view this group of entrepreneurs and the entrepreneurial actions they take. The "joias" (which are recognized by entrepreneurs and townspeople alike) seek to preserve and express the unique culture of the region in their products and services. They also take a long-term orientation to the business, and tend to be compliant with tax and other state regulations which are frequently ignored in Brazil.

The views and actions of the "joia" entrepreneurs contrast sharply with another distinct category of entrepreneur found in Tiradentes. These individuals are not motivated by the small town lifestyle, but instead see their business as a profit maximizing endeavor that is formed in response to perceived opportunities, like the existence of an underserved market that flourished during the 1990s when tourist traffic to the town increased considerably. This group of entrepreneurs frequently used financial and investment language in our interviews and spoke often of business growth and superior financial returns. The quote below contains the admiring description of a colleague by one local owner that is indicative of entrepreneurs that fall in this second category:

> She [a bijuteria owner] has a restaurant and now she's building a convention center for two thousand people, and a heliport. She already has a hall for big events that will hold 1500 people. She has an excellent industrial kitchen. During the gastronomy festival some of the world's best chefs came to her property. She has a furniture store, a bath and bed store, a craft store, anything you could want. She sells everything. She has the best hotel in town and you can buy the sheets right off your bed. She grew very quickly and occupied a bunch of different market niches. (Informant 28, Female, Nonnative, Joia Owner)

A less somewhat less admiring description of the same person by a native describes the same style:

> She has excellent commercial sense. Anything she touches turns to gold. But she is methodical and cold. Her workers are only valued for what they can produce. She doesn't let anything or anybody hold her back. She goes out and gets what she wants. That's why she grows. (Informant 31, Female, Native, Bijuteria Owner)

Clearly, the actions of this entrepreneur reflect a very different ideal than the sentiments expressed by those in the "joia" category. These opportunity-focused entrepreneurs and their businesses are called "bijuteria," which means "trinket," or "costume jewelry." Costume jewelry has an aesthetic purpose, but because it is not expensive or rare, it is considered a copy of the original, or an item that may hold attraction but not value. Here again, the symbolism contained in the term "bijuteria" is descriptive of how informants view these individuals and their actions. Specifically, the "bijuteria" businesses are often well managed, efficient, and have excellent service or product quality, but do so without any particular effort to preserve the identity or cultural legacy of the town. They use start-up models that are growth oriented, volume focused, and market driven and thus engage in aggressive promotion and management of activities that increase tourist traffic and bring customers to the area. These entrepreneurs may or may not comply willingly and rigorously with local laws and regulations.

The distinct differences in identity between the "joia" and "bijuteria" entrepreneurs are further reflected in the leadership and personal interactions found in the businesses. We found that the "joia" entrepreneurs emphasized personal relations with customers, community members, and emphasized the personal development of employees. In comparison, the "bijuteria" entrepreneurs emphasized efficiency in the execution of tasks. The "joia" businesses attempted to develop their personnel far beyond what was required by their immediate task environment. For example, "joia" business owners frequently enrolled their employees in literacy programs, made sure that workers stayed in school and even helped pay for college education in some cases. As a result, their businesses often experienced lower turnover and managers were frequently promoted from the ranks of loyal long-term staff. Formalized standards and policies were uncommon except for those required to comply with Brazilian labor laws. Entrepreneurs in the "bijuteria" category favored a less personal work environment, stressing deadlines, explicit performance standards, evaluation and reward systems based on explicit norms, and the use of formal hierarchy to monitor employee behavior. In this regard, they broke with the tradition of personalistic, long-term relations and reciprocity that are typical of Tiradentes in particular and small communities in Brazil generally. They also preferred to hire migrants from outside the region because they viewed them as better workers. The following quotes are expressive of differences in the discourses of the two categories. The first quote is from a prosperous "bijuteria" entrepreneur who owns a sizable hotel, the second from "joia" entrepreneur who owns a small but exclusive pousada:

> *Bijuteria Owner:* For example, we have a particular way of working. We work like a corporation. You don't see employees out shooting the breeze at work. Everyone is working, producing. The employees that are from Tiradentes don't really care ... We don't have many local employees, but the ones we have don't want to be subordinates,

they want to work on their terms. That's why I say we need to modernize, there needs to be a more qualified workforce here. We need to work on service, discipline, and hierarchy. We started an employee campaign called "Giants of the Hotel" with a special shirt. Today it's that girl over there in green shirt. (Informant 7, Female, Native, Bijuteria Owner)

Joia Entrepreneur: So our hotel was the first in town where everyone is registered officially with a right to holidays and profit sharing, everything. In terms of working climate we're outstanding, so much so that we have a retired worker who won't stop coming to work. This is like their home. Here they feel valued and respected. When they leave there is a real void in their lives .... I have a major concern and that is first not to be subservient and not to permit subservience to our guests or to ourselves as owners. We seek respect for our employees and we respect their legal rights. (Informant 20, Male, Nonnative Joia Owner)

This contrasts to the begrudging compliment rendered by a bijuteria owner who sees a future competitor in one of her subordinates:

Bijuteria Owner: One of my less educated employees does very well. He started waiting tables and in no time, he's leading the others. Clients ask for him by name. It won't be long before he starts his own business and I'm sure he'll do quite well. (Informant 4, Female, Native, Bijuteria Owner)

These comments illustrate two very different perspectives on the purpose of the business, and the way in which people should be treated. All of this appears to be heavily influenced by the social culture of the community and both constrain and facilitate certain types of behavior. For example, the "bijuteria" entrepreneur appears to feel constrained by the fact that local Tiradentes people do not really care and do not want to be subordinates. Yet, this same attitude facilitates the "joia" entrepreneur's business practices are based on not being subservient to customers. In both cases, the sociocultural fabric of the community is influencing the actions entrepreneurs take as they attempt to develop their business in a manner that fits their identity and vision. By extension, these actions feed into community dynamics via an ad-hoc and slow evolution that in the case of Tiradentes has been rather divisive. This has led to opposing views (by entrepreneurs and townspeople alike) regarding the future economic development of Tiradentes. We call these opposing viewpoints "preservation" versus "exploitation."

Collective Preservation versus Individual Exploitation Mindset

All of the entrepreneurs, whether born in Tiradentes or not, were concerned in some way with the disorderly growth of the town and the tendency for development in the retail and restaurant sectors to over-shadow the historical, artistic, and cultural appeal of the community. They stressed the need to conserve local historic and cultural capital and distinguished between "simple growth" and "true prosperity." The idea of "true prosperity" involved quality of life generally and particularly environmental conservation, protection of the town's historical and cultural assets, and the promotion of educational, cultural, and artistic endeavors. As a result some entrepreneurs were more sensitive to and vocal about the community's problems and deficiencies in water supply and quality, sewage treatment, and waste management, among other community issues. They were not only vocal, they were also active in attempting to develop collective initiatives to solve local problems and develop the community in more strategic and sustainable manner.

At the other extreme were entrepreneurs who were more individualistic in their activities and more oriented to the maximization of individual financial performance as opposed to collective prosperity. Their business practices were less concerned with possible negative impacts on the historic ambiance of the town, its culture or the day to day lives of its residents. They tended to be less optimistic about the potential for collective action as a vehicle for community development and tended to see little benefit in supporting public causes. Some typical contrasting statements follow:

> This is a big issue, and I am more concerned because the hotel needs the town. There's no point in making it (the hotel) nice inside if the minute you cross the threshold, you're in a different world. Just down the street there is a business that's incompatible with the ambiance of the town, and that's not good for our hotel. So for us, the big challenge is the town itself. All of the businesspeople and townspeople, they all need to get it through their heads that the heritage of the town isn't for sale. (Informant 12: Female, Nonnative, Joia Owner)

> It's a pity. Tirdentes is becoming famous as a place to eat. They say it's turning into a big shopping center. That's what they say in Belo Horizonte (the capital city of the state). They come here to eat and shop. They say we have no cultural life. Of course that's not true. We have cultural activities but they are under publicized and underfunded. We have art but it needs patronage sponsorship. Without sponsorship it remains small scale and people from outside don't know about it. (Informant 21, Female, Nonnative, Joia Owner)

Contrast these quotes with the less "preservationist" orientations below:

> My partner is bringing a big event to town. He's going to transform Tiradentes into a city like you'd find in the Southern United States. We're going to bring creole food here. It will be a super big deal with a lot of money. (Informant 26, Male, Nonnative, Bijuteria Owner)

I have a couple of evens that I do internally here. We brought in three famous chefs. We made it like a class, just for the guests. I do one just for guests and one open to the public. The difficult thing is to get the town to close down the street for something because the mayor is against our vision. Politically, if you don't vote for them all the doors are closed. That's a problem because if it will be good for everybody the city should support it despite any personal misgivings. That's the way I think at least. (Informant 7, Female, Native, Bijuteria Owner)

We've been trying to get the horse carriages out of the plaza for a long time, but we can't. We should have cafes and shops there, but with the horses it stinks to high heaven. It is tradition, but it's really bad for the tourist trade. (Informant 34, Female, Native, Bijuteria Owner)

The clear, polarized cognitive and social distance between these entre-preneurs is accompanied by a degree of mistrust, animosity, and tension, which prevents effective coordination and collective action among entrepre-neurs. This is compounded by the isolation of the entrepreneurs from the traditional family dynasties in the town, which control the political machine, and which with few exceptions, are not involved in local busi-nesses. There have been several attempts to organize a chamber of com-merce, bureau of tourism, or similar commercial associations, but none of them yielded a surviving organization. One entrepreneur, who had been prominent in attempts to organize two or three local associations, was quite bitter about his experience:

I had the formal role of president, which really means court jester (*bobo da corte*) for a bunch of clowns. I spent several thousands of personal funds for start-up expenses. I never got a penny reimbursed. No one was willing to lift a finger for the common good. We wanted to certify local businesses as complying with a code of conduct and principles, but a lot of owners balked at the idea of committing to faithfully pay their taxes. I finally got tired of taking it in the shorts. (Informant 3, Male, Nonnative, Joia Owner)

Another lamented the difficulty of getting any formal initiative through the political machine:

Traditionally there were basically two families that controlled the local government. Nothing happened without their OK. We were able to break this monopoly to a degree but to this day things are still done very informally. Nothing in writing, everything verbal, no laws. (Informant 8, Female, Native, Bijuteria Owner)

Based on the quotes and observations above, it is clear that the mindsets — a disposition that influences a person's interpretation and response to a situation (MacGrath, 2000) — of the collective preservation minded are radically different from those of the individual exploitation minded in Tiradentes. The "collective preservationists" tend to be located downtown and are primarily "joia" entrepreneurs who see their business as central to their lifestyle and hence see the long-term prosperity of the community as being achieved through preservation of its local flavor. Alternatively the "individual exploitationists" are "bijuteria" business owners, who are typically located in the periphery, are profit oriented, and who view progressive changes as the key to future economic success in Tiradentes. Naturally, there are exceptions to this pattern, especially among nonnatives who arrived too late and/or too poor to acquire downtown property. However, our investigation suggests that these two categories capture many of the principal mindsets of the entrepreneurs in this community.

The degree to which these oppositional themes covary and mutually reinforce each other can be illustrated by examining the association between memberships in different categories. Table 2 contains cross tabulations of all possible combinations of the four oppositional categories: Joia-Bijuteria with Center-Periphery; Native-Nonnative with Center-Periphery; Individualism-Collectivism with Center-Periphery; Native-Nonnative with Joia-Bijuteria, Native-Nonnative with Joia-Bijuteria; Joia-Bijuteria with Individualism-Collectivism. We include values of phi which provide some indicator of the strength of association between different variables. Table 2 makes clear that, as our narrative above stresses, membership in one category tends to predict status in others. Joia enterprises tend to be located in

Table 2. Associations between Oppositional Categories for 29 Tiradentes Enterprises.

	ET	Worm		Joia	Bijuteria
Center	15	6	*Center*	15	6
Periphery	3	5	*Periphery*	2	6
	Phi = .31			*Phi = .42*	

	ET	Worm		ET	Worm
Joia	15	2	*Individualistic*	4	9
Bijuteria	3	9	*Collectivistic*	13	2
	Phi = .64			*Phi = .56*	

	Joia	Bijuteria		Individualistic	Collectivistic
Individualistic	2	11	*Center*	8	13
Collectivistic	12	1	*Periphery*	5	3
	Phi = .73			*Phi = .21*	

the center, and owned by nonnatives with a collectivistic orientation. Conversely, Bijuteria enterprises tend to be located outside of the center, and owned by natives with individualistic orientations.

Differences in the strengths of these associations are also instructive. Among other observations that could be made, both the strongest and weakest associations have to do with individualism-collectivism. The weakest association is between center-periphery and individualism-collectivism (Phi = .21). The strongest association is between Joia-Bijuteria and Individualism-Colectivism (Phi = .73). Thus while geographic location is a weak predictor of community orientation, entrepreneurial type is highly determinate, suggesting that in Tiradentes at least, an entrepreneur's type and mindset is much more constraining than location in how she/he relates to the broader community.

SUMMARY OF FINDINGS

Taken together, the history and development of Tiradentes, the sociocultural fabric that has emerged as a result of that development, variance between entrepreneurs found within that environment, and the mindsets and actions these individuals take provide us with a unique perspective on the sociocultural-individual interaction and the effects of that interaction on entrepreneurship. As such, it is useful to concisely summarize our findings before further developing these insights by engaging the relevant literature and elaborating existing theory. We summarize the following major findings which underpin the conceptual model illustrated in Fig. 1.

Finding 1: The community has developed a unique sociocultural fabric that is reflected in a vocabulary shared by local entrepreneurs and this vocabulary expresses the major social tensions created by the town's history, rapid development, geography of that development, and departure from its historical roots.

Finding 2: The recursive relationships between the sociocultural fabric of the community, the entrepreneur's native or nonnative perspective, and the entrepreneur's social identity result in two distinctive types of entrepreneurs.

Finding 3: Joia and Bijuteria entrepreneurs have different identities, perspectives, and goals for the development of their enterprise, as well as the development of the community.

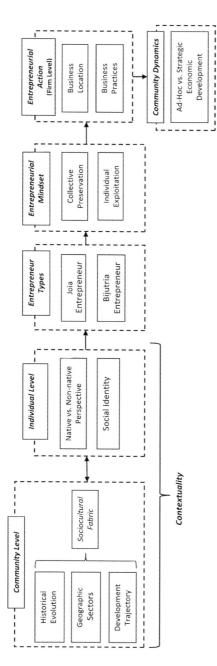

Fig. 1. Conceptual Model of Sociocultural-Individual Interaction-Driven Entrepreneurship.

Finding 4: In the context of the sociocultural fabric, the differences between Joia and Bijutria entrepreneurs result in distinctive entrepreneurial mindset that correlate with the entrepreneur's type.

Finding 5: In the context of the sociocultural fabric in which they reside, entrepreneurial mindsets constrain and facilitate the geographic and social spaces entrepreneurs occupy.

Finding 6: In the context of the sociocultural fabric, entrepreneurial mindsets influence the models of start-up thinking and action (i.e., business practices) entrepreneurs employ.

Finding 7: Entrepreneurs' support for collective preservation versus individual exploitation ideology prevents entrepreneurs from pursuing common goals, thus creating ad-hoc economic development.

Finding 8: Counter intuitively, nonnative Joia entrepreneurs are the most collective preservation minded and therefore the most supportive of strategic economic development designed to preserve the history, culture, and architecture of the town.

DISCUSSION

Engaging Relevant Literature and Theory

We believe that our field study of entrepreneurship in Tiradentes offers a reasonably complete view of many entrepreneurs' backgrounds, identities, mindsets, and how these influence models of start-up thinking and action, as well as what entrepreneurs in Tiradentes think of when they think about their community. We were struck by the ease and frequency with which those we studied discuss their internally generated thoughts and feelings and the actions they advocate and sometimes take as a function of their external environment. For the entrepreneurs we studied, these appear to be inextricably linked and this suggests that the distinctions scholars make between the external and internal explanations for entrepreneurial thinking and action are in many ways artificial. That said we also believe that it is analytically important to identify and relate the different levels of analysis we faced in the field as we attempt to engage in *theory elaboration* (Lee, Mitchell, & Sabylinski, 1999). As a first step in this process we have developed a figure (see Fig. 1) which organizes the relationships advanced in our summary propositions by unit of analysis in somewhat the same fashion of

Lepoutre and Valente's (2012) study of a community of entrepreneurs in the Belgian horticultural industry.

At the community level, the historical evolution of the town created distinct geographic sectors and a unique trajectory for economic development. This set the stage for the emergence of a unique set of circumstances that both facilitated and constrained entrepreneurs' perceptions of the start-up models available as well as the actions that flow from them. Businesses located in the downtown area, for example, are expected to be small-scale operations that add charm to the town by integrating local history and culture into their business. Thus the social norms associated with geographic sectors serve as a guide for "appropriate" start-up models and tension rises when the guide for what constitutes an attractive model is marginalized or ignored. Similar dynamics were documented in Jobes' (2000) study of Bozeman, Montana, which contains many references to local business owners and their role in the community. Much like Tiradentes, Bozeman residents are sharply divided by differences in positions on environmental and historic preservation and the desirability of unfettered economic growth. These dynamics are not universal, however, as Chiles, Meyer, and Hench's (2004) study of the development of Branson Missouri highlight. These authors report that Branson experienced a rather smooth developmental trajectory in which local entrepreneurs, associations, and government worked in concert to attract retiring traditional Nashville acts, and later prominent pop stars, in a series of actions that increased the scale of local enterprises without significant damage to the regions' conservative, family-oriented culture. All of this suggests that while community contexts vary, there are common variables, like geographic enclaves, historical evolution, and local culture that both facilitate and constrain entrepreneurial thinking and action. The implication is that prior theoretical explanations for entrepreneurial thinking and action hold less explanatory power in bounded communities because they fail to include community level variables along the lines of those articulated in our model.

Moving to the individual level, the connection between our study and extant thinking emerges from the realization that the entrepreneurs' backgrounds (native vs. nonnative) and social identities come together with the sociocultural fabric of the community to spawn distinct types of entrepreneurs who share common mindsets. Specifically, we observed the "bijuteria" entrepreneur who is typically a native and growth oriented and applies corporate organizational models to bring scale to the town. In contrast, "joia" entrepreneurs are typically nonnative, conservative, and focused on minimally invasive business practices that preserve the architecture and heritage of the community. Clearly, joia and bijuteria entrepreneurs have very different mindsets and our findings inform the literature that asserts individuals take action because they have developed an "entrepreneurial mindset" (Haynie et al., 2009; McMullen, Wood, & Palich, 2014). However, our findings suggest that there may be many different types of "entrepreneurial mindsets" and these are not only a function of the individual (internal), but also a function of the circumstances (external). This suggests a need for more research on the various types of entrepreneurial mindsets that might exist across a range of contexts. Given that we document the relationship between the type of mindset and the start-up model utilized (i.e., location and type of action taken), investigations along these lines are likely to further bridge the internal/external perspectives and thereby advance our understanding of the role of mindset as an explanation for the ways in which entrepreneurs pursue the start-up process and later run their businesses.

One of the advantages of using inductive techniques is the ability to capture cross-level interactions. In our case, we document a recursive relationship that exists between community level and individual level variables (e.g., Finding 2). We are struck by how closely interactions between entrepreneurs and the sociocultural fabric found in Tiradentes align with Anthony Gidden's (1984) theory of structuration. Gidden's argument is that people's actions are constrained, at least in the near term, by social traditions and norms. We suggest that the idea of constraints has not been well accounted for in current theories of start-up thinking and action and as we begin to elaborate existing theory by integrating social constraints, our findings are insightful because they point to the potential validity of "contextuality" – interactions in specific time and space given actors co-present and their communications (Giddens, 1984) – as bridge between the external and internal perspectives on entrepreneurial action. We find ample evidence of dynamics indicative of contextuality as our observations and interviews revealed how the sociocultural fabric, native or nonnative perspective, and identities coalesce in recursive ways to influence mindsets and ultimately the type of start-up model selected in ways that facilitate the reproduction of long standing practices, such as opening boutique type shops in historical buildings. However, in some cases we find that the process of contextuality leads individuals to believe they are "change agents" (Khavul, Chavez, & Bruton, 2013) and thus ignore convention by opening large-scale businesses in Tiradentes. Therefore *contextuality* appears to be an important part of the community – individual nexus and thus we suggest that it is a construct that future research may find useful in attempts to integrate the external and internal perspectives using the community or other specific action contexts as bridge.

In the spirit of the contextuality idea, we found that as sociocultural fabric and individual entrepreneurs in Tiradentes become intertwined, entrepreneurs are confronted with matching their identity, mindset, and business practices to the norms of the geographic sector. In that respect, natives and nonnatives have very different views on alignment. Entrepreneurs who are nonnative seem to understand that the downtown area contains a unique and limited store of historical and cultural assets and that opening a business in the central district comes with the responsibility to fit with the historic and cultural traditions of the town. Natives seem to be less constrained by this expectation, perhaps because they have always lived around these buildings and practices, and the local culture did not assign any special value to them. When these conflicting expectations met, we observed a pattern similar to what Jobe found in Bozeman, Montana. Social tension increased within the community — especially in the case of large-scale businesses attempting to operate downtown. These dynamics emerge from what is to us a counterintuitive relationship. We were surprised to find that it was the nonnatives that were focused on preserving the town's architecture and cultural heritage while the natives were less concerned with this. For insights on this phenomenon we turned to Merton's (1957) work on the concepts of "local" and "cosmopolitan" orientation.

In the 1940s Merton conducted a study funded by Time Magazine. In the process of finding out what kinds of opinion leaders in a small town subscribed to Time Magazine and what kinds did not, Merton observed two broad types of leaders — the local and the cosmopolitan. The locals were tightly integrated into the community social structure through many strong ties and focused their interest and attention on local gossip and on the affairs of people similar to themselves. Cosmopolitans by contrast tended to possess expert or professional skills which could be executed without particular reference to the idiosyncrasies of the community. Their motivations for association and action followed broad principles often related to or derived from their professional identity, ethical orientation, and intellectual interests. Cosmopolitans tended to be seen by locals as "interesting-idea people whose feet were not entirely on the ground." Cosmopolitans tended to view locals as having a narrow world view and rather philistine interests. One of the principal differences between locals and cosmopolitans was their point of reference, with locals' experience and knowledge coming from the community and community contacts while the cosmopolitan's experience and knowledge came from outside the community and a much broader set of contacts.

Viewing the Tiradentes case from Merton's perspective suggests that the nonnatives in Tiradentes reflect "cosmopolitan" characteristics. It is the nonnative Joia entrepreneurs with their broader education, life experience, and sophistication who have an idealistic view of the community and its cultural heritage. In contrast, the native Bijuteria entrepreneurs reflect a "local" mindset because they seem to be interested principally in profit and scale and do fully not appreciate the value of the idiosyncratic resources and culture found in Tiradentes. Perhaps this is because, as one informant put it: "they [natives] have never been to Rio, never seen the ocean." It appears that like those in the Time Magazine study, the natives rely on local knowledge and experience while the nonnatives rely on knowledge and experience derived from a much broader set of life experiences and contacts. It is our view, then, that the nonnatives have a cosmopolitan perspective that allows them to see the unique features of Tiradentes in a way that the natives cannot. Hence, the natives are less concerned about preservation and more focused on profit because they have not developed a worldview that allows them to contrast Tiradentes with other communities they have visited or lived. These differences in worldview and mindset are exacerbated by the fact that nonnatives who have moved to the community and stayed (many outsiders move to Tiradentes and then leave) have made a conscious, materially and psychologically expensive decision to live in a different context from that in which they were born. The implications of an active decision to choose a new context, is, to our understanding, not considered explicitly in either Merton or Giddens' work nor in the entrepreneurship literature that we have read. As such, it suggests a new avenue for inquiry into the origins of entrepreneurial thinking and action where researchers consider the idea that those who self-select into a given community are qualitatively different from those who remain where they have always been. Clearly, more research is needed in other domains to better understand if the nonnative cosmopolitan's caring more about preserving history and culture than native locals is unique to Tiradentes or is part of a broader phenomenon found in other communities. Research along these lines is especially important because to our knowledge, the dichotomy of cosmopolitans versus locals are absent from entrepreneurial studies yet appear relevant as researchers begin to integrate community level and individual level variables into explanations for models of start-up thinking and action.

Future Research

Several major themes that emerged from our study – center-periphery, native versus nonnative, preservation versus exploitation for example – were not foreshadowed in the literatures we reviewed. This indicates that settings such as the community, which the mainline research has not yet fully explored, may have unique attributes and suggest new perspectives. More significant still for us was the fact that dynamics seen as varying by nation in the literature (e.g., individualism vs. collectivism) were clearly present within the entrepreneurial class of a small community within the same country. This suggests that cultural variance within countries is not homogenous, but instead varies along very distinct lines. This is an important point because it parallels observations in the study of organizational culture (Nelson & Gopalan, 2003), but has received less attention in entrepreneurship. The implication, then, is that the social fabric of the community (much like the culture of an organization) can explain some of the variance in within country entrepreneurship. A dynamic that we believe is worth further investigation by interested researchers.

Another notable theme is the departure of our research focus and results from those of an influential stream of community ecology research which focuses on the dynamics of new industries. In the community ecology research, supplier ties, vertical integration, competitive moves, and resource flows between actors have been shown to be significant drivers of entrepreneurial thinking and action (Freeman & Audia, 2006; Mezias & Kuperman, 2001; Owen-Smith & Powell, 2004). Because our focus was different – we studied a specific community based on the physical space – we found that competition, supply relationships, and resource flows were of little significance in terms of the tensions and issues identified by entrepreneurs in the region. Rather, differences in personal experience, identities, mindsets, and resulting start-up models selected drove entrepreneurial behavior and led to conflicting positions about the future economic development of the town. Thus instead of the evolution of the community being bound up in competitive dynamics, it is bound up in the conflicting mindsets of "joia" and "bijuteria" entrepreneurs and others. While there is little doubt that resources and competition are important drivers of thinking and action, our findings add to the growing research that suggests social dynamics may trump traditional strategic considerations. This suggests that research is needed taking a closer look at when and why the sociocultural fabric of the start-up context trumps considerations of things like competition and resources.

Another area for future research comes from our findings that the conflicting mindsets of entrepreneurs in Tiradentes resulted in a lack of collective action. This intriguing given Chiles, Meyer, and Hench's (2004) observation that collective action was the key to success in the development of the tourist enclave in Branson, Missouri. Yet in Tiradentes it appears that the lack of collective action has engendered important benefits to the community. Specifically, if the community of Tiradentes had not harbored an initial stock of historical buildings in a more or less unspoiled location, it is unlikely that the "collective preserving" entrepreneur would be attracted to or find a place in the community. If the second category, the "individual exploitation" minded entrepreneur had been absent, it is unlikely that the current volume of tourist traffic would have been attained because the preserving entrepreneurs' business models are ill suited for economies of scale. However, if the individual exploitation minded entrepreneurs were to dominate Tiradentes, the town would likely lose much of its current appeal as the degradation of historical and cultural assets would ensue. Our sense is that for the present at least, the current mixture of two types of mindset permits the town as a whole to successfully address two market segments, probably doubling its income. Thus the community ecology of Tiradentes permits the coexistence of different entrepreneurial types and benefits from both until such time as one faction becomes dominant. This suggests a line of inquiry that explores the relationship between collective action (or lack thereof) and entrepreneurial outcomes across a range of contexts.

A final opportunity for future research afforded by our study comes from calls for more entrepreneurship research in contexts outside of North America and Europe. Bruton et al. (2008, p. 1), for instance, point out that "little is known of entrepreneurship in emerging economies" and the studies that do exists tend to focus on culture while ignoring other dynamics. Our study takes a step towards addressing this gap by providing insight from a community in the developing country of Brazil. But just as entrepreneurs vary, countries and communities also vary. Tiradentes, for example, is in a developing country where organizations and industries are not well organized and this means economic develop often happens, as it has in Tiradentes, in an unfocused and uncoordinated manner. In the absence of strong political institutions and mechanisms for citizen participation in local government decisions, this can cause major tension within the community as some constituencies come to view the consequences of entrepreneurial progress quite negatively. Much more research is needed to better understand how variations in communities that reside in both developed and developing countries influence models of entrepreneurial thinking and action and how those actions feedback into economic, political, and social development of the community.

Limitations

The findings from our study should be viewed in light of a number of limitations, many of which are inherent to qualitative research and have been discussed in detail elsewhere (cf., Eisenhardt, 1989; Eisenhardt & Graebner, 2007). In our case, an additional potential limitation of our study is that our theory is in many ways "local" (i.e., it has greater explanatory value and application for the specific situation studied). That said our findings parallel themes found in other studies conducted in communities such as Branson, Missouri and Bozeman, Montana that are very different from Tiradentes, Brazil but also have a heavy focus on tourism. As such, we believe that the Tiradentes case touches on themes in ways that current entrepreneurship theory has not recognized. To that end, we note that some of the dynamics observed in Tiradentes parallel those seen in developed economies, yet others have not been noted in the literature. As such we suspect that other communities in developed and developing economies harbor similarly complex sociocultural context – entrepreneur interactions. This is likely especially true of those communities that experience rapid growth. As such, we believe that our study provides in-depth insight into how communities and individuals come together to spawn distinct types of entrepreneurs and mindsets and why these differences play an important role in models of entrepreneurial thinking and action.

CONCLUSION

Although macroeconomic and historical forces set the stage for the development of Tiradentes as a tourist enclave, a variety of individual actors, each with their own backgrounds and mindsets played determining roles in what made different start-up approaches attractive to particular types of entrepreneurs, ultimately setting the tone for the town. Initial historical and economic accidents created a configuration of physical resources that was unique and fortunate in many ways. What happened next, however, was much more dependent on the actions of individual actors and today this is manifest in the distinct types of entrepreneurs we found in Tiradentes. Specifically, the "joia" entrepreneurs are conservation minded, whereas the "bijuteria" entrepreneurs, by contrast, are exploitation minded and typically less concerned with preserving the historical culture of the town as they seek robust growth for their enterprises. As such, the start-up thinking and actions of the "bijuteria" entrepreneurs have the potential to fundamentally change the nature of the community to something substantially different from what initially attracted visitors. In other words, the time capsule feel of Tiradentes may soon be lost. Having said that, because the mindsets of these actors are so different, no formal or informal coordination mobilizes the town's business owners, and this currently prevents the "bijuteria" from destroying the town's charm, or the "joia" from moving the town away from large-scale tourism. However, in the absence of strong political and regulatory frameworks, the fear is that this variance among entrepreneurs in Tiradentes will result in actions that will contribute to the eventual loss of its position as premium tourist destination. Ultimately, this chapter of the story has yet to unfold but it is clear to us that in addition to accounting for macrolevel outcomes (e.g., employment growth and GDP) scholars need to pay more attention to how the models of start-up thinking and action utilized by entrepreneurs influence other outcomes such as architectural and cultural change at the community level.

REFERENCES

Baker, T., & Nelson, R. (2005). Creating something from nothing: Resource construction through entrepreneurial bricolage. *Administrative Science Quarterly, 50*, 329–366.

Baron, R. A., & Ensley, M. D. (2006). Opportunity recognition as the detection of meaningful patterns: Evidence from comparisons of novice and experienced entrepreneurs. *Management Science, 52*, 1331–1344.

Benbasat, I., Goldstein, D., & Mead, M. (1987). The case research strategy in studies of information systems. *MIS Quarterly, 11*(3), 369–386.

Bowen, G. (2006). Grounded theory and sensitizing concepts. *International Journal of Qualitative Methods, 5*(3), 1–9.

Brandstätter, H. (2011). Personality aspects of entrepreneurship: A look at five meta-analyses. *Personality and Individual Differences, 51*(3), 222–230.

Brockhaus, R. (1980). Risk taking propensity of entrepreneurs. *Academy of Management Journal, 23*(3), 509–520.

Bruton, G. D., Ahlstrom, D., & Obloj, K. (2008). Entrepreneurship in emerging economies: Where we are today and where should the research go in the future. *Entrepreneurship Theory and Practice, 32*(1), 1–14.

Carland, J. C., Carland, J. W., & Stewart, W. (1996). Seeing what's not there: The enigma of entrepreneurship. *Journal of Small Business Strategy, 7*(1), 1–20.

Carland, J. W., & Carland, J. C. (1992). Managers, small business owners, entrepreneurs: The cognitive dimension. *Journal of Business and Entrepreneurship, 4*(2), 55–66.

Chiles, T. H., Meyer, A. D., & Hench, T. J. (2004). Organizational emergence: The origin and transformation of Branson, Missouri's musical theaters. *Organization Science, 15*(5), 499–519.

Collins, O., & Moore, D. (1964). *The enterprising man.* East Lansing, MI: Michigan State University Press.

Companys, Y. E., & McMullen, J. S. (2007). Strategic entrepreneurs at work: The nature, discovery, and exploitation of entrepreneurial opportunities. *Small Business Economics, 28*(4), 301–322.

Corbett, A. (2005). Experiential learning within the process of opportunity identification and exploitation. *Entrepreneurship Theory and Practice, 29,* 473–491.

Daft, R. L., & Weick, K. (1984). Toward a model of organizations as interpretation systems. *Academy of Management Review, 9*(2), 284–295.

Dana, L. P. (1995). Entrepreneurship in a remote sub-arctic community. *Entrepreneurship Theory and Practice, 20,* 57–72.

Denzin, N. K. (1997). *Interpretive ethnography: Ethnographic practices for the 21st century.* Thousand Oaks, CA: Sage.

Denzin, N., & Lincoln, Y. (2000). *Handbook of qualitative research* (2nd ed.). Thousand Oaks, CA: Sage.

Dey, I. (2007). Grounding categories. In Bryant & Charmaz (Eds.), *The SAGE handbook of grounded theory.* Los Angeles, CA: Sage.

Dimov, D. (2010). Nascent entrepreneurs and venture emergence: Opportunity confidence, human capital, and early planning. *Journal of Management Studies, 47*(6), 1123–1153.

Eisenhardt, K. (1989). Building theories from case study research. *Academy of Management Review, 14,* 532–550.

Eisenhardt, K., & Graebner, M. (2007). Theory building from cases: Opportunities and challenges. *Academy Management Journal, 50*(1), 25–32.

Emerson, R., Fretz, R., & Shaw, L. (1995). *Writing ethnographic fieldnotes.* Chicago, IL: University Chicago Press.

Fauchart, E., & Gruber, M. (2011). Darwinians, communitarians, and missionaries: the role of founder identity in entrepreneurship. *Academy of Management Journal, 54*(5), 935–957.

Flick, U. (2009). *An introduction to qualitative research.* London: Sage.

Freeman, J. H., & Audia, P. G. (2006). Community ecology and the sociology of organizations. *Annual Review of Sociology, 32,* 145–169.

Freytag, A., & Thurik, R. (2010). *Entrepreneurship and culture.* Berlin: Springer Verlag.

Frota, L. C., & Peterson, C. (1993). *Tiradentes: Retrato de uma cidade.* Campos Gerais: Rio.

Gaglio, C. M., & Katz, J. (2001). The psychological basis of opportunity identification: Entrepreneurial alertness. *Small Business Economics, 16,* 95–111.

Giddens, A. (1979). *Central problems in social theory.* Berkeley, CA: University of California Press.

Giddens, A. (1984). *The constitution of society: Outline of the theory of structuration.* Cambridge: Cambridge University Press.

Giola, D. A., & Thomas, J. B. (1996). Identity, image, and issue interpretation: Sensemaking during strategic change in academia. *Administrative Science Quarterly, 47,* 370–403.

Glaser, B. (1978). *Sensitivity: Advances in the methodology of grounded theory*. Mill Valley, CA: Sociology Press.

Glaser, B. (1992). *Basics of grounded theory analysis: Emergence vs. forcing*. Mill Valley, CA: Sociology Press.

Glaser, B., & Strauss, A. (1967). *The discovery of grounded theory: Strategies for qualitative research*. New York, NY: Aldine de Gruyter.

Greenwood, R., & Suddaby, R. (2006). Institutional entrepreneurship in mature fields: The big five accounting firms. *Academy of Management Journal, 49*(1), 27–48.

Grégoire, D. A., Corbett, A. C., & McMullen, J. S. (2011). The cognitive perspective in entrepreneurship: An agenda for future research. *Journal of Management Studies, 48*(6), 1443–1477.

Gregory, K. L. (1983). Native view paradigms: Multiple cultures and culture conflicts in organizations. *Administrative Science Quarterly, 28*, 359–376.

Hagan, E. (1962). *On the theory of social change: How economic growth begins*. Homewood, IL: Dorsey.

Hammersley, M., & Atkinson, P. (1983). *Ethnography: Principles in practice*. London: Routledge.

Haynie, J., Shepherd, D., & McMullen, J. (2009). An opportunity for me? The role of resources in opportunity evaluation decisions. *Journal of Management Studies, 46*(3), 337–361.

Hebert, R. F., & Link, A. N. (1988). *The entrepreneur: Mainstream views and radical critiques*. New York, NY: Praeger.

Hindle, K. (2010). How community context affects entrepreneurial processes. *Entrepreneurship and Regional Development, 22*, 599–647.

Hogg, M. A., & Terry, D. I. (2000). Social identity and self-categorization processes in organizational contexts. *Academy of Management Review, 25*(1), 121–140.

Holcombe, R. (2003). The origins of entrepreneurial opportunities. *The Review of Austrian Economics, 16*(1), 25–43.

Hornaday, J. A., & Bunker, C. S. (1970). The nature of the entrepreneur. *Personnel Psychology, 21*(1), 47–54.

Hull, D., Bosley, J., & Udell, G. (1980). Renewing the hunt for the heffalump: Identifying potential entrepreneurs by personality characteristics. *Journal of Small Business Management, 18*(1), 11–18.

Hwang, H., & Powell, W. (2009). The rationalization of charity: The influences of professionalism in the nonprofit sector. *Administrative Science Quarterly, 54*, 268–298.

Jobes, P. C. (2000). *Moving nearer to heaven: The illusions and disillusions of migrants to scenic rural places*. Westport, CT: Greenwood Publishing Group.

Kelle, U. (2004). Computer assisted qualitative data analysis. In D. Silverman, G. Gobo, C. Seale, & J. F. Hubrium (Eds.), *Qualitative research practice* (pp. 473–489). London: Sage.

Kelle, U. (2005). Emergence versus forcing of empirical data: A crucial problem of grounded theory reconsidered. *Forum: Qualitative Social Research, 6*, 27.

Kenney, M. (2000). *Understanding Silicon Valley: Anatomy of an entrepreneurial region*. Stanford, CA: Stanford University Press.

Khavul, S., Chavez, H., & Bruton, G. (2013). When institutional change outruns the change agent: The contested terrain of entrepreneurial microfinance for those in poverty. *Journal of Business Venturing, 28*(1), 30–50.

Klein, P. G. (2008). Opportunity discovery, entrepreneurial action, and economic organization. *Strategic Entrepreneurship Journal, 2*(3), 175–190.

Koh, H. C. (1996). Testing hypotheses of entrepreneurial characteristics: A study of Hong Kong MBA students. *Journal of Managerial Psychology, 11*(3), 12–25.

Lee, C. M., Miller, W., Hancock, M., & Rowan, H., (Eds.). (2000). *The Silicon Valley edge: A habitat for innovation and entrepreneurship.* Stanford, CA: Stanford University Press.

Lee, T. W., Mitchell, T. R., & Sablynski, C. J. (1999). Qualitative research in organizational and vocational psychology, 1979–1999. *Journal of Vocational Behavior, 55*(2), 161–187.

Lepoutre, J. M., & Valente, M. (2012). Fools breaking out: The role of symbolic and material immunity in explaining institutional nonconformity. *Academy of Management Journal, 55*(2), 285–313.

Lessinger, J. (1987). The emerging region of opportunity. *American Demographics, 9*, 33–68.

Locke, K., & Golden-Biddle, K. (1997). Constructing opportunities for contribution: Structuring intertextual coherence and "problematizing" in organizational studies. *Academy of Management Journal, 40*(5), 1023–1062.

MacGrath, R. G. (2000). *The entrepreneurial mindset: Strategies for continuously creating opportunity in an age of uncertainty.* Boston, MA: Harvard Business Press.

McKelvie, A., Haynie, J. M., & Gustafsson, V. (2011). Unpacking the uncertainty construct: Implications for entrepreneurial action. *Journal of Business Venturing, 26*, 273–292.

McMullen, J., & Shepherd, D. (2006). Entrepreneurial action and the role of uncertainty in the theory of the entrepreneur. *Academy of Management Review, 31*, 132–152.

McMullen, J. S., Wood, M. S., & Palich, L. E. (2014). Entrepreneurial cognition and social cognitive neuroscience. *Handbook of Entrepreneurial Cognition*, 316–363.

Merton, R. (1957). Patterns of influence: Local and cosmopolitan influentials. *Social theory and social structure* (pp. 387–420). Glencoe, IL: Free Press.

Mezias, S. J., & Kuperman, J. (2001). Economic action and social structure: The problem of embeddedness. *American Journal of Sociology, 91*(3), 481–510.

Miles, M., & Huberman, A. (1994). *Qualitative data analysis. An expanded sourcebook* (2nd ed.). Thousand Oaks, CA: Sage.

Ministerio de Turismo. (2009). *Habitos de consumo do turismo brasileiro.* Retrieved from www.tourismo.gov.br

Navis, C., & Glynn, M. A. (2010). How new market categories emerge: Temporal dynamics of legitimacy, identity, and entrepreneurship in satellite radio, 1990–2005. *Administrative Science Quarterly, 55*(3), 439–471.

Nelson, R. E., & Gopalan, S. (2003). Do organizational cultures replicate nacional cultures? *Organization Studies, 24*, 115–152.

Owen-Smith, J., & Powell, W. W. (2004). Knowledge networks as channels and conduits: The effects of spillovers in the Boston biotech community. *Organization Science, 15*, 5–21.

Padgett, D. K. (2004). Coming of age: Theoretical thinking, social responsibility and a global perspective on qualitative research. In D. K. Padgett (Ed.), *The qualitative research experience.* Belmont, CA: Wadsworth/Thompson Learning.

Patton, M. (1990). *Qualitative evaluation and research methods.* Newbury Park, CA: Sage.

Rauch, A., & Frese, M. (2007). Let's put the person back into entrepreneurship research: A meta-analysis on the relationship between business owners' personality traits, business creation, and success. *European Journal of Work and Organizational Psychology, 16*(4), 353–385.

Sarasvathy, S. (2012). Worldmaking. In A. Corbett & J. Katz (Eds.) *Entrepreneurial action* (Vol. 14, pp. 1–24). Advances in Entrepreneurship, Firm Emergence and Growth. Bingley, UK: Emerald Group Publishing Limited.

Schumpeter, J. (1942). *Capitalism, socialism and democracy*. New York, NY: Harper.

Selsky, J. W., & Smith, A. (1994). Community entrepreneurship: A framework for social change and leadership. *Leadership Quarterly, 5*, 277–296.

Shackle, G. L. S. (1979). *Imagination and the nature of choice*. Edinburgh: Edinburgh University Press.

Shane, S. (2003). *A general theory of entrepreneurship: The individual-opportunity nexus*. Cheltenham: Edward Elgar.

Stewart, W. H., & Roth, P. L. (2001). Risk propensity differences between entrepreneurs and managers: A meta-analytic review. *Journal of Applied Psychology, 86*(1), 145.

Stinchfield, B., Nelson, R., & Wood, M. (2012). Learning from Levi Strauss' legacy: Art, craft, engineering, bricolage, and brokerage in entrepreneurship. *Entrepreneurship Theory and Practice, 37*(4), 889–921.

Strauss, A. (1987). *Qualitative analysis for social scientists*. Cambridge: Cambridge University Press.

Strauss, A., & Corbin, J. (1998). *Basics of qualitative research: Techniques and procedures for developing grounded theory* (2nd ed.). Thousand Oaks, CA: Sage.

Venkataraman, S., Sarasvathy, S. D., Dew, N., & Forster, W. R. (2012). Reflections on the 2010 AMR decade award: Whither the promise? Moving forward with entrepreneurship as a science of the artificial. *The Academy of Management Review, 37*(1), 21–33.

Vignoles, V. L., Chryssochoou, X., & Breakwell, G. M. (2000). The distinctiveness principle: Identity, meaning, and the bounds of cultural relativity. *Personality and Social Psychology Review, 4*(4), 337–354.

Wood, M., & McKinley, W. (2010). The production of entrepreneurial opportunity: A constructivist perspective. *Strategic Entrepreneurship Journal, 4*(1), 66–84.

Wood, M. S., McKelvie, A., & Haynie, J. M. (2013). Making it personal: Opportunity individuation and the shaping of opportunity beliefs. *Journal of Business Venturing, 29*(2), 252–272.

Zhao, H., & Seibert, S. E. (2006). The big five personality dimensions and entrepreneurial status: A meta-analytical review. *Journal of Applied Psychology, 91*(2), 259.

CHAPTER 3

NEW VENTURE PLANNING AND LEAN START-UP ACTIVITIES: A LONGITUDINAL EMPIRICAL STUDY OF ENTREPRENEURIAL SUCCESS, FOUNDER PREFERENCES AND VENTURE CONTEXT

Benson Honig and Christian Hopp [*]

ABSTRACT

In this chapter, we examine two theorized approaches to entrepreneurial activity: experiential versus prediction based strategies. We empirically assess the comparative performance of several commonly recommended approaches — researching customer needs, researching the competitive landscape, writing a business plan, conceptually adapting the business plan or experimentally adapting the primary business activity. We found

[*] Both authors contributed equally to this manuscript and are listed alphabetically.

Models of Start-up Thinking and Action: Theoretical, Empirical and Pedagogical Approaches
Advances in Entrepreneurship, Firm Emergence and Growth, Volume 18, 75–108
Copyright © 2016 by Emerald Group Publishing Limited
All rights of reproduction in any form reserved
ISSN: 1074-7540/doi:10.1108/S1074-754020160000018003

that the majority of nascent entrepreneurs began with a business plan, but only about a third adapted their plan in later stages. We also found that talking with customers and examining the competitive landscape were normative activities. Those who started a plan were more likely to create a venture, although the effects much stronger for those who changed their plan later on, as well as for those who researched customer needs.

Our results show that the selection of these activities is both ubiquitous and driven by pre-start-up experience and new venture characteristics. The activities themselves do not robustly link with successful new venture foundation. Hence, pre-start-up experiences, venture characteristics, and the institutional environment are more important in explaining successful performance than recommended activities. Implications for research, practice, and pedagogy are discussed.

Keywords: New venture organizing; business planning; experimentation; prediction; PSED II

INTRODUCTION

Considerable debate continues to rage in the entrepreneurship literature regarding the relevance of planning (Brinckmann, Grichnik, & Kapsa, 2010; Davidsson, 2015; Dimov, 2010; Honig, 2004; Honig & Samuelsson, 2014, 2015; Mintzberg, Ahlstrand, & Lampel, 2005). Much of this work assumes that nascent entrepreneurs are homogenous vis-à-vis planning, as the limited longitudinal studies conducted fail to distinguish between different entrepreneurial approaches or persuasions (Brinckmann et al., 2010; Honig & Karlsson, 2004; Honig & Samuelsson, 2012). The idea that "one planning size fits all" not only appears to be embedded in the entrepreneurial literature, but represents an assumption rarely discussed or adequately studied. Questions concerning business planning activities are far from academic, as they represent a very significant investment advocated by incubators, instructors, activists, and investors (Honig & Martin, 2014).

More recently, we are witnessing a new approach associated with entrepreneurship promotion: the "lean startup" (Ries, 2011) and the business model canvas (Osterwalder & Pigneur, 2010). These works represent the latest efforts to endorse a widely adopted under-researched paradigm.

Scholarship often follows publicity, as we scholars explore the intricacies involved in basking under the media's limelight (Maxwell, Jeffrey, & Lévesque, 2011; Maxwell & Lévesque, 2011). Unfortunately, stage lights are rather fickle, and tend to move from place to place according to the fashions of the time (Abrahamson, 1991). As Andy Warhol predicted, we collectively seem to strive for our 15 minutes of fame, whether it be a business plan competition or an elevator pitch contest.

Commensurate with our media strivings are the accomplishments of the entrepreneurial gurus of the day. We were once mesmerized by Peter's and Waterman's "In Search of Excellence" (1982; now largely discredited, see Guest, 2001). Unfortunately, their work was not grounded in empirical research or theory − in fact, many of the supposedly "excellent" firms they highlighted went on to eventual failure.

Similarly, it is difficult to evaluate the measured effectiveness of the "lean startup" and the business model canvas tools/paradigms in terms of instruction or entrepreneurial success (Osterwalder & Pigneur, 2010; Ries, 2011). Though they are quite popular and appear to be widely endorsed, they lack theoretical underpinnings and thus, grounds for empirical testing. In fact, the wide disparity of applications and the absence of theoretical foundations and empirical verifications raise professional concerns. As scholars, we should be asking ourselves under what conditions are these tools most suitable, if indeed they are useful? Rather, we seem to get on the "bandwagon" of implementation, much like the previous (and now increasingly considered passé) era whereby we promoted the institution of business planning (Honig, 2004; Honig & Samuelsson, 2012; Karlsson & Honig, 2009).

We therefore wish to examine the following research questions: Are entrepreneurs that rely on experimentation or on validated learning techniques (researching customer needs and doing competitor analyses) more successful in founding a new venture? Do entrepreneurs utilize prediction and planning from different perspectives, either as legitimating activities only, or alternatively, as road maps for organizational progress? Do initial plans impact future success, regardless of whether or not they are modified? Do plans change as nascent entrepreneurs go about their gestation activities?

We believe that the existing studies suffer from several shortcomings that make it impossible to assess whether certain recommended activities limit or abet new venture creations. Firstly, we argue that studies examining within-process heterogeneity in entrepreneurship have been lacking, in particular longitudinal research that examines the evolution of relationships between core activities and performance. Failing to account for heterogeneity invites the risk of drawing conclusions based on the population of entrepreneurs that are, in fact, limited to only a subset of their population. It would seem to be impossible to identify an ideal educational intervention in a highly heterogeneous population. The result may lead to naïve generalizations. By gathering data over time, our work contributes to the understanding of how entrepreneurship evolves (McMullen & Dimov, 2013), filling an important research gap in our knowledge of these processes, and informing us regarding how best to prepare and educate potential entrepreneurs.

Secondly, we found significant differences in the way entrepreneurs approach exploitive activities such as business planning, researching customer needs and that of competitors, and explorative activities such as experimenting with their primary business activity. Some entrepreneurs engage in deliberate variations of the business plan while others refrain from doing so. Studying these antecedents is important to help us understand the relationship between gestation activities, planning, and venture outcomes, particularly because the merits and perils of specific activities − as well as the order and consequence of gestation behaviors − are heavily debated.

We strongly believe that process, planning and performance research questions are important due to a practical need to provide guidance to nascent entrepreneurs on how best to structure their foundation processes and in which activities to invest their efforts. By identifying activities that maximize the benefits for several approaches, our study provides practical implications for entrepreneurs interested in minimizing opportunity costs. Instructors and support institutions wishing to facilitate and accelerate entrepreneurial activities may also gain insight. Our findings question global recommendations for all entrepreneurs and highlight the importance of recognizing heterogeneity that allows for the tailoring of recommendations according to strategic trajectories. Thus, our results may reconcile some previously ambiguous findings on the role of new venture start-up activities at the nascent pre-formation stage, and instead strengthen the need for a mediation approach to entrepreneurial activities (Brinckmann et al., 2010; Burke, Fraser, & Greene, 2010; Karlsson & Honig, 2009).

In this chapter, we examine the actual behavior of nascent entrepreneurs longitudinally. We compare those that were prone to plan, to research customer needs and competitors, with those that were not, as well as those that made significant changes to their initial plans or experimented with their strategies, with those that did not. One of our objectives in conducting this exercise is to understand to what extent any particular paradigm can be universally applied to a normal distribution of nascent entrepreneurs.

By examining both the heterogeneity of entrepreneurs, and their outcomes, we believe we provide important evidence highlighting the contingent nature of entrepreneurial activities, and thus, the contingent impact of any particular support policy.

In sum, we help fill an important research gap by evaluating nascent entrepreneurs and several ubiquitous start-up activities employed longitudinally, measuring important performance criteria over time with respect to their heterogeneity, research largely absent from existing scholarship.

We use a representative population of nascent entrepreneurs surveyed for between five to seven years. By focusing on entrepreneurial heterogeneity, ubiquitous activities, and a range of alternative outcomes over time, we contribute to the literature by carefully examining contextual and contingent decision-making and performance relationships. We also enhance the debate regarding both entrepreneurial heterogeneity, and the advantages in accounting for variation when making process oriented recommendations and when designing curricula (Neck & Greene, 2011). Taken together, our findings provide insight into understanding the processes involved in entrepreneurial emergence, with significant implications for both the pedagogy of entrepreneurship education and the support of entrepreneurial activity.

THEORETICAL BACKGROUND AND RESEARCH QUESTION

Just as the specific definition of entrepreneurship continues to be disputed (Sørensen, 2008), so varies the recommended curriculum. Despite the fact that heterogeneity in entrepreneurship is well established (Carayannis, Kaloudis, & Mariussen, 2008; Davidsson & Honig, 2003; Spilling, 2008), pedagogical approaches tend to ignore the heterogeneity in entrepreneurial behavior and focus instead on common processes, often demonstrating a "one-size fits all" method of instruction (Neck & Greene, 2011). This perspective is an outcome of research that frequently lumps entrepreneurial activity into one discrete category or process.

Advocates of prediction based strategies cite the importance of organization, opportunity recognition and systematic approaches to the development of a new idea (Delmar & Shane, 2003; Gruber, 2007), as well as the importance of fine tuning business models and eliminating costly mistakes (Doganova & Eyquem-Renault, 2009; Morris, Schindehutte, & Allen, 2005). Critics point to the impossibility of future prediction (Bhidé, 2000;

Mintzberg, 1991, 1994) the lack of performance related outcomes (Honig & Karlsson, 2004) and the institutionalization of business planning as a "myth and ceremony" (Karlsson & Honig, 2009). A comprehensive meta-analysis of the relationship between planning and performance yielded weak positive results regarding planning and performance for early stage ventures – although the average time frame for "young" entrepreneurial firms in the analysis was over seven years (Brinckmann et al., 2010).

Some entrepreneurs – perhaps those most suitable for a lean startup model – pursue a contingent approach. They examine their own capabilities and resources, and based upon those attributes, attempt to iteratively design a course of action. Drawing on March (1991), and March and Simon (1958), much has been written regarding Sarasvathy's perspective (2001), that divides entrepreneurial activities into two groups, one that focuses on controlling, the other on predicting. Sarasvathy provides a set of conjectures: effectuating entrepreneurs are less likely to use traditional marketing surveys or techniques, and are more likely to "jump right into it." Effectuating entrepreneurs are also less likely to use long-term planning. All in all, a great theoretical and empirical divide persists as to which activity best links with successful new venture creation.

Entrepreneurial Heterogeneity: On Pursuing Prediction versus Experimental Strategies

While there may be numerous general strategic clusters that entrepreneurs follow, one increasingly relevant categorization allows for the difference between those that rely on prediction and those that rely on experimentation. Following in the tradition of Simon (1959), March (1991), and March and Simon (1958), Sarasvathy (2001) used a grounded theory approach to differentiate two theories of entrepreneurial strategy: Causation and effectuation. Causally oriented entrepreneurs are those who acquire means to implement effects, while effectual entrepreneurs are those who take their means a given, and adjust their effects with a given set of means. From a theoretical perspective, causal entrepreneurs should be more enamored of planning and planning routines, while effectual entrepreneurs should be more hesitant to engage directly in comprehensive planning. Causal entrepreneurs first begin by identifying an opportunity. They follow this by identifying goals and formulating a plan to accomplish those goals (perhaps producing a complete formal business plan). Entrepreneurial education is typically oriented toward a causal mode, and the lean startup model is a recent abbreviated variant that has become an increasingly popular component of the contemporary curricula. The lean startup model presumes entrepreneurs (and students) will conduct research activities, however abbreviated (Ries, 2011). While the business model canvas emphasizes research activities before engaging in entrepreneurial activities (Osterwalder & Pigneur, 2010), the lean start-up emphasizes relying on understanding customer needs first, before moving the venture forward and cycling around what the customer may want or need. Thus, both the lean startup and the business model canvas approach encourage entrepreneurs to endeavor to obtain the sufficient resources that their plan dictates, before implementing their business model and going to market. In this way, they present a variation of the prediction approach. They vary from the effectual model presented by Sarasvathy, whereby an entrepreneur examines their current resources and maximizes the available opportunities given their current means.

Effectual entrepreneurs pursue more of a contingent approach. From a learning theory perspective, they are more experimental by nature, following pedagogical models advocated by Vygotsky and Piaget (Piaget, 1974; Vygotsky, 1980). They examine their own capabilities and resources, and based upon those attributes, attempt to iteratively design a course of action. They are, by nature, less specific in their approach. Their resulting market activities are not fixed according to ex-ante beliefs, rather, they reflect a process whereby the entrepreneur slowly identifies a method of obtaining comparative advantage based on existing available resources. What Sarasvathy initially overlooked, however, is that knowledge itself is a resource, and the iterative learning that takes place in an effectual model represents a new accumulation of superior opportunities based on that increasingly valuable resource (Sarasvathy, 2001). While the importance of the learning opportunity was somewhat addressed in subsequent work (Dew, Read, Sarasvathy, & Wiltbank, 2009), entrepreneurial heterogeneity (including personal preference) has been largely overlooked. For example, cultural biases are likely to influence both the effectiveness and the suitability of one style over another.

Research Lacunae and Implications for Future Theorizing and Empirical Research

The underlying question for either of these approaches then becomes how the entrepreneur identifies the market opportunity or how she perceives her new venture idea. One natural staring point might be an understanding of customer needs or a deeper knowledge of the competitive landscape. Entrepreneurs following a more predictively oriented approach place importance on identifying an opportunity and developing a solution before proceeding. This resembles what Chandler defined as business strategy "the determination of the basic long-term goals and objectives of an enterprise and the adoption of courses of action and the allocation of resources for carrying out these goals" (Chandler, 1990). Once this solution has been recognized, these entrepreneurs move ahead with a step-by-step plan to operationalize their new-found opportunities. They do this either with careful and often meticulous business planning, based on the recognized strategy affixed to their business plan, or with more ad hoc approaches, that help them focus on a few particular strategies (e.g., the customer for the lean startup, or a missing element highlighted in the business model canvas).

Seeing into the future is impossible, but using imagination may provide a glimpse into how the future might look. Individuals can think about what is likely and how they want things to be (Taylor, Pham, Rivkin, & Armor, 1998). They can run through a series of mental exercises and imagine scenarios "[...] in concrete and specific form (Taylor et al., 1998, p. 430), as if these events were true." It is important to note that although mental simulations require imaginative activities, they are not magic or mystical (Kahneman & Miller, 1986), or hinge on improbable or fantastic steps; rather they focus on what might be doable, thus eliminating the improbable (Taylor et al., 1998). As a result, new venture organizing processes may, at times, be relatively planned and focused. Those that prefer to plan are more likely to create a successful new business by adopting predictive capacities reflected in changes to their business plans. These entrepreneurs would be more successful systematically pursuing a strategy based on their plan because they believe in a predictable future and will systematically gather and analyze information. Such entrepreneurs are unlikely to make radical changes in the way they proceed, because changing their strategy upturns their carefully-prepared step-by-step implementation. New business models would only hamper their efficiency and performance and it would be unwise for a predictive entrepreneur to rely on iterative variations or leap to other opportunities

Yet, a careful reading of Drucker (1996) and Mintzberg (1990, 1991, 1994) reveals that while the future is unquestionably an uncertain task, developing contingencies may provide a useful framework even for entrepreneurs engaging in predictive activities (Honig, 2004). In particularly turbulent environments, later – rather than earlier – planners seem to have more persistence (Liao & Gartner, 2006). Individuals with a predictive preference should be more likely and more willing to adapt their plan to changing circumstances. The perceived opportunity is effectively enacted by modifying parameters. Thus, if planning by entrepreneurs leads to performance improvements, it should do so particularly when their plans are modified. Hence, these theoretical considerations will imply different strategies that could prove beneficial. As such, based on a thorough understanding of what the venture might look like and the competition may allow, these entrepreneurs envision their venture and move forward accordingly.

On the other hand, at the heart of experimental approaches to new venture creation lies the notion of experimenting with different strategies, where choices are frequently made foregoing one option in favor of others. This transformation is iterative, indicating that new alternatives are adopted when they arise, or become possible after a new learning resource is acquired. These entrepreneurs adjust their activities, iteratively experimenting with the marketplace. They focus on iterative learning activities and how they can solve various problems with existing resources, rather than systematically searching for the resources they lack. In doing so they need to regularly modify their business activity, evolving it to match their changing goals and the reaction of the environment. By iteratively experimenting, these entrepreneurs should be more efficient because they integrate their learning into their activity and change their business strategy to reflect their new-found learning.

Research in experimental nascent activities itself is a nascent field of study (Perry, Chandler, & Markova, 2012). Quantitative research attempts to operationalize these theoretical perspectives have proven difficult. The firms studied already passed through enumerable stages of conceptualization and possible predictive or experimental reasoning, on their way to becoming fully fledged recognized organizations (Chandler, DeTienne, McKelvie, & Mumford, 2011). Similar weaknesses exist for explicit studies of effectuation (Perry et al., 2012; Read, Song, & Smit, 2009). Thus, a limitation with most entrepreneurship studies that examine prediction and experimentation is that the data is heavily biased towards existing up and running firms (Chandler et al., 2011; Perry et al., 2012; Read et al., 2009). This presents problems because entrepreneurship theory is meant to examine firm emergence under conditions of uncertainty, in contrast with firm maintenance of existing organizations that may have somewhat more predictable growth prospects (Perry et al., 2012). If entrepreneurs believe they are dealing with relatively unpredictable phenomena, they will try and gather information through experimental and iterative learning techniques aimed at first discovering the underlying distribution of the future (Sarasvathy, 2001, p. 252).

Considering Entrepreneurial Heterogeneity as Antecedents to Founding Approaches

Entrepreneurial education has been developed to both enhance the prospects of nascent entrepreneurs, as well as to increase their density (Vanevenhoven & Liguori, 2013). One of the most ubiquitous elements of entrepreneurship education is the development of the business plan. Courses world-wide examine and promote plans, competitions exist to identify startups with the most potential, and mass media is replete with programming focusing on venture capitalists who evaluate business plans and presentations. The assumption is that good planning leads to good performance, and that entrepreneurship is a process whose steps and techniques can be taught (Neck & Greene, 2011). Examining the relationship between planning and performance highlights a near universal orientation. Those who adhere to the importance of planning expect organizations to be rational, to collect relevant information, confer, evaluate, and decide so as to provide a maximum of efficiency (Fredrickson & Iaquinto, 1989). Much the same argument has been made in support of strategic planning for existing organizations (Ansoff, 1991). Empirical research that explores this view has a well-documented history (Delmar & Shane, 2003, 2004; Eisenhardt, 1989; Gruber, 2007; Matthews & Scott, 1995; Miller & Cardinal, 1994; Zollo & Winter, 2002).

However, theory also highlights the limitations in the ability of organizations to learn, due to biases imposed by actors' preferences (March & Olsen, 1975) by the perception of failure (McGrath & MacMillan, 2000) the inability to accurately forecast future events (Mintzberg, 1990, 1994) or the problem of locking into predefined world views (Honig, 2004). Alternatives to the rational perspective focus on inherent limitations regarding accurately and efficiently arriving at organizational decisions. These arguments, first put forward by March and Simon (1958) focus on the inherent time and logistical limitations of making effective organizational decisions (Mintzberg, 1991). They also highlight the organizational routines utilized in arriving at decision making under typical environments of limited rationality (Cyert & March, 1963; Mintzberg, 1994; Sarasvathy, 2001). Empirical research that explores "non-rational" views is also well documented (Bhidé, 2000; Honig & Karlsson, 2004; Karlsson & Honig, 2009).

Yet, an important and largely overlooked gap in the new venture activities-performance literature is the implication of heterogeneity and entrepreneurship; this is the area our study seeks to address. Various theoretical and empirical studies have highlighted the importance and implications of heterogeneity, including resources, opportunities (Alvarez & Busenitz, 2001; Davidsson & Honig, 2003; Kirzner, 1997), who may contingently either benefit from, or be sidetracked by planning, depending upon the type of business and their environmental conditions (Burke et al., 2010). Other studies have focused on cognitive variations in entrepreneurial approaches (Baron, 1998; Busenitz & Barney, 1997; Sarasvathy, 2001), as well as the impact of different team member approaches over time (Vanaelst et al., 2006). Thus, there is more than ample research and theory highlighting entrepreneurial heterogeneity.

The conundrum that persists is whether the strategies chosen prove valuable, considering that there are individuals making deliberate choices for either approach given their personal characteristics or the circumstances they find themselves in. As March and Olsen (1975, p. 168) state: "As we have come to recognize the limitations on rational calculation, planning, and forecasting as bases for intelligence in many organizations, interest in the potential for organizational learning has increased. That interest, however, tends to underestimate the extent to which adaptive rationality is limited by characteristics of human actors and organizations. The problems are similar to, and probably as profound as, the limits on calculated rationality."

We would argue, that neither approach yields benefits by itself and for all and sundry, but is affected by who decides to take which approach given the situation he is in. We postulate that while some individuals might be cognitively inclined to plan, this group is not necessarily a majority of the nascent entrepreneurial population. We question whether their decision-making style is beneficial for all and sundry and whether this style is consistent during a firm's emergence. For example, entrepreneurial planning and prediction should not be undertaken to eliminate risk; rather, it should be used to estimate the impact of current decisions, essentially to better understand the future risk of contemporary decision-making. When conducted effectively, it may help some entrepreneurs with their current decision-making. By contrast we maintain that estimating decisions that may be needed in an uncertain future is of little value to entrepreneurs. Because some markets are more dynamic than others, entrepreneurs will need to continually adapt to existing environmental conditions, including (but not limited to) turbulence. Starbuck (1992) makes this point regarding the implications of new information. A need for refinement and adaptation comes into play when the venture matures. Entrepreneurs may then have to deal with new information that arises and subsequently determine how to act, given the changed circumstances.

In sum, theory implies that one of two essential strategies of entrepreneurial emergence may occur: One, a predictive model, where various types of planning and appropriate resource collection and allocation will yield increasing returns and productive outcomes; the other, an experimental model, where careful planning is either deferred or ignored, in favor of experimentation, adaptation, and iterative learning whereby experience becomes a valuable resource through knowledge acquisition. Accordingly, the entrepreneurial field should be populated with heterogeneity as individuals pursue either of these basic strategies, so individuals should choose the strategies that best fit their needs.

The research questions we are therefore interested in, is whether an experientially or a prediction based strategy yields a comparative performance benefit and whether the components (researching customer needs, researching the competitive landscape, writing a business plan, conceptually adapting the business plan or experimentally adapting the primary business activity) are predictive of success, or simply reflective of the entrepreneur, new venture characteristics, or the institutional environment.

DATA AND METHODS

Sample Description

To empirically test our research questions, we drew on the Second Panel Study of Entrepreneurial Dynamics (PSED II) dataset. The PSED II is a representative survey of entrepreneurial activities in the United States that portrays individuals during their business creation process. The dataset describes the characteristics of nascent entrepreneurs, documents the sequences of the organizing activities, summarizes the types and quantities of resources committed and characterizes the new ventures.

In late 2005 and early 2006 individuals were identified for PSED II and undertook four recurrent follow-up interviews, each subsequently taking place after 12 months. The last wave was completed in 2011. For this phase the sample of active nascent entrepreneurs was taken from an overall group of 31,845 individuals. Out of this probability group 1,214 active nascent entrepreneurs were identified in an initial interview. A process was developed to establish those eligible to take part. The study was looking for entrepreneurs involved with an ongoing but not yet operational start-up. Interviewees were chosen through screening questions that asked whether they were intending to start a new firm, had carried out at least one start-up activity in past years, expected to own part of the firm and did not already run an operational business. The early stage screening was also employed to ensure the data was representative and, more importantly, to reduce distortions caused by potential survivorship biases.

The number of respondents falls – as is common with longitudinal data (Davidsson & Gordon, 2012) – across successive waves: 972 for Wave B and 746, 526, 435 and 375 for Waves C–F, respectively. Throughout the data collection process respondents gave affirmative answers concerning a package of start-up activities that revealed their progress in becoming operational. With re-interviewing over the course of five years, the resulting longitudinal structure gave monthly indications of activities started and finished that allowed for inferences on the process of organizing activities and facilitated discovery inferences among dependent and independent variables.

Sample Composition

Yang and Aldrich (2012) identify that one of the potential issues with using PSED II data – particularly when the focus is on temporal issues – is that these data may be prone to left and right censoring biases. Left censoring occurs when an event (e.g., creating a new venture) has occurred before enrolment in a study. This is not an issue with PSED II since it only samples nascent entrepreneurs that are at the time of the first interview in 2005 (Wave A) actually trying to build a new venture. Nonetheless, at Wave A it is possible that some nascents may have already spent time and completed one or several venture creation activities prior to the interview.

We resolve these truncation issues in several ways. First, like Yang and Aldrich (2012) we truncate our sample to those nascents whose gestation activities began 120 months (10 years) prior to Wave A. Excluding these nascents reduces our sample from 1,214 to 1,106 nascents. To control for right censoring biases (i.e., when a subject, e.g., a nascent entrepreneur, leaves the study without the study being able to identify what happened to them, e.g., venture viability/disbandment), we follow Dimov (2010) and Yang and Aldrich (2012) and treat these subjects as "still trying" to create a new venture at the time of the last activity reported. In overall terms, our approach follows that of Yang and Aldrich (2012). Having controlled for left and right censoring issues we have a sample of 1,106 nascents of which we had incomplete information on 18 entrepreneurs, leaving us with a sample of 1,088 nascent entrepreneurs.

Dependent Variable

To assess venture outcomes we use the occurrence of the first positive cash flow (PSED II: question A35). This measurement follows Kim et al. (2015) and Yang and Aldrich (2012). In our main analysis, we compare nascent entrepreneurs that create a viable venture against those that disband their venture or report ongoing activities as per Wave F. We define venture disbandment as occurring when all those identified as working on the venture stop their entrepreneurial activities (*A43*). This includes both the focal entrepreneur and any potential team member.

We complement the binary measure of venture outcomes by providing further granularity to our outcome measures. This is in response to Davidsson and Gordon (2012) advocate that the conceptualization and operationalization of venture start-up should be more fined grained and consider those "still trying." Hence, we use a multinomial and ordered logit framework for a trichotomous dependent variable – venture creation, "still trying" and disbandment – to further assess the impact of business planning activities on venture outcomes. We only account for activities before the venture becomes operational or disbands. Secondly, all business planning activities always precede success/disbandment.

Explanatory Variables

We measure whether or not nascent entrepreneurs began preparations for a business plan using question D1 from the PSED that reads as "(Have/Had) you already begun preparation of a business plan for this new business, (will you prepare one in the future), or (is/was) a business plan not relevant for this new business (before your involvement ended)?"

Research also highlights the need for conceptual adaptation involving experimentations with the primary business activity and the formal business plan. To measure the impact of changes to the business plan we consider the answer to questions D30, respectively, that asks "Since last year, (has/had) the business plan been modified or updated (before your involvement ended)?" To measure the impact of changes to the primary business activity we consider the answer to questions A12 in waves B-E, respectively this question asks "Last year, you told us that your business, [A3 BUSINESS NAME], (was engaged in/was) (a/the) [NATURE OF BUSINESS ACTIVITY]. (Is/Was) this still an accurate description of the business activity (before your involvement ended)?" The variables are labeled "changes to the business plan" and "changes to the primary business activity."

Moreover, to proxy for more ubiquitous activities that form the basis of the business model canvas (researching before engaging) as well as the lean startup (researching the customer's needs), we examined question D 22 "Has an effort been made to collect information about the competitors of this new business?" and D 20 "Has an effort been made to talk with potential customers about the product or service of this new business?," respectively. We label these variables "Talked to Customers" and "Collect Competitor Information."

We follow the extant literature (Delmar & Shane, 2003; Dimov, 2010; Gruber, 2007) and administer all of the above variables in dichotomous form. All activities are measured in Waves A–E while the dependent variables are measured until Wave F. This ensures that our independent variables precede our success measures to avoid reverse causality.

Control Variables

In terms of venture characteristics, we draw on Dahlqvist and Wiklund (2012) who assess the innovative venture characteristics through a three point scale (S1:3 = all, 2 = some, 1 = no customers … are unfamiliar with the new product/service) and measure competitive pressures (S2: 3 = there are many; 2 = there are some; 1 = there are no … other businesses offering the same product/service). Further, because planning may be a reflection of the need to access financial capital (Honig & Karlsson, 2004) we follow (Reynolds, 2011) and use two measures of external finance: if nascent entrepreneurs were actually seeking financial capital (E2: 1 = yes; 0 = otherwise); and how important their personal resources were to the venture (Q4–Q10: Total dollar amount invested of personal savings and other sources) (Reynolds, 2011). In sum, about one-third of nascent entrepreneurs were seeking external finance.[1] We also control for the generic

(educational attainment: H6) and specific human capital (sectoral experience: H11; prior entrepreneurial experience: H13). We control for these by
equating educational attainment with years of schooling and identifying sectoral (in years) and entrepreneurial experience (number of other ventures).
Furthermore, following on from Dimov (2010), we control for ability expectations (PSED II: Q.AY4-AY8; scales inverted so that higher values indicate
higher levels of ability expectations; Cronbach's alpha: 0.68), start-up commitment (Cronbach's alpha: 0.71, comparable to Dimov, 2010), work
experience (H20: years), team size (AG2: number of founders), time spent
on the nascent venture (H16:1 = 35 h or greater; 0 = otherwise), sector
(dummies of service, retail and manufacturing (base category)) and, following on from Lichtenstein, Carter, Dooley, and Gartner (2007), a measure of
early gestation activity summing the activities undertaken before nascent
entrepreneurs thought about their business.[2]

Estimation Strategy

In non-experimental situations such as ours, Li (2013) and Aguinis and
Edwards (2014) argue that a powerful way of controlling for endogeneity
and selection effects is to use propensity score matching. Propensity score
matching is now widely used in the social sciences (Kaiser & Malchow-
Møller, 2011; Rosenbaum & Rubin, 1983) particularly in situations – like
ours – that use longitudinal observational data sets that are likely to be
biased by selection effects.
    Overall, we follow the agenda proposed by Aguinis and Edwards (2014)
and use propensity score matching to estimate the probability to makes
changes to the business plan or business strategy conditional on matching
entrepreneur characteristics (e.g., education, prior entrepreneurial experience) and venture contexts (e.g., nature of competitive environment, innova-
tiveness of the venture). This allows us to level out differences in
entrepreneur and context characteristics allowing for the identification of the
relationship between different adaptation strategies and venture outcomes.

RESULTS

We organize our results in seven tables. Table 1 presents summary statistics
and correlation. Table 2 presents the unadjusted results of adaptations on
new venture creation and also reports the antecedents to either new venture

Table 1. Summary Statistics and Correlation Matrix.

	Mean	SD	1	2	3	4	5	6	7	8	9	10	11	12	13	14	15	16	17	18	19	20	21	22
1 Successful foundation	0.22	0.41																						
2 Disbandment	0.40	0.49	-0.43																					
3 Stiu-trying	0.38	0.49	-0.42	-0.64																				
4 Started business plan	0.74	0.44	0.08	-0.08	0.01																			
5 Changes to business plan	0.36	0.48	0.16	-0.15	0.02	0.44																		
6 Changes to primary business activity	0.17	0.38	0.10	-0.17	0.09	0.05	0.18																	
7 Talked to customers	0.86	0.35	0.13	-0.06	-0.05	0.20	0.19	0.05																
8 Collected competitor information	0.74	0.44	0.08	-0.01	-0.05	0.18	0.22	0.09	0.22															
9 Education	14.48	2.11	0.08	0.00	-0.07	0.08	0.15	0.07	0.12	0.12	0.17													
10 Sectoral experience	8.37	1.11	0.12	-0.16	0.05	0.00	0.07	0.03	0.05	0.05	0.01	0.09												
11 Full time work experience	20.24	0.77	0.02	0.00	-0.03	0.04	0.07	0.09	0.04	0.04	0.09	0.18	0.23											
12 Entrepreneurial experience	0.33	0.36	0.01	-0.03	0.02	0.01	0.06	0.06	0.10	0.10	0.15	0.00	0.12	0.12										
13 Novelty to competitors	1.64	0.74	-0.07	0.02	0.03	0.01	0.08	-0.03	-0.03	-0.05	0.05	-0.10	-0.03	0.07										
14 Novelty to customers	1.32	0.77	0.03	-0.01	-0.04	-0.03	-0.07	-0.04	0.04	-0.01	-0	0.01	-0.03	-0.05	-0.27									
15 Personal savings	4.42	4.27	0.06	-0.08	0.03	-0.13	-0.03	0.00	-0.03	0.00	0.03	0.01	0.02	-0.01	-0.08	0.13								
16 Seeked outside financing	0.28	0.45	0.12	-0.10	0.00	0.15	0.19	0.07	0.09	0.09	0.07	0.05	0.01	0.07	-0.02	0.06	0.00							
17 35 h on venture (d)	0.30	0.46	0.15	-0.16	0.04	0.05	0.12	-0.06	0.06	0.06	0.00	0.07	0.02	-0.01	-0.01	0.01	0.07	0.10						
18 Team size	1.81	1.55	0.01	-0.02	0.01	0.08	0.06	0.00	0.01	0.01	0.05	0.08	0.04	0.15	0.15	-0.05	-0.05	0.16	0.00					
19 Ability expectation (self-efficacy)	4.35	0.51	0.07	-0.09	0.04	0.11	0.13	-0.03	0.07	0.10	0.10	0.21	0.01	0.00	0.03	0.01	0.00	0.06	0.14	-0.06				
20 Commitment (startup motivation)	4.10	0.86	0.02	-0.07	0.06	0.08	0.08	-0.04	-0.02	-0.01	-0.19	0.08	0.00	-0.08	0.03	-0.04	0.02	0.05	0.13	-0.06	0.46			
21 Early activities	0.31	1.00	0.03	-0.04	0.02	0.05	0.07	0.09	0.01	0.01	-0.03	0.10	0.05	0.04	-0.01	-0.01	-0.04	0.01	0.10	0.00	0.00	0.05		
22 Retail	0.19	0.39	-0.05	0.05	-0.01	0.04	0.01	0.01	0.00	0.03	-0.06	-0.11	0.01	0.02	0.06	-0.06	-0.09	-0.02	0.00	-0.02	-0.02	0.02	-0.01	
23 Services	0.64	0.48	0.07	-0.02	-0.04	0.03	0.02	-0.06	0.04	-0.01	0.10	0.00	-0.05	-0.04	0.01	0.03	0.04	-0.03	-0.02	0.00	0.02	-0.04	-0.01	-0.64

Summary statistics and correlation matrix are based on 1,088 observations.

Table 2. Antecedents to Venture Creation and Activities.

	(1) Venture creation	(2) Venture creation	(3) Venture creation	(4) Venture creation	(5) Venture creation	(6) Started business plan	(7) Changes to business plan	(8) Changes to business activity	(9) Talked to customers	(10) Collected competitor information
Started business plan (d)	0.062** (0.026)									
Changes to business plan (d)		0.103*** (0.000)								
Change in business activity (d)			0.117*** (0.002)							
Talked to customers (d)				0.135*** (0.000)						
Collected competitor information (d)					0.052* (0.063)					
Education	0.011* (0.070)	0.009 (0.144)	0.011* (0.066)	0.010 (0.101)	0.011* (0.083)	0.020*** (0.003)	0.033*** (0.000)	0.009 (0.109)	0.015*** (0.004)	0.032*** (0.000)
Sectoral experience	0.040*** (0.001)	0.038*** (0.002)	0.038*** (0.002)	0.037*** (0.002)	0.040*** (0.001)	-0.017 (0.175)	0.010 (0.486)	-0.003 (0.804)	0.008 (0.402)	-0.020 (0.129)
Entrepreneurial experience	0.004 (0.911)	0.001 (0.977)	-0.004 (0.913)	-0.008 (0.824)	-0.003 (0.938)	-0.024 (0.536)	0.031 (0.472)	0.037 (0.227)	0.099*** (0.008)	0.088** (0.031)
Innovative product services	-0.033* (0.074)	-0.037** (0.043)	-0.031* (0.091)	-0.032* (0.081)	-0.031* (0.093)	-0.010 (0.580)	0.037* (0.079)	-0.022 (0.175)	-0.012 (0.379)	-0.045** (0.016)
Competitive pressures	0.003 (0.878)	0.005 (0.753)	0.007 (0.688)	-0.001 (0.953)	0.002 (0.891)	-0.007 (0.696)	-0.034* (0.091)	-0.028* (0.074)	0.015 (0.278)	-0.003 (0.865)
Private savings	0.005* (0.082)	0.005 (0.106)	0.004 (0.128)	0.005 (0.100)	0.004 (0.144)	-0.014*** (0.000)	-0.003 (0.361)	0.000 (0.905)	-0.003 (0.214)	-0.000 (0.975)
Seeking external finance (d)	0.083*** (0.005)	0.073*** (0.013)	0.085*** (0.004)	0.084*** (0.004)	0.088*** (0.003)	0.125*** (0.000)	0.182*** (0.000)	0.061** (0.025)	0.049** (0.019)	0.073*** (0.012)
35 h on venture (d)	0.113*** (0.000)	0.105*** (0.000)	0.123*** (0.000)	0.108*** (0.000)	0.116*** (0.000)	0.040 (0.168)	0.093*** (0.006)	-0.060*** (0.010)	0.047** (0.020)	-0.013 (0.654)

Team size	−0.000	−0.000	0.002	0.001	0.000	0.032**	0.007	−0.007	−0.002	0.011
	(0.958)	(0.991)	(0.854)	(0.920)	(0.975)	(0.025)	(0.482)	(0.355)	(0.713)	(0.297)
Ability expectation	0.020	0.016	0.026	0.016	0.019	0.073**	0.086**	−0.004	0.047**	0.107***
	(0.487)	(0.579)	(0.381)	(0.586)	(0.523)	(0.012)	(0.015)	(0.869)	(0.030)	(0.000)
Work experience	−0.009	−0.011	−0.012	−0.009	−0.010	0.018	0.024	0.041**	−0.002	0.032*
	(0.579)	(0.515)	(0.483)	(0.602)	(0.560)	(0.308)	(0.237)	(0.015)	(0.856)	(0.066)
Early activities	0.003	0.002	0.000	0.004	0.004	0.026*	0.026*	0.028***	0.002	0.008
	(0.829)	(0.880)	(0.989)	(0.746)	(0.759)	(0.083)	(0.081)	(0.004)	(0.867)	(0.518)
Retail (d)	0.029	0.031	0.037	0.032	0.035	0.107***	0.059	−0.029	0.033	0.047
	(0.517)	(0.499)	(0.419)	(0.487)	(0.451)	(0.003)	(0.260)	(0.382)	(0.257)	(0.269)
Services (d)	0.074**	0.074**	0.083***	0.072**	0.078**	0.095**	0.052	−0.060*	0.042	0.009
	(0.022)	(0.021)	(0.009)	(0.025)	(0.015)	(0.010)	(0.200)	(0.058)	(0.131)	(0.804)
Start-up commitment	−0.005	−0.006	−0.001	−0.000	−0.001	0.031*	0.032	−0.009	−0.017	−0.015
	(0.780)	(0.710)	(0.936)	(0.996)	(0.930)	(0.067)	(0.114)	(0.529)	(0.213)	(0.395)
Chi-square	71.21	78.57	75.56	71.68	67.69	82.35	103.86	40.53	39.56	66.04
p > Chi-square	0.000	0.000	0.000	0.000	0.000	0.000	0.000	0.000	0.001	0.000
Observations	1,088	1,088	1,088	1,088	1,088	1,088	1,088	1,088	1,088	1,088

$*p < 0.1$, $**p < 0.05$, $***p < 0.01$; coefficients correspond to the marginal effects for the independent variables calculated at the mean levels of the remaining variables. p-Values are shown in parentheses.

organizing activity. Tables 3–7 present the results for the adjusted effect new venture organizing activities on new venture creations.

Table 1 shows that 22 percent of nascent entrepreneurs had created a viable venture (237 observations), with 38 percent "still trying" and 40 percent having disbanded their attempt (418 and 433 observations, respectively). These outcomes are similar to other US new venture studies (Reynolds, 2011; Spletzer, Faberman, Sadeghi, & Talan, 2004). Table 1 reports that some 75 percent began preparations for a business plan, and some 36 percent of the nascent entrepreneurs engage in adaptations to their business plan (that equates to about 50 percent of those that start preparations for a plan) while some 17 percent experiment by making changes to their primary business activity. In addition, four out of five entrepreneurs engage in talks with customers and three out of four research the competitive landscape while organizing the new venture. Hence, our activity spectrum is very reflective of experimental (and thus less frequent activities) to ubiquitously employed activities.

In terms of entrepreneur characteristics, Table 1 shows that nascent entrepreneurs typically have at least a high school degree, that the average sectoral experience is nine years, and that one-in-three have prior entrepreneurial experience. Nascent entrepreneurs also identify that, on average, competitive pressures are modest whilst some of them have innovative product/services. Moreover, about one-third of nascent entrepreneurs were seeking external finance.

The first part of Table 2 (models 1–5) reports the unadjusted estimates from a regression using the new venture organizing activities as explanatory variables and new venture creation as the outcome variable. We find that those that start preparations for a business plan are more likely to successfully create a new venture ($\beta = 0.062$, $p < 0.05$). Moreover, conceptual adaptations involving changes to the business plan also relate positively to new venture creation ($\beta = 0.103$, $p < 0.01$) and experimentations with the primary business activity leads to successful new venture creation ($\beta = 0.117$, $p < 0.01$). Researching customer needs reveals the largest coefficient among the activities ($\beta = 0.135$, $p < 0.01$), while researching the competitive landscape exhibit the smallest coefficient ($\beta = 0.052$, $p < 0.1$) and is only significant at the 10 percent level. All in all, we find overwhelming evidence that all new venture activities depicted positively affect new venture creation.

However, the second part of Table 2 reports the antecedents to either new venture organizing activity. Noticeably, education is positively associated with beginning preparations for a business plan ($\beta = 0.02$, $p < 0.01$),

Table 3. Average Treatment Effect on the Treated — Started Business Plan.

Estimation Model	Outcome: Venture Creation	
	Average treatment effect on the treated	
	Coefficient	S.E.
Logit model	0.047	0.052
Multinomial logit	0.045	0.048
Ordered logit	0.016	0.037
Generalized ordered logit	0.016	0.037

*$p < 0.1$, **$p < 0.05$, ***$p < 0.01$.

with making changes to the business plan ($\beta = 0.033$), researching customer needs ($\beta = 0.015$), and researching the competitive landscape ($\beta = 0.032$). Similarly, all activities are positively affected by the search for external finance. Those that seek for financing are more likely to start planning ($\beta = 0.125$), change plans ($\beta = 0.182$), change their primary business activity ($\beta = 0.061$), research customer needs ($\beta = 0.049$), and research the competitive landscape ($\beta = 0.073$). Effects are sizeable and highly significant. Hence, there is evidence that speaks in favor of new venture organizing activities being reflective of institutionalized learning and isomorphic pressures (Honig & Karlsson, 2004). Also we find that those with more entrepreneurial experience are more likely to research customer needs ($\beta = 0.099$), and research the competitive landscape ($\beta = 0.088$). Those with innovative products are more likely to change their business plan ($\beta = 0.037$) and less likely to research the competitive landscape ($\beta = -0.045$), while competitive pressures reduce the likelihood of changing the business plan ($\beta = -0.034$) and changing the primary business activity ($\beta = -0.028$). Lastly, the likelihood of engaging in these new venture organizing activities of also reflective of effort exerted (whether or not someone puts in more than 35 h on the venture) and the ability expectation of the respective entrepreneur.

All in all, the results present clear evidence that the new venture organizing activities under investigation are endogenous to the endowments of the entrepreneur and may not necessarily by themselves relate to new venture creations. In fact, the presence of several antecedents presents room for biases related to endogeneity. Hence, without appropriate controls for selection effects, endogeneity (that occurs when predictor

Table 4.   Average Treatment Effect on the Treated – Changes to
Business Plan.

Estimation Model	Outcome: Venture Creation	
	Average treatment effect on the treated	
	Coefficient	S.E.
Logit model	0.074	0.050
Multinomial logit	0.076	0.053
Ordered logit	0.034	0.040
Generalized ordered logit	0.034	0.040

$*p < 0.1; **p < 0.05; ***p < 0.01.$

Table 5.   Average Treatment Effect on the Treated – Changes to Primary
Business Activity.

Estimation Model	Outcome: Venture Creation	
	Average treatment effect on the treated	
	Coefficient	S.E.
Logit model	0.122*	0.063
Multinomial logit	0.095	0.071
Ordered logit	−0.030	0.052
Generalized ordered logit	0.131*	0.072

$*p < 0.1; **p < 0.05; ***p < 0.01$

variables correlates with the error term) in the propensity to follow either
new venture organizing activity may subsequently distort our estimates in
favor of predictor variables (adoption of a type of activity) and simultaneously affecting the dependent variable (venture creation). We therefore
follow the suggestions in Li (2013) and estimate the effect of following a
certain new venture organizing activity conditional on the very selection
into these very activities; that is accounting for the theorized heterogeneity in selection.

Firstly, we analyze in Table 3 how the impact of business plan preparations on new venture creation changes, when taking into consideration the
antecedents to planning. Table 3 presents the average treatment effect that
is conditional on predicted selection probability. We present four variants

Table 6. Average Treatment Effect on the Treated – Talk to Customers.

Estimation Model	Outcome: Venture Creation	
	Average Treatment Effect on the Treated	
	Coefficient	S.E.
Logit model	0.050	0.045
Multinomial logit	0.044	0.033
Ordered logit	0.037	0.023
Generalized ordered logit	0.037	0.023

$*p < 0.1; **p < 0.05; ***p < 0.01.$

Table 7. Average Treatment Effect on the Treated – Collect Competitor Information.

Estimation Model	Outcome: Venture Creation	
	Average treatment effect on the treated	
	Coefficient	S.E.
Logit model	0.036	0.043
Multinomial logit	0.035	0.040
Ordered logit	0.039	0.030
Generalized ordered logit	0.039	0.030

$*p < 0.1; **p < 0.05; ***p < 0.01.$

of these results. First, we present results from a logit model comparing those that created a new venture successfully with those that did not. Here we can see that the previously positive effect becomes insignificant. Second, to mitigate problems with model uncertainty (due to differential distributions in our propensity score matching), we report additional models based on more granular outcomes. Following Davidsson and Gordon (2012) who advocate that the conceptualization and operationalization of venture start-up should consider those "still trying," we consider three outcomes – venture viability, "still trying" and disbandment – to further assess the impact of planning activities on these outcomes (Table 3, row 2). The multinomial model reports again an insignificant treatment effect. The same holds for the outcome of the ordered logit and the generalized logit model. There is no evidence confirming the initial positive effect once we control for the selection into the approach given the entrepreneurial hetero-geneity and preferences for each founding approach.

We turn now to the impact of conceptual adaptation involving those that indicate changes to the business plan. First, results from a logit model in Table 4 show that despite the positive effect reported in Table 2, making changes to the plan are not significantly related to new venture creation when accounting for differences in predictor variables. Second, the multi-nomial model reports again an insignificant treatment effect. Similar results are reported for the outcome of the ordered logit and the generalized logit model. In neither model can we confirm the initial positive effect reported in Table 2 that making changes to the business plan positively affects new venture creation.

In addition, we repeat this exercise for the entrepreneurs that decide to change their primary business activity. Row 1 in Table 5 reports the results for the logit model. We can confirm a positive coefficient of changing the primary business activity on new venture creation. Yet, this effect vanishes for the multinomial and ordered logit model. However, as the model violates the parallel lines assumption of either model, these results should be treated with a certain note of caution. In fact, when accounting for non-parallel lines in outcomes, we find an effect for making changes to the primary business activity on new venture creation ($\beta = 0.131$, $p < 0.1$), yet, the effect is significant at the 10 percent level. So all in all, it appears that the effect of making changes to the primary business activity is only marginally significant, and only remotely robust.

Similarly, we inspected the effect of other new venture organizing activ-ities that are frequently highlighted in practitioner publications in Tables 6 and 7. Firstly, the results on the treatment effect for those engaging in research on customer needs are insignificant. Also, the multinomial model again reports an insignificant treatment effect. The same holds true for the outcome of the ordered logit and the generalized logit model. In neither model can we confirm the initial positive effect. Hence, conditional on selection, we do not find any evidence that eliciting customers' needs affects new venture outcomes positively.

We repeat the exercise for researching the competitive landscape and also find that neither in the logit model, nor in any of the ordered logistic or multinomial models the initial positive coefficient can be confirmed. In sum, when controlling for selection of those that research the competi-tive landscape, we find that they are not more likely to successfully create a new venture.

Taken together we do not find an effect of business plan preparations on successfully founding a new venture. This effect is primarily driven by entrepreneurial heterogeneity steering the chances to engage in this very activity, but the activity itself does not affect performance. Neither can we confirm a positive effect for conceptual adaptations that involve changing the business plan on the chances to successfully create a new venture. For experimenting with the primary business activity, we find a small effect on new venture creation. However, it is much less significant than without appropriate controls for entrepreneurial heterogeneity, and is only modest. Lastly, the results also report that neither researching customers' needs nor researching the competitive landscape affects new venture creation positively, despite effects reported in the unadjusted models. All in all, our results highlight that antecedents to new venture creation activities are important, yet the activities by themselves do not create value.

DISCUSSION

In this chapter, we empirically examined two ubiquitous approaches to entrepreneurial activity: experiential versus prediction based strategies. We empirically assess the comparative performance impact (defined as obtaining positive cash flow) of several commonly recommended components of these very approaches. Above and beyond the planning paradigm, we explicitly touch on two recently popular pedagogical strategies – the lean startup, and the business model canvas, both of which advocate experimentation and validated learning techniques (researching customer needs and doing competitor analyses) rather than focusing on elaborate planning activities.

Our trichotomous dependent variable compares a positive outcome with still trying and disbandment, offering a unique longitudinal perspective for nascent entrepreneurial studies. Our predictor (independent) variables (as well as controlling for experience and education) consisted of business planning in the early stages, a change in business planning in later stages, as well as efforts to collect both customer information and competitive information. The latter two were selected because these activities are heavily endorsed by the lean startup and business model canvas advocates.

We found that the majority of nascent entrepreneurs began with a business plan, but only about a third adapted their plan in later stages. Thus, about half of those that planned later amended their plans. Overall, we found that 22 percent of the nascents had created a viable business activity with the 4–5 year window sampled, 38 percent were still trying, and 40 percent disbanded. We also found that talking with customers was quite normative (four out of five) as well as examining the competitive landscape (three out of four). Note that these activities took place before the lean startup and business model canvas were commonly advocated.

Next, we ran models examining the probabilities of antecedents impacting venture creation outcomes. Surprisingly, we found that those who started a plan were more likely to create a venture, although the coefficient was much stronger for those who changed their plan later on, as well as for those who researched customer needs. Importantly, we were not testing for having completed a formal business plan as in many other studies, rather, we were asking if they had begun preparation of a plan, of if they believed a plan was relevant to their success. In other words, a naïve analysis would suggests that even a back of the envelope plan might have produced a positive response. We also found that education, larger teams, and seeking external finance were good predictors of who would plan and who would change their plan. Similarly, and attesting to the normative nature of the phenomenon, education, seeking funding and previous entrepreneurial experience were all drivers regarding who would talk to customers or collect competitive data.

As we continued to evaluate a range of antecedents, we found that, sectoral experience, seeking capital, working over 35 h a week, and pursuing a service business were all statistically significant factors leading to emergence.

Prescriptions for or against several new venture organizing activities continue to dominate the entrepreneurial landscape, both from a pedagogical perspective, as well as from empirically observed and applied activities. Peter Drucker, one of the century's most prolific business thinkers, questioned the utility of planning vis-à-vis entrepreneurship in very stark terms, stating "Planning, as the term is commonly understood is actually incompatible with an entrepreneurial society and economy ... innovation, almost by definition, has to be decentralized, ad hoc, autonomous, specific, and micro-economic" (Drucker, 1996, p. 505). In a chapter insightfully titled "Strategic planning: The entrepreneurial skill," he further points out that planning is "not a box of tricks, a bundle of techniques. It is analytical thinking and commitment of resources and action" (Drucker, 1996, p. 123).

Thus, our task as scholars and researchers, in understanding the role and characteristics of entrepreneurial activities, is to discern the conditions under which formulaic practice is cast aside in favor of analysis and insight, and under which conditions entrepreneurial experimentation is more relevant. Entrepreneurial prediction activities, such as planning routines, should not be undertaken to eliminate risk, rather, they should be used to estimate the impact of current decisions – essentially, to better understand the future risk of contemporary decision making. When done effectively, these activities should help with current decision making, but they are of little use in estimating decisions that might take place in an uncertain future. Some elements may serve useful for individual or organizational goals but they may not by itself create value, especially not for all and sundry. Developing contingencies may provide a useful framework for certain individual entrepreneurs (Honig, 2004). The proactive personality, for example, has been shown to lead to successful career activity (Seibert, Kraimer, & Crant, 2001). Ex-ante, our assumption was that significant heterogeneity exists among nascent entrepreneurs, and that this heterogeneity can not only be observed, but also provide a useful method of diagnosing entrepreneurial strategic activity, such as planning preferences and behavior. Neither of these perspectives offers an unqualified advantage or disadvantage, rather, it becomes a question of maximum suitability – matching an individual's preferences and learning styles with their pursuits, styles, and organizational routines.

Our results also showed that only when not accounting for antecedents (entrepreneur and venture level characteristics) one would find that initial planning efforts and subsequent plan changes impact performance. Yet, when taking into consideration that certain individuals may have a planning preference or are coerced to plan, planning becomes only reflective of these variables. The same applies for validated learning techniques, such as researching customer needs and doing competitor analyses.

While certain individuals are more likely to engage in these new venture organizing activities, the activities themselves appear to be only reflective of personal skill and trait endowments and normative pressures. Hence, pre-start-up experiences and the external environment in which activities take place are more important in explaining successful performance than the actual activities undertaken. When studying which activities proved to be useful for a successful entrepreneur, it is important to bear in mind who the entrepreneur is and why she chooses a certain path in the first place.

Interestingly, entrepreneurs that experimented with their primary business activity were more successful than those that did not, though they would have to tradeoff these effects against a higher risk of still-trying ($\beta = 0.13$ for being successful, and $\beta = 0.17$ of still-trying).

This may provide an interesting explanation regarding Gimeno, Folta, Cooper, and Woo's (1997) finding of the existence of under-performing new ventures. Not realizing that a business idea is potentially flawed, and instead of abandoning the idea altogether focusing on experimentations or iterations of the idea, appears to increase persistence but may not necessarily lead to successful venture creation. A failure to appropriately adapt may thus provide confused signals about venture viability (Chwolka & Raith, 2012) and lead to a "foolish escalation of commitment" (Davidsson & Gordon, 2012, p. 7).

LIMITATIONS

As with all research, this study is not without limitations. One important relationship we were unable to study was the stability of entrepreneurial strategies. For example, we have no idea when entrepreneurs begin to exploit, and if they persist, in being exploitive. They may change mid-stream and begin following an exploration strategy. Unfortunately, our data were unable to systematically examine the possibility of such transition, if indeed they do exist. In addition, our study is based on a nation-wide sample of American nascent entrepreneurs. It could be the case that our observations are biased by the highly individualistic nature of US entrepreneurship. We call for more cross-national research in order to enhance our understanding of entrepreneurial strategic orientation.

CONCLUSION

The continued prevalence of one-size fits all entrepreneurial startup-activity solutions are ubiquitous. They range from researching opportunities and competitive landscapes before engaging (as in the business model canvas), to researching customer's needs (as in the lean start-up approach), business model experimentations (as in effectuation), as well as meticulous business planning and business plan competitions. These recommendations are widely evident in entrepreneurship literature, in pedagogy at multiple levels, and in the institutional environment (Honig, 2004; Neck & Greene, 2011). An extensive debate continues to rage regarding the merits or perils of planning, though primarily in academic journals. Yet, at the very same time, the business model canvas and lean startup models are gaining traction in practice by emphasizing very similar start-up activities that concurrently raise skepticism in academia.

We believe this study demonstrates important insight into these directions. We found that some individuals were likely to be attracted to planning, to experiment, to research, though they were not necessarily more effective and efficient at carrying out these routines. Another group of entrepreneurs, in comparison, were (slightly) more successful when they modified their business model.

The consequence of recognizing different organizational paths to venture emergence, particularly as entrepreneurs and firms attempt to learn from their environment, is an important, and perhaps the most critical element of the entrepreneurial journey. Thus, it may not be the new venture organizing activities that entrepreneurs engage in, per se, that lead to success, but rather who (given the skill and trait endowments) engages in those activities that may differentiate the successful firms (Steve Jobs at Apple) from the unsuccessful firms (Adam Osborne at Osborne computers). How this learning takes place – whether the entrepreneur follows an exploitative approach (Simon, 1991) or explorative approach (March, 1991) may be critical in explaining the outcomes of entrepreneurial activity.

In this study we document that advice needs to be appropriately researched and subsequently tailored to entrepreneurial situations. The advice for predictive activities should not be purely prescriptive. Understanding when predictive or experimental activities are needed and for which purposes, is crucial in empirically disentangling performance impacts and providing practical advice.

Advocates should consider the contextual nature of entrepreneurship. For example, business plans may serve a specific purpose, either for learning and guidance of the entrepreneur or for third parties to attract outside capital, suggesting that different forms of planning might be beneficial for different types of entrepreneurs. Selling advice on a "one-size-fits-all" menu offering a "silver bullet" for entrepreneurship promotion may only serve to disappoint and squander limited resources. Rather, developing an adaptive consultative approach that considers personal and cultural characteristics and circumstances could well increase the chances of helping entrepreneurs to stand the test of time.

NOTES

1. In PSED II, only 97 ventures received venture capital funding (Reynolds, 2011). On average, ventures reported funding to be $144,661, compromised of $22,165 in equity and $121,893 in debt finance) this is higher than informal capital ($102,696) and SBA guaranteed loans ($12,308) usage.

2. Our approach also allows us to control for other effects that may in their own right influence venture viability. This is because, by controlling for selection effects,

we are not only able to robustly identify the planning-performance relationship, we are also able to identify the independent impact of a range of control (entrepreneurial and venture characteristics) variables. In other words – to return to the medical example – someone's age (control variable) has an effect on the outcome variable (heart attack) even if we have controlled for age differences between the treated and untreated groups.

REFERENCES

Abrahamson, E. (1991). Managerial fads and fashions: The diffusion and rejection of innovations. *Academy of Management Review, 16*(3), 586–612.

Aguinis, H., & Edwards, J. R. (2014). Methodological wishes for the next decade and how to make wishes come true. *Journal of Management Studies, 51*(1), 143–174.

Alvarez, S. A., & Busenitz, L. W. (2001). The entrepreneurship of resource-based theory. *Journal of Management, 27*(6), 755–775.

Ansoff, H. I. (1991). Critique of Henry Mintzberg's "The design school: Reconsidering the basic premises of strategic management". *Strategic Management Journal, 12*(6), 449–461.

Baron, R. A. (1998). Cognitive mechanisms in entrepreneurship: Why and when entrepreneurs think differently than other people. *Journal of Business Venturing, 13*(4), 275–294.

Bhidé, A. (2000). *The origin and evolution of new businesses.* New York, NY: Oxford University Press.

Brinckmann, J., Grichnik, D., & Kapsa, D. (2010). Should entrepreneurs plan or just storm the castle? A meta-analysis on contextual factors impacting the business planning–performance relationship in small firms. *Journal of Business Venturing, 25*(1), 24–40.

Burke, A., Fraser, S., & Greene, F. J. (2010). The multiple effects of business planning on new venture performance. *Journal of Management Studies, 47*(3), 391–415.

Busenitz, L. W., & Barney, J. B. (1997). Differences between entrepreneurs and managers in large organizations: Biases and heuristics in strategic decision-making. *Journal of Business Venturing, 12*(1), 9–30.

Carayannis, E. G., Kaloudis, A., & Mariussen, A. (Eds.). (2008). *Diversity in the knowledge economy and society: Heterogeneity, innovation and entrepreneurship.* London: Edward Elgar Publishing.

Chandler, A. D. (1990). *Strategy and structure: Chapters in the history of the industrial enterprise.* Cambridge, MA: MIT Press.

Chandler, G. N., Detienne, D. R., Mckelvie, A., & Mumford, T. V. (2011). Causation and effectuation processes: A validation study. *Journal of Business Venturing, 26*(3), 375–390.

Chwolka, A., & Raith, M. G. (2012). The value of business planning before start-up – A decision-theoretical perspective. *Journal of Business Venturing, 27*(3), 385–399.

Cyert, R. M., & March, J. G. (1963). *A behavioral theory of the firm* (Vol. 2). Englewood Cliffs, NJ: Prentice-Hall.

Dahlqvist, J., & Wiklund, J. (2012). Measuring the market newness of new ventures. *Journal of Business Venturing, 27*(2), 185–196.

Davidsson, P. (2015). Data replication and extension: A commentary. *Journal of Business Venturing Insights, 3*, 12–15.

Davidsson, P., & Gordon, S. R. (2012). Panel studies of new venture creation: A methods-focused review and suggestions for future research. *Small Business Economics*, *39*(4), 853–876.

Davidsson, P., & Honig, B. (2003). The role of social and human capital among nascent entrepreneurs. *Journal of Business Venturing*, *18*(3), 301–331.

Delmar, F., & Shane, S. (2003). Does business planning facilitate the development of new ventures? *Strategic Management Journal*, *24*(12), 1165–1185.

Delmar, F., & Shane, S. (2004). Legitimating first: Organizing activities and the survival of new ventures. *Journal of Business Venturing*, *19*(3), 385–410.

Dew, N., Read, S., Sarasvathy, S. D., & Wiltbank, R. (2009). Effectual versus predictive logics in entrepreneurial decision-making: Differences between experts and novices. *Journal of Business Venturing*, *24*(4), 287–309.

Dimov, D. (2010). Nascent entrepreneurs and venture emergence: Opportunity confidence, human capital, and early planning. *Journal of Management Studies*, *47*(6), 1123–1153.

Doganova, L., & Eyquem-Renault, M. (2009). What do business models do? Innovation devices in technology entrepreneurship. *Research Policy*, *38*(10), 1559–1570.

Drucker, P. (1996). The executive in action, the effective executive. New York, NY: Harper Business.

Eisenhardt, K. M. (1989). Making fast strategic decisions in high-velocity environments. *Academy of Management journal*, *32*(3), 543–576.

Fredrickson, J. W., & Iaquinto, A. L. (1989). Inertia and creeping rationality in strategic decision processes. *Academy of Management Journal*, *32*(3), 516–542.

Gimeno, J., Folta, T. B., Cooper, A. C., & Woo, C. Y. (1997). Survival of the fittest? Entrepreneurial human capital and the persistence of underperforming firms. *Administrative Science Quarterly*, *42*(4), 750–783.

Gruber, M. (2007). Uncovering the value of planning in new venture creation: A process and contingency perspective. *Journal of Business Venturing*, *22*(6), 782–807.

Guest, D. (2001). Right enough to be dangerously wrong. *Organizational Studies: Modes of Management*, *1*, 347.

Honig, B. (2004). Entrepreneurship education: Toward a model of contingency-based business planning. *Academy of Management Learning & Education*, *3*(3), 258–273.

Honig, B., & Karlsson, T. (2004). Institutional forces and the written business plan. *Journal of Management*, *30*(1), 29–48.

Honig, B., & Martin, B. (2014). Entrepreneurship Education. In F. Alain (Ed.), *Handbook of research on entrepreneurship* (pp. 127–146). Northampton MA: Edward Elgar Publishing.

Honig, B., & Samuelsson, M. (2012). Planning and the entrepreneur: A longitudinal examination of nascent entrepreneurs in Sweden. *Journal of Small Business Management*, *50*(3), 365–388.

Honig, B., & Samuelsson, M. (2014). Data replication and extension: A study of business planning and venture-level performance. *Journal of Business Venturing Insights*, *1*(2), 18–25.

Honig, B., & Samuelsson, M. (2015). Replication in entrepreneurship research: A further response to Delmar. *Journal of Business Venturing Insights*, *3*, 30–34.

Kahneman, D., & Miller, D. T. (1986). Norm theory: Comparing reality to its alternatives. *Psychological Review*, *93*(2), 136.

Kaiser, U., & Malchow-Møller, N. (2011). Is self-employment really a bad experience?: The effects of previous self-employment on subsequent wage-employment wages. *Journal of Business Venturing*, *26*(5), 572–588.

Karlsson, T., & Honig, B. (2009). Judging a business by its cover: An institutional perspective on new ventures and the business plan. *Journal of Business Venturing, 24*(1), 27–45.

Katz, J. A. (2003). The chronology and intellectual trajectory of American entrepreneurship education: 1876–1999. *Journal of Business Venturing, 18*(2), 283–300.

Kim, P. H., Longest, K. C., & Lippmann, S. (2015). The tortoise versus the hare: Progress and business viability differences between conventional and leisure-based founders. *Journal of Business Venturing, 30*(2), 185–204.

Kirzner, I. M. (1997). Entrepreneurial discovery and the competitive market process: An Austrian approach. *Journal of Economic Literature, 35*(1), 60–85.

Li, M. (2013). Using the propensity score method to estimate causal effects a review and practical guide. *Organizational Research Methods, 16*(2), 188–226.

Liao, J., & Gartner, W. B. (2006). The effects of pre-venture plan timing and perceived environmental uncertainty on the persistence of emerging firms. *Small Business Economics, 27*(1), 23–40.

Lichtenstein, B. B., Carter, N. M., Dooley, K. J., & Gartner, W. B. (2007). Complexity dynamics of nascent entrepreneurship. *Journal of Business Venturing, 22*(2), 236–261.

March, J. G. (1991). Exploration and exploitation in organizational learning. *Organization Science, 2*(1), 71–87.

March, J. G., & Olsen, J. P. (1975). The uncertainty of the past: Organizational learning under ambiguity. *European Journal of Political Research, 3*(2), 147–171.

March, J. G., & Simon, H. A. (1958). Organizations.

Matthews, C. H., & Scott, S. G. (1995). Uncertainty and planning in small and entrepreneurial firms: An empirical assessment. *Journal of Small Business Management, 33*(4), 34.

Maxwell, A. L., Jeffrey, S. A., & Lévesque, M. (2011). Business angel early stage decision making. *Journal of Business Venturing, 26*(2), 212–225.

Maxwell, A., & Lévesque, M. (2011). Technology incubators: Facilitating technology transfer or creating regional wealth? *International Journal of Entrepreneurship and Innovation Management, 13*(2), 122–143.

McGrath, R. G., & MacMillan, I. C. (2000). *The entrepreneurial mindset: Strategies for continuously creating opportunity in an age of uncertainty* (Vol. 284). Boston, MA: Harvard Business Press.

McMullen, J. S., & Dimov, D. (2013). Time and the entrepreneurial journey: The problems and promise of studying entrepreneurship as a process. *Journal of Management Studies, 50*(8), 1481–1512.

Miller, C. C., & Cardinal, L. B. (1994). Strategic planning and firm performance: A synthesis of more than two decades of research. *Academy of Management Journal, 37*(6), 1649–1665.

Mintzberg, H. (1990). The design school: Reconsidering the basic premises of strategic management. *Strategic Management Journal, 11*(3), 171–195.

Mintzberg, H. (1991). Learning 1, planning 0 reply to Igor Ansoff. *Strategic Management Journal, 12*(6), 463–466.

Mintzberg, H. (1994). *Rise and fall of strategic planning.* New York, NY: The Free Press.

Mintzberg, H., Ahlstrand, B., & Lampel, J. (2005). *Strategy safari: A guided tour through the wilds of strategic management.* Toronto, ON: Simon and Schuster.

Morris, M., Schindehutte, M., & Allen, J. (2005). The entrepreneur's business model: Toward a unified perspective. *Journal of Business Research, 58*(6), 726–735.

Neck, H. M., & Greene, P. G. (2011). Entrepreneurship education: Known worlds and new frontiers. *Journal of Small Business Management, 49*(1), 55–70.

Osterwalder, A., & Pigneur, Y. (2010). *Business model generation: A handbook for visionaries, game changers, and challengers.* Hoboken, NJ: Wiley.

Perry, J. T., Chandler, G. N., & Markova, G. (2012). Entrepreneurial effectuation: A review and suggestions for future research. *Entrepreneurship Theory and Practice, 36*(4), 837–861.

Peters, T., & Waterman, R. (1982). *In search of excellence: Lessons from America's best-run corporations.* New York, NY: Warner.

Piaget, J. (1974). *Der Aufbau der Wirklichkeit beim Kinde.* Stuttgart: Klett-Cotta.

Read, S., Song, M., & Smit, W. (2009). A meta-analytic review of effectuation and venture performance. *Journal of Business Venturing, 24*(6), 573–587.

Reynolds, P. D. (2011). Informal and early formal financial support in the business creation process: Exploration with PSED II data set. *Journal of Small Business Management, 49*(1), 27–54.

Ries, E. (2011). *The lean startup: How today's entrepreneurs use continuous innovation to create radically successful businesses.* Crown Business, New York: Random House LLC.

Rosenbaum, P. R., & Rubin, D. B. (1983). The central role of the propensity score in observational studies for causal effects. *Biometrika, 70*(1), 41–55.

Sarasvathy, S. D. (2001). Causation and effectuation: Toward a theoretical shift from economic inevitability to entrepreneurial contingency. *Academy of Management Review, 26*(2), 243–263.

Seibert, S. E., Kraimer, M. L., & Crant, J. M. (2001). A longitudinal model linking proactive personality and career success. *Personnel psychology, 54*(4), 845–874.

Simon, H. A. (1959). Theories of decision-making in economics and behavioral science. *The American Economic Review, 49*(3), 253–283.

Simon, H. A. (1991). Bounded rationality and organizational learning. *Organization Science, 2*(1), 125–134.

Sørensen, B. M. (2008). 'Behold, I am making all things new': The entrepreneur as savior in the age of creativity. *Scandinavian Journal of Management, 24*(2), 85–93.

Spilling, O. R. (2008). 7. Entrepreneurship and heterogeneity. *Diversity in the Knowledge Economy and Society: Heterogeneity, Innovation and Entrepreneurship (The Gwu Nifu Step Series on Science, Innovation, Technology and Entrepreneurship),* 140.

Spletzer, J. R., Faberman, R. J., Sadeghi, A., & Talan, D. M. (2004). Business employment dynamics: New data on gross job gains and loss. *Monthly Labor Review, 127*(4), 29–42.

Starbuck, W. H. (1992). Learning by knowledge-intensive firms. *Journal of Management Studies, 29*(6), 713–740.

Taylor, S. E., Pham, L. B., Rivkin, I. D., & Armor, D. A. (1998). Harnessing the imagination: Mental simulation, self-regulation, and coping. *American Psychologist, 53*(4), 429.

Vanaelst, I., Clarysse, B., Wright, M., Lockett, A., Moray, N., & S'jegers, R. (2006). Entrepreneurial team development in academic spinouts: An examination of team heterogeneity. *Entrepreneurship Theory and Practice, 30*(2), 249–271.

Vanevenhoven, J., & Liguori, E. (2013). The impact of entrepreneurship education: Introducing the entrepreneurship education project. *Journal of Small Business Management, 51*(3), 315–328.

Vygotsky, L. S. (1980). *Mind in society: The development of higher psychological processes.* Boston, MA: Harvard University Press.

Yang, T., & Aldrich, H. E. (2012). Out of sight but not out of mind: Why failure to account for left truncation biases research on failure rates. *Journal of Business Venturing*, *27*(4), 477–492.

Zollo, M., & Winter, S. G. (2002). Deliberate learning and the evolution of dynamic capabilities. *Organization Science*, *13*(3), 339–351.

CHAPTER 4

A DESIGN THINKING-BASED CONCEPTUALIZATION OF THE "HOW" AND "WHAT" OF NASCENT SOCIAL VENTURE DEVELOPMENT

Aparna Katre

ABSTRACT

Social entrepreneurs who use market mechanisms to solve wicked problems (Rittel & Webber, 1973) may benefit from practices based on design thinking. Design thinking offers approaches to work iteratively on both problem and solution spaces collaboratively with multiple diverse stakeholders, which is characteristic of innovating for social change. This research conceptualizes designing as a construct formed by three practices: making improvements, generating creative leaps, and problem-solving. Using Boland and Collopy's (2004) conception of a sense-making manager, it proposes "how" nascent social entrepreneurs take actions and also proposes "what" specific activities they undertake for the development of the venture. A conceptual model proposing "what" it is that social entrepreneurs do and "how" they go about their activities affecting new venture development is tested using structural equation modeling. Preliminary support for the predictive capability of the model

Models of Start-up Thinking and Action: Theoretical, Empirical and Pedagogical Approaches
Advances in Entrepreneurship, Firm Emergence and Growth, Volume 18, 109–143
Copyright © 2016 by Emerald Group Publishing Limited
All rights of reproduction in any form reserved
ISSN: 1074-7540/doi:10.1108/S1074-754020160000018004

is encouraging, suggesting that practices based on design thinking may be further developed in order to advance theoretical understanding of the application of design thinking for social entrepreneurship.

Keywords: Social venture; entrepreneurial actions; design thinking; start-up; improvements; creative connections, problem-solving

INTRODUCTION

Societal issues cannot be adequately addressed by simply using models of the past; today's problems are complex, highly interconnected, and characterized by ambiguity, and it is not always possible to conclusively formulate the problem and the solution independent of each other. Innovating solutions for contemporary societal issues involves the birth of ideas, their development, and their utilization through products and services (Westley, 2008), all along generating an agreement between multiple agencies on both the issues and the solutions (Hagoort, Thomassen, & Kooyman, 2012). In many ways, entrepreneurship for social innovation is similar to commercial entrepreneurship; however, it differs in its focus on producing social change, but with a potential payoff (Guo & Bielefeld, 2014).

Despite mounting calls to improve the theoretical foundation of social entrepreneurship (Alvord, Brown, & Letts, 2004; Haugh, 2005; Nicholls, 2006), the formation and early development of social entrepreneurial ventures has been the subject of very few empirical studies (Gras, Mosakowski, & Lumpkin, 2011). Start-up research has primarily focused on the entrepreneur (Dees & Elias, 1998; Haugh, 2005) and the process of social entrepreneurship (Guclu, Dees, & Anderson, 2002; Perrini, Vurro, & Costanzo, 2010) with scant empirical studies on start-up practices.

Design thinking, which involves an active iterative search for a fit between the problem and possible solutions (Buchanan & Margolin, 1995; Cross, 1995; Margolin, 1995), is better suited than practices based on other approaches such as business plan development. Design thinking provides methods to gain insights, broaden and continually refine our understanding of the problem while generating insights and remaining alert for emergent solution ideas. Commercial new venture research has progressed from the personality traits of entrepreneurs, a focus on start-up processes and entrepreneurial cognition, to a more recent focus on entrepreneurial practices

(Neck & Greene, 2011). Pursuing this line of inquiry around practices, this research tries to answer the research question: Can entrepreneurial practices based on design thinking predict the development of nascent social ventures?

First, a conceptual model consisting of practices based on design thinking is developed. Hypotheses on the effect of "how" social entrepreneurs go about developing the venture and "what" (tasks and activities) they undertake to develop the venture are formulated. The hypotheses are tested using structural equation modeling using self-administered survey data. Preliminary results are encouraging and show support for the predictive capability of design thinking-based practices for social venture development. Three approaches – taking a problem-solving approach when dealing with micro-level issues, making changes in the form of improvements to gain insights, and generating creative leaps – collectively represent "how" entrepreneurs create possibilities for problem–solution. Entrepreneurs use this knowledge to choose among possibilities. The completion of specific tasks, that is, "what" they do, coupled with "how" they go about completing the tasks affects the development of nascent social ventures.

Next, a review of pertinent literature is performed to help conceptualize the model.

WHAT IS SPECIAL ABOUT SOCIAL VENTURES?

Rittel and Webber (1973) define "wicked problems" as those with no definitive statement of the problem; where there are many stakeholders who care about how the problem is solved; where the constraints on the solution change over time; and finally, the problem-solving process ends when one runs out of resources rather than when an optimal solution is found. Social innovation is similar to dealing with wicked problems, wherein innovators have to engage in an iterative process of idea generation until a solution agreeable to all collaborators is developed (Brown & Wyatt, 2010; Sarasvathy & Simon, 2000; York, Sarasvathy, & Larson, 2009). Social innovators need to be comfortable with ambiguity and uncertainty, must have the skills of negotiation and persuasion, and must stay focused on the long-term sustained change. This requires knowledge of and capabilities drawn from the discipline of design thinking (Hagoort et al., 2012).

Social entrepreneurs have the vision to affect social change through an enterprise utilizing business practices (Dart, 2009; Dees, Emerson, & Economy, 2002). Like nonprofits, producing sustainable social change often requires social entrepreneurs to align goals with stakeholders who are connected with the issue in one or more ways, and to engage in win—win actions (King, 2004). Cooperation among stakeholders leads to resource sharing and complementing each other's skills to constitute full systems change. However, commercial entrepreneurs often require win—lose action orientation and need to be proactive, competitive, innovative, and take risks in order to compete in the marketplace. These behaviors conflict with those of cooperation among stakeholders. Using business for social change, therefore, needs entrepreneurs to straddle these conflicting requirements while not losing sight of the bigger whole which constitutes the social issue. It also requires attending to a diverse body of stakeholders (Han & McKelvey, 2009), each with varying requirements, skills, competencies, and resources, all of which are essential to solving the social issue. Involvement of a wide array of stakeholders with these complexities makes social change a wicked problem.

Since social change occurs over an extended duration, it requires long-term involvement of stakeholders wherein requirements of the stakeholders and their skills and resource base might change over time. Similarly, the skills, expertise, and resources of the individuals and organizations leading the social change can evolve, suggesting revisions to stakeholder involvement, or even the need to engage new stakeholders. Social entrepreneurs may experience constant shifts giving rise to ambiguities and multiple interpretations of needs, capabilities, and possibilities associated with the social change, those that are typical of wicked problems.

For complex societal issues, the path an individual or an organization will traverse to conceptualize, initiate, and affect social change cannot be based on analysis and prediction or planning (Rittel & Webber, 1973). Instead, it is likely that the path is shaped or co-created with stakeholders, based on factors such as the knowledge, skills, expertise, and networks of the stakeholders, the entrepreneurs, and the participating organizations (Read, Sarasvathy, Dew, Wiltbank, & Ohlsson, 2011; Read, Song, & Smit, 2009; Sarasvathy, 2001). The specifics of the solution, that is, the paths traversed for social change, are unique to the individuals and organizations, and are known only when the solution has been created in concert with the stakeholders (Dorst, 2006). This suggests that not only are there multiple solutions to a specific social problem in a given societal context, but also that a solution which has worked in one instance may not necessarily work in another context. Therefore, there is not one right solution to bring about social change supporting its wicked nature.

In summary, these characteristics of business for social change, where (a) the solution has to address conflicting stakeholder requirements, (b) the problem is surrounded by uncertainties, (c) the solution is context sensitive, and good or bad, but not optimal, and (d) specifics of the problem are not known until an agreeable solution is found, make it a wicked problem to solve.

START-UP PRACTICES

Start-up practices, for the purposes of this research, refer to actions and decisions required for new venture creation. New venture creation literature presents multiple approaches such as business planning, feasibility analysis, business model canvas, and lean start-up. Business planning assumes that start-ups are smaller versions of companies emphasizing linear thinking and business plan based processes. Start-up processes, in this case, are thought of as sequential steps based on opportunity recognition, product development, market segmentation, and targeting and positioning. More recently, these are seen as providing no advantage to start-ups (Sarasvathy, 2008).

Contrarily, approaches based in creation recognize that start-ups are human institutions designed to create new products under conditions of extreme uncertainty (Reis, 2011) and that start-up entails a search for a business model, that is, how one creates and captures value. Examples of approaches based in the creation logic include effectuation, lean start-up, and business model canvas. These approaches provide entrepreneurs with methods − skills, tools, and practices − to influence the ways in which start-ups' uncertainties resolve, and also to guide decisions. Creation suggests that entrepreneurs "search," that is, take action or experiment in order to find answers to questions, demystify the unknowns or validate their assumptions at each step of development. Since the outcomes of a search cannot be predicted entrepreneurial decisions and subsequent actions are consequential depending on how they make sense of the outcomes. *Search* also suggests that the process is iterative continuing until most important questions are answered, and assumptions are (in)validated. Although the purpose of the iterative search is to generate convergence, entrepreneurial learning may lead to the formation of new goals, generating new means, forming new assumptions, and sometimes lead to critical pivot decisions. It is also likely that search may not result in convergence, and the entrepreneurs may call off the new venture creation.

Search-driven frameworks for new venture creation are a recent phenomenon where business model search lacks inductive empirical research and theory building is still in its early stages (Lambert & Davidson, 2013).

PRACTICES BASED IN DESIGN THINKING

Wicked problems cannot be solved using predictive approaches involving problem definition, analysis, and series of sequential steps (Dorst & Cross, 2001; Rittel & Webber, 1973). Instead, practices based in design thinking are useful in such cases (Buchanan & Margolin, 1995; Cross, 1995; Dorst, 2011). Next, key practices anchored in design thinking and central for social venture start-up are discussed.

Addressing Problems in Search for Solutions

Design thinking suggests that social entrepreneurs may decompose the overarching problem of "business for social change" into micro-level problems to solve. For example, consider the issue of breaking the cycle of poverty for low-skilled workers in a given community. The social transformation issue can be decomposed to a set of problems such as conceptualizing income generating products or services, identifying customer segments, figuring out product-market fit, determining the role of beneficiaries (producers, consumers, or both), identifying and forging nonprofit and business partnerships, and designing programs for the impoverished among others. The final solution to the problem is built from a combination of actions taken for the micro-level problems (Dorst, 2006; Simon, 1996). Actions for each micro-level problem can result in changes to circumstances, which the development of other components must take into account. For example, while searching for nonprofit partnerships, entrepreneurs may strike a partnership with a nonprofit which has the capability to deliver client programming. As a result, there may no longer be the need to develop those capabilities impacting subsequent venture development.

In many regards, solving the macro-problem entails assemblies of such components, that is, those that solve the micro-level problems. Entrepreneurs can use design thinking to gain intelligence about the micro-level problems and generate alternative solutions resulting in clarity of the problem and the solution. To succeed in the search objectives, successful entrepreneurs view problems, the resources, skills, and constraints as opportunities rather than being restricted by them (Sarasvathy, 2008). In addition, as good designers, they set aside personal preferences and conduct a balanced search for alternatives (Fricke, 1996). These arguments suggest that problem-solving as characterized above might help the development of new ventures.

Improving to Gain Insights and Stakeholder Support

Design thinking involves entrepreneurs leading a multi-stakeholder dialog with the hope of gaining insights, broadening understanding of macro- and micro-level problems, and continually refining the problem definition in search of emergent solutions (Woodbury, 2010). This collaborative stakeholder dialog is a process of deliberation, that is, conversations, argumentation and negotiation, and resolving issues rather than a search for optimal solution. It involves sharing ideas, points of views, and prototypes to gain newer insights and information as well as expert opinion. Each step of deliberation can be viewed as an improvement during the multi-stakeholder dialog. When improvements are demonstrated, they can be used as an instrument of power to negotiate stakeholder support (Buchanan & Margolin, 1995). When applied iteratively, deliberation can lead to concrete suggestions to acquire resources, gain stakeholder support, and together, shape the future of the venture. This process of problem—solution directed argumentation and negotiations generate improvements at each micro-step in venture creation. Improvements resulting from iterative deliberations focus on reducing the unknowns, and generating greater clarity on the problem—solution and the improvements in turn result in stakeholder support. Such iterative improvements (Baum & Bird, 2010) are a result of highly intertwined (rather than distinct) analytic-synthetic loops (Michlewski, 2008) and enable entrepreneurs to consolidate and reconcile various stakeholder objectives.

Generating "Creative Leaps"

Entrepreneurs as designers in search of problem—solution focus the deliberations on generating new possibilities rather than wait for sudden illumination or the "aha" moment. The act of deliberating described earlier often leads to new insights shifting the focus to a new part of the solution space

(Cross, 2006). These insights may occur as a "sudden flash" but more importantly, they have the potential to form a bridge across the requirements and solution features. Deliberation provides opportunities for the designer-entrepreneur to use previously held knowledge in new ways to make creative connections while also systematically venturing into new areas in search of generating new options. A critical component of such creativity then is to proactively seek information and constantly expand one's knowledge base, and thereafter use it in naturally occurring interactions. Creative solutions embodying novel features emerge when the possibilities are regarded as apposite by stakeholders. Initial stakeholder recognition and acceptance of the solution possibility can evolve and turn into one that is seen as a "creative leap" (Cross, 2006). Thus, while creativity is central to designing, it is opportunistic, iterative, and evolutionary, and often occurs by making creative connections across disparate and unrelated information in the form of reflexive actions.

The Formative Nature of these Practices

The above-mentioned practices describe "how" entrepreneurs might perform the actions. These practices based on design thinking, also called "designing" hereafter, can be summarized as consisting of:

(a) Problem-solving: taking a problem-solving approach to search solutions for the decomposed micro-level problems;
(b) Improving: focus on continuous improvements through deliberations; and
(c) Generating creative leaps: conceptualizing new forms and generating new possibilities by making creative connections between disparate information.

Boland and Collopy's (2004) framework of managing by design describes how managers acquire intelligence, analyze, and synthesize the information and act on the knowledge. These actions do not occur as distinct steps, but instead are reflexive in the moment actions. Preceding discussion about the three components pertains to how entrepreneurs acquire new knowledge and synthesize and generate alternatives to better understand the problem—solution space. This research proposes that designing is a formative measure.

Designing as a Formative Construct

Formative measures provide a means of modeling complex phenomena from a diverse and disparate set of observable items (Chin & Gopal, 1995; Diamantopoulos & Siguaw, 2006; Gefen & Straub, 2005); they also facilitate the aggregation of disparate indicators to the level of a holistic, single construct, which improves parsimony and enhances the predictive value of a measurement model (Cenfetelli & Bassellier, 2009). Jarvis, Mackenzie, Podsakoff, Mick, and Bearden (2003) suggest four primary guidelines for specifying formative constructs:

(1) The theoretical causal direction suggests that the formative measure (in this case, designing) is causing rather than being caused by the latent variables such as problem-solving;
(2) An examination of the interchangeability of latent variables allows the researcher to ascertain those which are not easily interchangeable and actually reflect different content themes;
(3) The latent variables are not multicollinear, that is, correlation among them is less than 0.7 (Hair, Black, Babin, & Anderson, 2010);
(4) The latent variables have different antecedents and consequences.

Criteria 1, 2, and 4 are explored and validated below; criterion 3, on the other hand, will be validated as a part of the data analysis in this research.

Causal Direction
Improvement actions based on stakeholder feedback allows products and processes to be modified, and the problem–solution space under design to evolve so as to meet the expectations of the external environment. The creative visualization to conjure a possibility for the future reality (Arnheim, 1980) is facilitated by making connections between unconnected information. Making connections is central to creative thinking in the design process and leads to newer, modified problem–solution space. Constraints during problem-solving can limit the actions of the designer and are treated as fundamental to the design process. However, deliberations involve identifying and negotiating the meanings of constraints, challenging them, and leveraging them in order to turn them into opportunities to produce solutions with greater acceptability in the environment (Vandenbosch & Gallagher, 2004). Therefore, in each of these cases, designing the problem–solution is caused by the three factors and validates the first criterion for a formative measure.

Interchangeability of Latent Variables
Next, the three factors are distinct and not interchangeable. Social entrepreneurs get to know their environment by investigating, trying, testing, or examining, and through the feedback they receive as a result (Frese, 2007; Thomke, 1998). On the mission side, human services social ventures are often employers of their beneficiaries and need to involve them in the production or service delivery processes. Through trials and pilots, they can determine the skills deficit and determine a subsequent course of action, such as selecting different products/services or training the employees. On the business side, this involves actions such as demonstrating a prototype of the product/service to prospective customers, seeking their feedback on its features, and understanding needed improvements (utility, price) in order that the product/service is viable. Improvement-oriented actions are emergent (Mintzberg & Waters, 1985), wherein trials are in-the-moment focused on practical issues.

Contrary to this, social ventures' common exclusion from conventional funding sources (Certo & Miller, 2008; Datta, 2011) may be overcome by being alert to the environment, picking up on opportunities to make connections to gain access to important financial, human, and political resources. Successful entrepreneurs scan the environment to acquire new knowledge, detect and leverage opportunities, both opportunistically (Frese, 2007) and intentionally. Central to such actions is connecting information which may have been disparate, perhaps unrelated, so as to generate alternatives for exploration with stakeholders.

Furthermore, entrepreneurs may resolve the uncertainty and ambiguity associated with nascent ventures through problem-solving, which is distinctly different from the two factors discussed above. Successful entrepreneurs as designers are not deterred by the limitations associated with nascent ventures; instead, they look at limitations as micro-level problems to solve, generate new possibilities to arrive at a legitimate response (Tolbert & Zucker, 1983). Therefore, improvement actions, generating creative leaps, and problem-solving are conceptually different and not interchangeable (Jarvis et al., 2003): each has a different focus when it comes to designing for problem—solution.

Different Antecedents and Consequences
Finally, the antecedents and consequences of the three factors are different. Intelligence (which can be gathered through prior experience, engaging with stakeholders, or previous trials) is the antecedent to *improvement actions*. Consequences, on the other hand, involve possible improvements

to products or processes which meet stakeholders' needs (Baum & Bird, 2010) and present problem–solution possibilities. *Generating creative leaps* requires maintaining continuous, broad, and undirected search for information, then creatively combining the information in new combinations (Tang, Kacmar, & Busenitz, 2011); the consequences involve product or process design of which entrepreneurs had not previously thought. Finally, an entrepreneur who is *problem-solving* is pursuing goals such as generating possible responses to micro-problem–solution and, thus, treats the accepted means with little regard, takes control in unstructured situations, challenges the rules, and has little respect for past custom. The entrepreneur may solve the problem independently or, in the case of complex problems, leverage social networks (Friedel & Hatala, 2010); when successful, the outcome is a legitimate problem–solution response. Therefore, the antecedents and consequences of the three factors are distinctly different and support the formative nature of *designing*.

This validation supports the proposal that *improving, generating creative leaps*, and *problem-solving* are distinctly different, but together constitute the formative measure: *designing*.

How Are Choices Made?

Actions based in design thinking strive to meet the demands of the environment. In doing so, social entrepreneurs are likely to generate opportunities to acquire resources pro bono or at lower-than-market rates, thereby keeping costs low. Designing (as described earlier) provides information and generates possibilities for problem–solution which entrepreneurs may use to judge the worthiness of each possibility, evaluate risks and potential losses associated with each possibility and decide with which alternative to proceed. Since most designing actions are in the moment and do not consist of distinct phases of gathering information and generating possibilities, this research proposes that entrepreneurs do not arrive at decisions (their preferred choice) to continue or change the direction of their actions based on research, detailed analysis, and deliberate logic; instead, they tend to be emergent, made "in the moment" (March & Simon, 1958; Mintzberg & Waters, 1985; Simon, 1996), based on the reality being designed. In a sense-making approach (Boland & Collopy, 2004; Weick, 1969), goals are understood retrospectively and the enactment of specific design-based actions is the primary driving force for the actions. This logic suggests that the *designing* is an antecedent to *choice*, rather than it being a factor of *designing*.

Hypothesis 1. Designing (which generates possibilities) is an Antecedent to Choice.

The decisions made directly contribute to the path the entrepreneur is taking for venture development. The choice of whether to proceed with a problem–solution possibility directly affects the venture's resource base, stakeholder support and advancement in the development of its products and processes among others. Due to its wicked nature social venture development during these early stages cannot be studied in absolute terms such as revenue and profits; instead, it is subjective, dependent on the entrepreneurs' and key stakeholders' conception of the venture and the perception of whether the venture will advance as a result of the decision. Therefore, this research focuses on perceived venture development, and suggests that it is a factor of how entrepreneurs' decide from possibilities they are presented with, that is, whether they are able to comprehend and identify those possibilities which can yield greater results for the perceived development of the venture. The better their ability to differentiate the possibilities and their potential outcomes, the greater is the development of the venture. Therefore:

Hypothesis 2. Choice Positively Impacts Perceived Venture Development.

Which and How Many Activities Are Completed?

Social venture start-up research has identified specific start-up activities during pre-launch and early development (Fisher, 2012; Haugh, 2007; Katre & Salipante, 2012). These include developing a social business concept, establishing legal entity, developing revenue models, developing product/service prototypes, securing funds (such as grants, donations, private investments), recruiting beneficiaries either as employees or as customers based on the social business concept, partnering with nonprofit, public, and private sector institutions, and making the first sale. The goal of these activities is to secure stakeholder commitments and advance venture development. Stakeholders indicate their support in the form of awarding non-financial resources (such as office space, free training, and other pro bono services), financial resources (such as project-related investments, grants, or donations), or by engaging in material resource exchanges (such as buying products/services). Resource acquisition and exchange enables completion of intermediate venture development tasks and activities demonstrating developmental progress which then allows stakeholders to award legitimacy to the start-up. Start-up activities undertaken and successfully completed at any point in time determine further development of the venture (Eckhardt, Shane, & Delmar, 2006). Commercial entrepreneurship research shows that specific start-up activities predict if a venture becomes real (Carter, Gartner, & Reynolds, 1996; Delmar & Shane, 2004; Gartner, Starr, & Bhat, 1999). This research postulates that the greater the number of social venture specific start-up activities completed, greater is the development of the nascent venture.

Hypothesis 3. Start-up Activities Completed Positively Impact Perceived Venture Development.

The formative nature of *Designing* and the hypotheses are depicted in the conceptual model in Fig. 1.

RESEARCH DESIGN

Measure Development and Survey Design

The conceptual model was tested using a self-administered survey methodology. Existing and validated measures were adapted wherever possible;

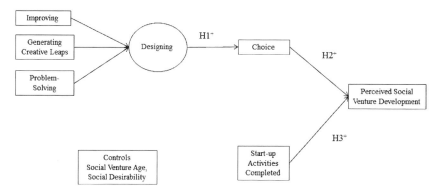

Fig. 1. Design Approach and Perceived Venture Development.

in other cases, new measures were defined. Refer to the appendix for survey wording, scales and items.

Improving: The five-item scale employed by Baum and Bird (2010) to measure multiple improvement actions for product/process enhancements most closely represented the phenomenon of design-based actions to make changes in order to meet stakeholder requirements. This scale items were reworded to suit the context of social entrepreneurship. Each item was measured on a five-point Likert scale anchored at the extremes by "1 – strongly disagree" and "5 – strongly agree."

Generating creative leaps: A review of measurement scales related to making creative connections using disparate and seemingly unrelated information led to the "connecting" dimension of the three element alertness scale by Tang et al. (2011). Items were reworded to suit the context of social entrepreneurship. Each item was measured on a five-point Likert scale anchored at the extremes by "strongly disagree" and "strongly agree."

Problem-solving: This dimension of designing had to do with not being constrained by the resources at hand and the predisposition to turn constraints into opportunities. Items from an existing, comprehensive proactiveness, scale (Bateman & Crant, 1993) best represented this phenomenon but were reworded to reflect actions which founders may have taken rather than generic indicators of problem-solving. Each item was measured on a five-point Likert scale anchored at the extremes by "strongly disagree" to "strongly agree."

Choice: Actions to evaluate situations for their potential in this case meant choices pertaining to acquiring pro bono resources, lowering costs, or acquiring new customers or partners among others. The evaluation and judgment dimension of the alertness scale (Tang et al., 2011) best represented this phenomenon. These items were adapted; each item was recorded and measured on a five-point Likert scale anchored at the extremes by "strongly disagree" to "strongly agree."

Start-up activities completed: The specific tasks and activities venture founders undertake to provide a measure of the lengths to which they will go to develop their new ventures. Commercial entrepreneurs engage in start-up activities such as attending training, forming legal entities, creating business plans, developing products/services, and making their first sales (Carter et al., 1996; Gartner et al., 1999); nonprofits, on the other hand, engage in defining the mission, recruiting board members and volunteers, developing client programs, and fundraising (Bobo, Kendall, & Max, 1996; Gartner, 1993). To assess such organizing tasks, a list of start-up activities undertaken by social ventures was developed from published social entrepreneurship research (Fisher, 2012; Guclu et al., 2002; Haugh, 2007; Katre & Salipante, 2012; Perrini et al., 2010). A score of "Low" was assigned if the number of activities completed was three or less; "Medium," if between four and six; and "High," otherwise.

One critical start-up activity is the financial support provided by external stakeholders to sustain the development of the venture. These may take the form of project-related investments and foundation grants as is the case with conventional nonprofits; in the case of business ventures, it may take the form of start-up capital from investors or "bootstrap" funds from family, friends, and social investors. These sources of financing are indicative of the entrepreneurs' ability to convince stakeholders and generate support for venture development. Therefore, financial support relative to the total operating budget was used as a measure on a three-point Likert scale of "Low," "Medium," and "High." This measure was retained as a distinct item and not included in the number of start-up activities completed. Therefore, the number of specific start-up activities completed (as described in the previous paragraph) and the financial support accumulated constituted the measure for start-up activities completed.

Perceived venture development: While there are some standard measures for business performance (revenue, profits, number of employees, growth rate), mission-performance scales are non-standard (Moxham, 2009) and primarily applicable to donor-based organizations. In addition, early development involves progressing from a raw idea to where the venture is real as perceived by the founders. Qualitative research (Haugh, 2007; Katre & Salipante, 2012) has suggested factors which entrepreneurs use to perceive their ventures as being real. This includes items such as whether they have begun serving the beneficiaries, been able to generate revenue from sales of products/services and if their venture is headed towards profitability. A scale using the above-mentioned items was developed to measure perceived venture development vis-à-vis the entrepreneur's initial vision for the start-up. Each item was measured on a three point Likert scale as "Low," "Medium," or "High,"

Controls: Older ventures have had more time and, thus, greater opportunities to undertake organizing activities, which in turn affects business venture growth and development (Carter et al., 1996; Gartner et al., 1999). The study was therefore controlled for venture age.

These measurement scales were refined through pretests and pilot testing using scale development guidelines (Churchill, 1979). Surveys were administered in-person using concurrent verbal-protocol content analysis (Bolton, 1993) to assess the survey quality. Additional pretests with 25 nonprofit practitioners and academicians involved written and verbal feedback. Finally, the survey design was further modified based on a pilot test with nascent social entrepreneurs.

Data Collection

A cross-sectional study was administered online from May 2011 to August 2011. The target population was (co)founders of social entrepreneurial ventures with no restrictions on age, gender, social mission, geographies served, or legal structure. As a result of targeting only early-stage ventures, 53% of those studied were less than five years old. In addition, the survey questions were worded to ensure that data were captured for the first five years, even if the ventures had been in existence for over five years.

The Social Venture Network, a practitioner network composed of the founders of social ventures throughout North America, provided access to their database of current members (486 in all). Additionally, membership-based networking forums such as the Social Enterprise Alliance (approximately 2,000 as stated by the listserv administrator), the Social Entrepreneur Empowerment Network (approximately 200 as stated by the listserv administrator), and the International Network of Socio-Eco Entrepreneurs (842 members) were leveraged to seek participants. The survey was emailed to a total of 3,528 members across these networks. All non-respondents were sent two follow-up reminders spaced three weeks apart, and several other measures were taken to ensure high response and completion rates: (a) a cover letter explained the need for scholarly research in the area and the critical role of practitioners in creating useful knowledge; (b) anonymity was assured, as well as individual and organizational confidentiality; and (c) respondents were informed they would have access to survey results upon completion of the study.

During the three months when the survey was administered, the inflow of responses was fairly consistent with a total of 450 responses received representing a response rate of 12.7%. A total of 196 were complete and usable for the analysis, resulting in a 37% completion rate. To test for unit non-response bias, the time trend extrapolation procedure suggested by Armstrong and Overton (1977) was employed; the presumption is that those who reply later to a survey are more likely to resemble non-respondents than early respondents. Incomplete responses were examined and it was discovered that 90% of such respondents had dropped out early after responding to about 5% of the survey. A one-way ANOVA revealed no significant differences between early and late respondents, except on two of the 43 items (4.6%); this indicates that responses can be regarded as broadly representative of the pooled sample. The sample size was deemed adequate. Characteristics of the sample are outlined in Table 1. The social purpose of ventures in the sample represented a mix of human services, education, and environmental issues, and more than 85% of the ventures' beneficiaries and customers were spread across North America, Africa, and Asia.

Data Screening and Analyses

Descriptive statistics for the study variables were analyzed. A few significant cases of univariate and multivariate outliers were identified but

Table 1.   Sample Characteristics.

Mission Purpose	Number	%	Main Business	Number	%
Human services	63	32	Manufacturing	14	7
Education	28	14	Retail and distribution	39	20
Environment	38	19	Services	93	47
Arts and crafts	4	2	Agriculture	5	3
Health	16	8	Real estate	6	3
Other	47	24	Other	39	20
Sales Geography	**Number**	**%**	**Beneficiaries' Geography**	**Number**	**%**
Africa	10	5	Africa	7	4
Asia	18	9	Asia	14	7
Europe	2	1	Europe	2	1
North America	109	56	North America	111	57
South America	2	1	South America	2	1
Global	55	28	Global	60	31
Legal Structure	**Number**	**%**	**Respondent's Gender**	**Number**	**%**
Nonprofit	69	35	Male	119	61
For-profit	124	63	Female	77	39
Mixed	3	2			

Total respondents 196

retained for further analysis. The tests for skewness and kurtosis using z-score tests (Hair et al., 2010) showed normality for all variables. The test for heteroscedasticity showed all relationships other than the one pair problem-solving and improving were heteroscedastic ($R^2 < 0.3$). Tests for linearity and multicollinearity did not show any significant threat, nor the need to remove any variables. The Durbin-Watson statistic was in the acceptable range (close to 2.0), indicating independence of the variables.

The research model was tested using Partial Least Squares, PLS-Graph, v3.0, Build 1060, (Chin & Frye, 1998). PLS was particularly well-suited for analysis given its flexibility in handling constructs with both reflective and formative indicators (Chin & Gopal, 1995). The PLS modeling approach involved two steps: validating the measurement model, then fitting the structural model. The former was accomplished primarily by reliability and validity tests of the measurement model; these were followed by testing the explanatory power of the overall model to explain variance and testing individual hypotheses in the structural model. A bootstrap resampling procedure (500 resamples) was conducted to test for significance of hypothesized relationships.

As noted earlier, and following the characterization by Diamantopoulos and Siguaw (2006) and Jarvis et al. (2003), the second-order formative construct *Designing* consists of reflective first-order components. Commonly espoused approaches to evaluating validity and reliability of first-order constructs were employed. Treating the sub-constructs as reflective constructs is appropriate, even though second-order constructs are formative (Cadogan, Souchon, & Procter, 2008). The dimensionality of each first-order construct in the research was verified using Confirmatory Factor Analysis (CFA) and ensuring that cross-loading of items was within acceptable limits. The CFA results, presented in Table 2, revealed high standardized regression weights (greater than 0.7) for all first-order constructs, confirming that the individual measures reflected the respective constructs. Further, internal consistency was observed, with composite reliability (CR) exceeding the recommended threshold of 0.70 (Tabachnick & Fidell, 2007).

Convergent validity, too, was established where the average variance explained (AVE) by each construct was greater than the measurement error (i.e., the AVE is at least 0.50). Further, discriminant validity was established by examining cross-loading of each item from a given construct on all of the other constructs, and by ensuring that maximum loadings were in fact appropriate to the construct to which each item belonged. As seen in Table 2, the AVE for all factors was less than the CR, suggesting discriminant validity of the factors (Fornell & Larcker, 1981).

Table 2. Results of CFA.

Construct and Items	Mean	Standard Deviation	Regression Weights	Critical Ratio	Composite Reliability	Average Variance Extracted
SVDev					*0.921*	*0.796*
M1T2	0.8418	0.0313	0.8363	27.6296		
B1T2	0.9198	0.0140	0.9210	61.9921		
B2T2	0.9099	0.0138	0.9174	79.6941		
Choice					*0.838*	*0.721*
AL1	0.8992	0.0208	0.8518	45.8986		
AL6	0.7911	0.0503	0.8518	45.8986		
Start-up Activities					*0.741*	*0.598*
B3T2	0.9076	0.0433	0.7816	34.1430		
ActDone	0.5977	0.1164	0.7816	34.1430		
GenCrLeap					*0.844*	*0.644*
AL2	0.8002	0.0340	0.8002	23.4092		
AL4	0.8254	0.0294	0.8233	26.8174		
AL7	0.7797	0.0470	0.7835	17.2560		
Improving					*0.881*	*0.553*
MIA1	0.7003	0.0518	0.6991	13.1910		
MIA3	0.7155	0.0449	0.7224	15.7608		
MIA4	0.7539	0.0414	0.7581	17.7265		
MIA5	0.7191	0.0644	0.7213	11.1786		
MIA6	0.7774	0.0437	0.7816	17.7848		
MIA7	0.7729	0.0533	0.7777	14.4963		
ProbSolve					*0.850*	*0.654*
PRO4	0.7424	0.0489	0.7527	17.2393		
PRO7	0.8812	0.0211	0.8817	43.0220		
PRO8	0.7866	0.0298	0.7868	24.0753		
Designing[a]					*0.879*	*0.398*[a]
GenCrLeap			0.3567	12.9214		
Improving			0.4770	17.7935		
ProbSolv			0.3696	12.6288		

[a]This is a formative construct.

Three of the four primary guidelines suggested by Jarvis et al. (2003) for the formative construct *Designing* were reviewed while proposing the construct. The fourth guideline, which pertained to multicollinearity, was analyzed to explore the lack of parsimony and conceptual overlap among the first-order constructs (Diamantopoulos & Siguaw, 2006). The data (Table 3) showed the shared variance was within acceptable range (less than 0.5) as suggested by Hair et al. (2010).

Checking for internal consistency of a formative construct is inappropriate, since each item of the construct is there for a theoretical reason: removing one component may adversely affect the overall meaning of the latent construct (Jarvis et al., 2003). PLS estimates the weights used to measure the contribution of each first-order latent construct to the variance of the latent variable. Following the suggestion of Petter, Straub, and Rai (2008), these weights were used as evidence of construct validity. When these are significant (by means of bootstrapping), item weights indicate that the first-order latent construct explains a significant portion of the variance in the formative construct (Roberts & Thatcher, 2009). As shown in Table 2, all latent constructs of the formative construct are significant ($p < 0.001$) and with acceptable values (Chin & Frye, 1998). Collectively, the analysis confirms that *Designing* is a higher-order formative construct made up of three lower-level reflective constructs, and can be used for hypothesis testing.

Common method bias was analyzed using the Marker Variable technique (Lindell & Whitney, 2001). Social desirability, a construct theoretically not correlated with other constructs, was introduced as a marker variable and showed a 0.22 correlation with all other latent constructs, indicating less than 5% maximum shared variance with other latent constructs. The data, therefore, did not demonstrate the presence of common method bias.

RESULTS

To test the hypotheses, the conceptual model in Fig. 1 was fitted using PLS, and each path in the causal model was tested for the significance of effect size and effect strength. The results (Table 4 and Fig. 2) provide evidence to support H1: *Designing* is an antecedent of, and is positively and significantly related to, *choice* ($\beta = 0.54$, $p < 0.001$). On the other hand, *choice* ($\beta = 0.29$, $p < 0.001$) was positively and significantly related to perceived venture development, confirming support for H2. In support of H3, *Start-up Activities* ($\beta = 0.40$, $p < 0.001$) had a significant and positive

Table 3. Correlations of Latent Variables.

	SVDev	Designing	Choice	Start-up Activities	GenCrLeap	ImprovActions	ProbSolve
SVDev	0.892						
Designing	0.121	0.630[a]					
Choice	0.281	0.539	0.849				
Start-up Activities	0.478	0.230	0.136	0.773			
GenCrLeap	0.017	0.750[b]	0.475	0.138	0.802		
Improving	0.066	0.870[b]	0.435	0.187	0.496	0.744	
ProbSolve	0.177	0.800[b]	0.430	0.190	0.416	0.599	0.809

[a]Designing is a formative construct.
[b]These latent constructs load on to Designing as a formative construct.

Table 4.   Structural Model Results.

Path	Regression Weight	Critical Ratio	p-Value	Support for the Hypothesis
H1: Designing → Choice	0.539	9.395	0.000***	Yes
H2: Choice → SVDev	0.260	3.559	0.000***	Yes
H3: Start-up Activities → SVPDev	0.401	6.405	0.000***	Yes
SVAge → SVDev	0.332	5.322	0.000***	

***$p < 0.001$.

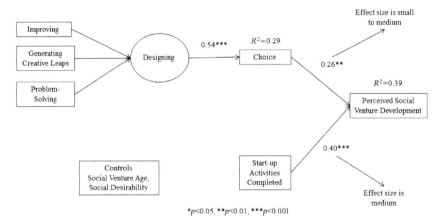

Fig. 2.   Results: Design Approach and Perceived Venture Performance.

relationship with perceived venture development. The coefficient of determination R^2 was evaluated and found to account adequately for variance in choice ($R^2 = 0.29$) and perceived venture development ($R^2 = 0.39$).

Predictive relevance and validity: In order to investigate the predictive power of each construct in the model, effect size tests as recommended by Chin and Frye (1998) were conducted. The f^2 statistic is based on the differences in R^2 between two models, with and without the particular construct whose effect strength is being measured. Cohen (1988) recommends that the effect size values of 0.02, 0.15, and 0.35 be viewed as an estimate of whether a predictor has a small, medium, or large effect at the structural level.

Table 5.   Path Effect Strength.

Path	R^2 Included	R^2 Excluded	f-Squared and Effect Significance
Choice → SVDev	0.386	0.341	0.08 (Small)
Start-up Activities → SVDev	0.386	0.256	0.21 (Medium)
SVAge → SVDev	0.386	0.294	0.16 (Medium)

The f^2 values for each hypothesized relationship are summarized in Table 5. Both *Designing* and *choice* were found to have a small- to medium-size effect on perceived venture development, whereas that of *start-up activities* was medium to large (Table 5). Thus, the conceptual model highlights that the "How?" (i.e., practices based on design thinking) and the "What?" (i.e., the *start-up activities*) explains perceived venture development. Finally, the model's predictive validity, Q^2, was verified according to the recommendation of Stone (1974) and Geisser (1975): a blindfolding procedure revealed that the Q^2-value estimate was greater than zero ($Q^2 = 0.05$), indicating that the model had predictive relevance.

DISCUSSION

The aim of this inquiry was to conceptualize and test a design thinking-based model for "what" social entrepreneurs do to create their ventures and "how" do they go about their start-up actions. Social entrepreneurs are dissatisfied with a social situation and are interested in bringing about a change in it. Designing, is in this case, not just about making decisions to formulate new products and services but is about describing, mapping, proposing, and reconfiguring complex services and systems to produce change (Jones, 2015). Design thinking-based practices facilitate the generation of insights and engagement of diverse group of stakeholders, as well as facilitate the synthesis of the conscious, the analytical and the intuitive, the functional and the emotional, and planning and creation (Buchanan & Margolin, 1995; Dorst, 2011). Designers' communication and visualization practices help make the intangible concepts tangible and facilitate iterative reflective conversation with the situation.

This research suggests that like commercial ventures, the development of social ventures can be predicted based on the nature and number of start-up activities completed, but is also dependent on how these activities are performed. The findings support recent research and recommendations on search-based approaches for new venture creation (Lambert & Davidson, 2013; Reis, 2011; Sarasvathy, 2008). For example, entrepreneurs may take different approaches to decide whether to engage clients as employees and/ or customers, an activity important for social ventures. Taking a predictive approach suggests conducting extensive industry, market and competitive research, and integrating the findings in a business plan in order to seek funding to launch the venture. Contrarily, search-based approach suggests treating the decision as a problem to solve, wherein entrepreneurs experiment with ideas, seek feedback, make improvements or make innovative connections between new information acquired to explore alternatives until they arrive at an acceptable idea (e.g., the social venture decides to employ clients but only as transitional employment). The designing construct formulated in this research suggests that such search-based approaches for various start-up activities together with the number of start-up activities completed (from a predefined list) can explain the extent of venture development.

Although commercial entrepreneurship and nonprofit organization research has each validated the predictive capabilities of their respective start-up activities, such knowledge is lacking for social ventures. Only recently have there been initiatives to measure social venture start-up activities (Gras, Moss, & Lumpkin, 2014). A validated scale consisting of 10 start-up activities shows that deciding early on whether to engage clients as employees and/or customers of the social venture, establishing nonprofit partnerships to provide additional clients services, while at the same time focusing on prototyping and testing the venture's product or service, attempting to generate sales, and securing funds are important predictors of social venture development. Activities such as creating a base of volunteers and making connections with the gatekeepers predict early stage survival of nonprofit organizations (Delehanty, 1996; Hager, Galaskiewicz, & Larson, 2004; McBrearty, 2007). Despite the exclusion of these activities, the rather high predictive capability of start-up activities in this research indicates that some of the activities typical for nonprofit survival may not be critical for social ventures.

The logic of proposing *designing* as a formative construct was based on design concepts (Boland & Collopy, 2004; Buchanan & Margolin, 1995; Cross, 2006; Rittel & Webber, 1973), and the causal relationships in the conceptual model were based on Boland and Collopy (2004) design approach of a "Sense-Making Manager." Actions representing the concept of *designing* were verified as a formative construct with adequate convergent, discriminant, and predictive validity. Given the tricky relationship between the "problem" and its "solution" (Cross, 2011), this research suggests that social entrepreneurs may explore its various dimensions by looking at start-up questions as problems to solve, repeatedly try out concepts with stakeholders and incorporate their suggestions, but also remain alert to new information acquired. For example, a social entrepreneur might look at coming up with product or service ideas to provide basic job skills for the incarcerated as a problem to solve. Simultaneously, based on prior knowledge, the entrepreneur can formulate service ideas such as lawn mowing and discuss with key stakeholders for feedback. While refining the idea if the entrepreneur remains open to ideas not thought of earlier, such as product/service possibilities with urban beekeeping, and incorporate it in the problem-solving process, then, creative and viable alternatives can be generated. Rather than linear analytical thought and action, this combined interactivity between problem-solving, trying out, making improvements, and remaining alert to possibilities can lead to solutions which no-one dreamed of.

Designing, which generates possibilities corresponding to various dimensions of the problem–solution relationships, was conceptualized as an antecedent to *choice*, representing the assessment and differentiation of alternatives which present greater value for the social venture. Continuing the above example, *choice* would mean assessing if urban beekeeping was a way to create greater value (for the clients, markets, and stakeholders engaged in the problem-solving process) than say lawn mowing. Sense-making manager approach suggests the generation of multiple alternatives to choose one among them to proceed with Boland and Collopy (2004). However, the high-level of connectedness of the three dimensions of *designing* presents the possibility that *choice* might be just another dimension where decisions are made as problem–solution possibilities emerge. To explore this possibility, a model where *choice* was a fourth *dimension* of designing was tested but did not find adequate support suggesting that social entrepreneurs first generate alternatives and then assess them to make decisions. Based on the instrument used to measure *choice*, it cannot be said with certainty as to whether evaluation happens by synthesizing the conscious (i.e., intellectual, analytical, and research based) and the intuitive (sensing and feeling at a subconscious level) as suggested by Papanek and Fuller (1972), or if entrepreneurs emphasize one over the other. The rather strong antecedent relationship may imply that *designing* is useful — to the extent that the actions involved in *designing* provide a real basis to judge an opportunity and arrive at decisions. They may also provide information as to the extent of stakeholder engagement required, responses from other nonprofits, and the market opportunity being shaped so as to arrive at a pragmatic decision (Simon, 1996) based on constructed reality (Giddens, 1984) rather than deliberate plans (Mintzberg & Waters, 1985).

The dimensions and components of *designing* is a unique and important contribution which adds to the scant knowledge pertaining to start-up stages of social entrepreneurship. Further, at nascent stages of theory testing, the effect size (small to medium) of *designing* (practices based in design thinking) on social venture development is promising. The Q^2 measure provides evidence of the predictive validity of the model. The research also provides a list of start-up activities with predictive capabilities which are unique for social entrepreneurship. Entrepreneurship literature, on the other hand, recognizes the value of design beginning with the pioneering work by Sarasvathy (2001) wherein entrepreneurship is considered as design, and entrepreneurial expertise and effectuation as a way of thinking and decision making. In an alternative conceptualization, entrepreneurship literature views design thinking as an approach to problem-solving, innovating new products and services, and to innovate business models (Ikem, Aponte, & Muffatto, 2015; Kovacevic et al., 2012). Research in these areas is largely conceptual or based on case studies and lacks a granular definition of practices which are empirically validated. This research contributes to the body of knowledge on the use of design thinking for entrepreneurship by precisely defining the nature of actions entrepreneurs might take regardless of the specific area − be it defining product or service, the business model, partnerships, or customer development.

LIMITATIONS

The research may not have covered the entire spectrum of social ventures. The domain of social entrepreneurship is broad and includes many types of enterprises: those undertaken by established nonprofits or operated by for-profit corporations, others with emerging legal structures such as L3C, and those originating in other parts of the world. Because the motives, approaches, and challenges associated with early development of each type may differ significantly, it is recommended that investigators exercise caution in generalizing the findings. Respondents in this study were from professional associations and special-interest groups with self-selected membership and, therefore, may not be representative of the broader population of social ventures.

Although the study was global and open to social ventures from all geographies, a significant percentage was from North America. Caution should be exercised in generalizing these findings to social ventures operating in other continents and countries. Furthermore, the study was focused on capturing actions, behaviors, and results pertaining to nascent stages (i.e., the initial five years). Since 47% of the ventures in the quantitative research had existed for more than five years, there is a need to recognize a potential time-bias wherein respondents may have had difficulty in recalling their actions. Although the study controlled for socially desirable responses, it is necessary to acknowledge that responses may represent prospective or hypothetical actions (Babbie, 2007) as opposed to the actions taken by the respondents. Finally, since the study did not capture the antecedents of *start-up activities*, there is a possibility that the observed effect may indeed be due to the antecedents.

IMPLICATIONS FOR RESEARCH AND PRACTICE

This research is one of the few to examine design thinking-based practices to create social ventures with emphasis on knowing, thinking, and doing. The research advances our understanding of design-based practices by identifying measures for specific practices in the context of social ventures. It also advances our understanding of design through (1) empirical validation of the design approach based on Karl Weick's "Sense-Making Manager" model and (2) providing a measurement for the components in the approach. Having survived a preliminary empirical exploratory investigation this research emphasizes the importance of the continued need to research the application of entrepreneurial actions based in design thinking for new venture creation.

There are several methodological and theoretical implications for future research. The research used existing measures from business entrepreneurship and nonprofit organization literature which accurately reflected the design concepts. The predictive reliability provides initial support for a positive relationship between this conceptualization of practices and nascent stages of venture development. This research should be treated as a starting point to further refine the measures and instruments relative to practices based on design thinking. The research also advances social entrepreneurship theory by providing specific actions founded in design thinking and constructivist principles for social innovation. The constructs are now available for further development in social venture research.

Finally, this research into venture development made a case for the use of a constructivist model rather than business planning models. The results show that, at a minimum, practices based in design thinking should be a complement to these latter models. The fact of small- to medium-effect sizes for design constructs leaves open the distinct possibility that predictive or planning logic may play a role. An exploration of planning for the venture configurations with specific venture activities may improve understanding of the relationship of designing to planning constructs.

The research also has several implications for practice. Sustainable social innovation is founded on designing cross-sector partnerships. Practices based in design thinking are based on stakeholder commitments; thus, they provide a pragmatic approach to the creation of sustainable social businesses. The conceptual model and measures use entrepreneurial vernacular, thereby providing a visualization of the venture creation actions for nascent social entrepreneurs. It highlights entrepreneurial actions essential to gaining micro-commitments from stakeholders, thus leading to the successful designing of venture products and processes. These include maintaining a high level of alertness to the information shared by others in day-to-day dealings, trying out improvements with stakeholders, and problem-solving to gain knowledge and acquire resources. But, most importantly, embedded in this conceptual model and its measures is the need to constantly review whether ventures should continue down their chosen paths – based on stakeholder commitments they may or may not secure.

REFERENCES

Alvord, S. H., Brown, L. D., & Letts, C. W. (2004). Social entrepreneurship and societal transformation. *The Journal of Applied Behavioral Science*, *40*(3), 260–282.

Armstrong, J. S., & Overton, T. S. (1977). Estimating nonresponse bias in mail surveys. *Journal of Marketing Research*, *14*(3), 396–402, Special Issue: Recent Developments in Survey Research.

Arnheim, R. (1980). A plea for visual thinking. *Critical Inquiry*, *6*(3), 489–497.

Babbie, E. (2007). *The practice of social research*. Belmont, CA: Wadsworth Publishing Inc.

Bateman, T. S., & Crant, J. M. (1993). The proactive component of organizational behavior: A measure and correlates. *Journal of Organizational Behavior*, *14*(2), 103–118.

Baum, J. R., & Bird, B. J. (2010). The successful intelligence of high-growth entrepreneurs: Links to new venture growth. *Organization Science*, *21*(2), 397–412.

Bobo, K. A., Kendall, J., & Max, S. (1996). *Organizing for social change: A manual for the activists in the 1990s* (2nd ed.). Santa Ana, CA: Seven Locks Press.

Boland, R. J., & Collopy, F. (Eds.). (2004). *Managing as designing*. Stanford, CA: Stanford University Press.

Bolton, R. N. (1993). Pretesting questionnaires: Content analyses of respondents' concurrent verbal protocols. *Marketing Science, 12*(3), 280–303.

Brown, T., & Wyatt, J. (2010). *Design thinking for social innovation.* Unpublished manuscript. Retrieved from https://openknowledge.worldbank.org/handle/10986/6068. Accessed on January 15, 2015.

Buchanan, R., & Margolin, V. (1995). *Discovering design: Explorations in design studies.* Chicago, IL: University of Chicago Press.

Cadogan, J. W., Souchon, A. L., & Procter, D. B. (2008). The quality of market-oriented behaviors: Formative index construction. *Journal of Business Research, 61*(12), 1263–1277.

Carter, N. M., Gartner, W. B., & Reynolds, P. D. (1996). Exploring start-up event sequences. *Journal of Business Venturing, 11*(3), 151.

Cenfetelli, R. T., & Bassellier, G. (2009). Interpretation of formative measurement in information systems research. *MIS Quarterly, 39*(4), 689–707.

Certo, S. T., & Miller, T. (2008). Social entrepreneurship: Key issues and concepts. *Business Horizons, 51*(4), 267–271.

Chin, W. W., & Frye, T. A. (1998). *PLS-graph, version 3.0.* Soft Modeling Inc.

Chin, W. W., & Gopal, A. (1995). Adoption intention in GSS. *ACM SIGMIS Database, 26*(2–3), 42–64.

Churchill, G. A., Jr. (1979). A paradigm for developing better measures of marketing constructs. *Journal of Marketing Research, 16*(1), 64–73.

Cohen, J. (1988). *Statistical power analysis for the behavioral sciences* (2nd ed.). Erlbaum, NJ: Hillsdale.

Cross, N. (1995). *Discovering design ability.* Chicago, IL: University of Chicago Press.

Cross, N. (2006). *Designerly ways of knowing.* Berlin: Springer.

Cross, N. (2011). *Design thinking: Understanding how designers think and work.* Oxford: Berg.

Dart, R. (2009). Charities in business, business in charities, charities and business. *The Philanthropist, 18*(3), 181–199.

Datta, P. B. (2011). Exploring the evolution of a social innovation: A case study from India. *International Journal of Technology Management & Sustainable Development, 10*(1), 55–75.

Dees, J. G., & Elias, J. (1998). The challenges of combining social and commercial enterprise. *Business Ethics Quarterly, 8*(1), 165–178.

Dees, J. G., Emerson, J., & Economy, P. (2002). *Enterprising nonprofits: A toolkit for social entrepreneurs.* New York, NY: John Wiley and Sons.

Delehanty, D. A. (1996). *Survival strategies: How social service nonprofits succeed and fail in the public arena (A case study of sexual assault and domestic violence centers).* Ph.D. Dissertation.

Delmar, F., & Shane, S. (2004). Legitimating first: Organizing activities and the survival of new ventures. *Journal of Business Venturing, 19*(3), 385.

Diamantopoulos, A., & Siguaw, J. A. (2006). Formative versus reflective indicators in organizational measure development: A comparison and empirical illustration. *British Journal of Management, 17*(4), 263–282.

Dorst, K. (2006). Design problems and design paradoxes. *Design Issues, 22*(3), 4–17.

Dorst, K. (2011). The core of 'design thinking' and its application. *Design Studies, 32*(6), 521–532.

Dorst, K., & Cross, N. (2001). Creativity in the design process: Co-evolution of problem–solution. *Design Studies, 22*(5), 425–437.

Eckhardt, J. T., Shane, S., & Delmar, F. (2006). Multistage selection and the financing of new ventures. *Management Science, 52*(2), 220–232.

Fisher, G. (2012). Effectuation, causation, and bricolage: A behavioral comparison of emerging theories in entrepreneurship research. *Entrepreneurship Theory and Practice, 36*(5), 1019–1051.

Fornell, C., & Larcker, D. F. (1981). Evaluating structural equation models with unobservable variables and measurement error. *Journal of Marketing Research, 18*(1), 39–50.

Frese, M. (2007). The psychological actions and entrepreneurial success: An action theory approach. In *The psychology of entrepreneurship*. Retrieved from http://www.evidence-based-entrepreneurship.com/content/publications/212.pdf

Fricke, G. (1996). Successful individual approaches in engineering design. *Research in Engineering Design, 8*(3), 151–165.

Friedel, C. R., & Hatala, J.-P. (2010). *Incorporating problem solving theory and social capital theory to improve entrepreneurial goal attainment*. Retrieved from http://www.socialnetworkaudit.com/articles/Social_Capital_Problem_Solving.pdf

Gartner, W. B. (1993). Organizing the voluntary association. *Entrepreneurship Theory and Practice, 17*(2), 103–106.

Gartner, W. B., Starr, J. A., & Bhat, S. (1999). Predicting new venture survival. *Journal of Business Venturing, 14*(2), 215–232.

Gefen, D., & Straub, D. (2005). A practical guide to factorial validity using PLS-graph: Tutorial and annotated example. *Communications of the Association for Information Systems, 16*(5), 91–109.

Geisser, S. (1975). The predictive sample reuse method with applications. *Journal of the American Statistical Association, 70*(350), 320–328.

Giddens, A. (1984). *The constitution of society: Outline of the theory of structuration*. Los Angeles, CA: University of California Press.

Gras, D., Mosakowski, E., & Lumpkin, T. (2011). Gaining insights from future research topics in social entrepreneurship: A content-analytic approach. In G. T. Lumpkin & J. A. Katz (Eds.), *Social and sustainable entrepreneurship* (1st ed., Vol. 13). Advances in Entrepreneurship, Firm Emergence and Growth. Bingley, UK: Emerald Group Publishing Limited.

Gras, D., Moss, T. W., & Lumpkin, G. (2014). The use of secondary data in social entrepreneurship research: Assessing the field and identifying future opportunities. In *Social entrepreneurship and research methods* (Vol. 9, pp. 49–75). Research Methodology in Strategy and Management. Bingley, UK: Emerald Group Publishing Limited.

Guclu, A., Dees, J. G., & Anderson, B. B. (2002). The process of social entrepreneurship: Creating opportunities worthy of serious pursuit. *Center for the Advancement of Social Entrepreneurship*, 1–15.

Guo, C., & Bielefeld, W. (2014). *Social entrepreneurship: An evidence-based approach to creating social value*. San Francisco, CA: John Wiley and Sons.

Hager, M. A., Galaskiewicz, J., & Larson, J. A. (2004). Structural embeddedness and the liability of newness among nonprofit organizations. *Public Management Review, 6*(2), 159–188.

Hagoort, G., Thomassen, A., & Kooyman, R. (2012). *Pioneering minds worldwide: On the entrepreneurial principles of the cultural and creative industries: Actual insights into cultural and creative entrepreneurship research*. Eburon Uitgeverij BV.

Hair, J. F., Black, W. C., Babin, B. J., & Anderson, R. E. (2010). *Multivariate data analysis* (7th ed.). Englewood Cliffs, NJ: Pearson-Prentice Hall.

Han, M., & McKelvey, B. (2009). *Emergence and performance of social entrepreneurship: A complexity science perspective.* Retrieved from http://www.billmckelvey.org/documents/working%20papers/2009%20Han,%20McKelvey(09)-Social%20Entrepreneurship–Jan.pdf

Haugh, H. (2005). A research agenda for social entrepreneurship. *Social Entrepreneurship Journal, 1*(1), 5–12.

Haugh, H. (2007). Community-led social venture creation. *Entrepreneurship Theory and Practice, 31*(2), 161–182.

Ikem, C., Aponte, A. S., & Muffatto, M. (2015). Design and innovation as drivers of modern entrepreneurship. Paper presented at the European Conference on Innovation and Entrepreneurship, 832.

Jarvis, C. B., Mackenzie, S. B., Podsakoff, P. M., Mick, D. G., & Bearden, W. O. (2003). A critical review of construct indicators and measurement model misspecification in marketing and consumer research. *Journal of Consumer Research, 30*(2), 199–218.

Jones, P. (2015). Design research methods for systemic design: Perspectives from design education and practice. Paper presented at the Proceedings of the 58th Annual Meeting of the ISSS-2014 United States, 1(1).

Katre, A., & Salipante, P. (2012). Start-up social ventures: Blending fine-grained behaviors from two institutions for entrepreneurial success. *Entrepreneurship Theory and Practice, 36*(5), 967–994.

King, N. K. (2004). Social capital and nonprofit leaders. *Nonprofit Management and Leadership, 14*(4), 471–486.

Kovacevic, A., Sharma, A., Rieple, A., Huber, A. M., Zidulka, A., Urrego, A. C., & Whicher, A. (2012). *Leading innovation through design: Proceedings of the DMI 2012 international research conference.*

Lambert, S. C., & Davidson, R. A. (2013). Applications of the business model in studies of enterprise success, innovation and classification: An analysis of empirical research from 1996 to 2010. *European Management Journal, 31*(6), 668–681.

Lindell, M. K., & Whitney, D. J. (2001). Accounting for common method variance in cross-sectional research designs. *Journal of Applied Psychology, 86*(1), 114–121.

March, J., & Simon, H. (1958). *Organizations.* Oxford: Blackwell Publishers.

Margolin, V. (1995). The product milieu and social action. *Discovering design: Explorations in design studies* (p. 122). Chicago, IL: University of Chicago Press.

McBrearty, S. (2007). Social enterprise – A solution for voluntary sector? *Social Enterprise Journal, 3*(1), 67–77.

Michlewski, K. (2008). Uncovering design attitude: Inside the culture of designers. *Organization Studies, 29*(3), 373–392.

Mintzberg, H., & Waters, J. A. (1985). Of strategies, deliberate and emergent. *Strategic Management Journal, 6*(3), 257–272.

Moxham, C. (2009). Performance measurement. *International Journal of Operations & Production Management, 29*(7), 740–763.

Neck, H. M., & Greene, P. G. (2011). Entrepreneurship education: Known worlds and new frontiers. *Journal of Small Business Management, 49*(1), 55–70.

Nicholls, A. (2006). *Social entrepreneurship: New models of sustainable social change.* New York, NY: Oxford University Press.

Papanek, V., & Fuller, R. B. (1972). *Design for the real world.* London: Thames and Hudson.

Perrini, F., Vurro, C., & Costanzo, L. A. (2010). A process-based view of social entrepreneurship: From opportunity identification to scaling-up social change in the case of San Patrignano. *Entrepreneurship & Regional Development, 22*(6), 515–534.

Petter, S., Straub, D., & Rai, A. (2008). Specifying formative constructs in information systems research. *MIS Quarterly, 31*(4), 623–656.

Read, S., Sarasvathy, S., Dew, N., Wiltbank, R., & Ohlsson, A. (2011). *Effectual entrepreneurship.* New York, NY: Routledge.

Read, S., Song, M., & Smit, W. (2009). A meta-analytic review of effectuation and venture performance. *Journal of Business Venturing, 24*(6), 573–587.

Reis, E. (2011). *The lean startup.* New York, NY: Crown Business.

Rittel, H. W., & Webber, M. M. (1973). Dilemmas in a general theory of planning. *Policy Sciences, 4*(2), 155–169.

Roberts, N., & Thatcher, J. (2009). Conceptualizing and testing formative constructs. *ACM SIGMIS Database, 40*(3), 9–39.

Sarasvathy, S., & Simon, H. A. (2000). Effectuation, near-decomposability, and the creation and growth of entrepreneurial firms. Paper presented at the First Annual Research Policy Technology Entrepreneurship Conference.

Sarasvathy, S. D. (2001). Causation and effectuation: Toward a theoretical shift from economic inevitability to entrepreneurial contingency. *The Academy of Management Review, 26*(2), 243–263.

Sarasvathy, S. D. (2008). *Effectuation: Elements of entrepreneurial expertise.* Cheltenham: Edward Elgar.

Simon, H. (1996). *The sciences of the artificial* (3rd ed.). Cambridge, MA: The MIT Press.

Stone, M. (1974). Cross-validatory choice and assessment of statistical predictions. *Journal of the Royal Statistical Society, Series B (Methodological), 36*(2), 111–147.

Tabachnick, B., & Fidell, L. (2007). Multivariate analysis of variance and covariance. In B. G. Tabachnick (Ed.), *Using multivariate statistics* (pp. 243–310). Boston, MA: Allyn & Bacon.

Tang, J., Kacmar, M., & Busenitz, L. (2011). Entrepreneurial alertness in the pursuit of new opportunities. *Journal of Business Venturing, 27*(1), 77–94.

Thomke, S. H. (1998). Managing experimentation in the design of new products. *Management Science, 44*(6), 743–762.

Tolbert, P. S., & Zucker, L. G. (1983). Institutional sources of change in the formal structure of organizations: The diffusion of civil service reform, 1880–1935. *Administrative Science Quarterly, 28*(1), 22–39.

Vandenbosch, B., & Gallagher, K. (2004). The role of constraints. In R. Boland (Ed.), *Managing as designing* (p. 198). Stanford, CA: Stanford University Press.

Weick, K. E. (1969). *The social psychology of organizing.* New York, NY: McGraw-Hill.

Westley, F. (2008). *The social innovation dynamic.* manuscript. Retrieved from http://sig.uwaterloo.ca/sites/default/files/documents/TheSocialInnovationDynamic_001.pdf

Woodbury, R. (2010). *Elements of parametric design* (1st ed.). New York, NY: Routledge.

York, J. G., Sarasvathy, S. D., & Larson, A. (2009). The thread of inchoate demand in social entrepreneurship. *Values and opportunities in social entrepreneurship* (p. 141). New York, NY: Palgrave Macmillan.

APPENDIX

Table A1. Survey and Scale Items.

Items	Social Venture Development
	We would like to know the *performance* of the venture *against your vision* for the first five years *(1 = Low, 2 = Medium, 3 = High, 4 = Not Applicable)*.
M1T2	Number of clients served in comparison with your vision
M2T2	Extent of improvement in clients' conditions in comparison with your vision (D)
M3T2	Additional programming and services offered to your clients (D)
B1T2	Revenues from sales of product/service in comparison with the total operating budget
B2T2	Extent of profitability

Items	Activities Done
	Tell us if you have *executed* the following activities for your venture in the first five years *(Y = Yes, N = No)*.
AE1	Develop a viable concept of the social business model
AE2	Explore services provided by other nonprofit, government and for-profit organizations
AE3	Secure funds from external funders
AE4	Establish a legal entity
AE5	Pilot and/or prototype revenue generating product/service
AE6	Make the first sales of product/service
AE7	Involve clients as employees and/or customers
AE8	Implement strategies to grow sales
AE9	Partner with nonprofits to provide additional services to clients
AE10	Stabilize operations for financial sustainability
	We would like to know the level of funds received *against your vision* for the first five years *(1 = Low, 2 = Medium, 3 = High, 4 = Not Applicable)*.
B3T2	Level of funds received (from investors, grants, and donors) in comparison with the total operating budget

Items	Choice
	Social entrepreneurs have many demands on their time and must *prioritize* their activities. Please tell us about your *choices for actions* during the initial development of your venture. Indicate the extent to which you agree with the following statements *(1 = Strongly Disagree to 5 = Strongly Agree)*.
AL1	I was able to distinguish high-value opportunities from low-value ones
AL6	I could distinguish between profitable and not-so profitable opportunities
AL9	I had a gut feeling for potential opportunities (D)

Table A1. *(Continued)*

Items	Generating Creative Leaps

Social entrepreneurs have many demands on their time and must *prioritize* their activities. Please tell us about your *choices for actions* during the initial development of your venture. Indicate the extent to which you agree with the following statements *(1 = Strongly Disagree to 5 = Strongly Agree)*.

AL2   I was able to see connections between previously unconnected domains of information

AL4   I was good at connecting dots

AL7   I saw links between seemingly unrelated pieces of information

Items	Problem-solving

The extent to which you agree with each of the *actions* listed below when you were creating your social venture *(1 = Strongly Disagree to 5 = Strongly Agree)*.

PRO4   If I saw something I didn't like, I would fix it

PRO7   When I had a problem, I tackled it head-on

PRO8   I was great at turning problems into opportunities

Items	Improving

Social entrepreneurs have many demands on their time and must *prioritize* their activities. Please tell us about your *choices for actions* during the initial development of your venture. Indicate the extent to which you agree with the following statements *(1 = Strongly Disagree to 5 = Strongly Agree)*.

MIA1   I frequently experimented with product and process improvements

MIA2   After I made decisions, I was good at monitoring the unfolding results (D)

MIA3   Continuous improvement in our products and processes was a priority

MIA4   I kept trying until I found a solution

MIA5   I regularly tried to figure out how to make everything work better

MIA6   I was constantly on the lookout for new ways to improve

MIA7   I was always looking for better ways to do things

Items	Social Desirability

Indicate if each of the following statements is true or false as it pertains to you personally, and beyond the development of the social venture *(1 = True, 2 = False)*.

SD1   By and large I do not hesitate to go out of my way to help someone in trouble

SD2   I have never intensely disliked anyone

SD3   I sometimes feel resentful when I don't get my way

SD4   There have been times when I felt like rebelling against people in authority even though I knew they were right

Table A1. (*Continued*)

Items	Social Desirability
SD5	I can remember "playing sick" to get out of something
SD6	When I don't know something I don't mind at all admitting it
SD7	Most often I am courteous, even to people who are disagreeable
SD8	I would rarely think of letting someone else be punished for my wrong-doings
SD9	There have been times when I was quite jealous of the good fortune of others
SD10	I am sometimes irritated by people who ask favors of me

Items	Controls
SVAGE	No. of years the social venture has been in existence (0−3 years, 3−5 years, over 5 years)

(D) = Items were dropped during CFA.

CHAPTER 5

THE EVOLUTION OF BUSINESS PLANS IN INTERNATIONAL BUSINESS PLAN COMPETITIONS

Charles Hofer

ABSTRACT

This chapter will describe and analyze the evolution of the structure, content, and other key parameters of business plans in international business plan competitions from the beginnings of such competitions in 1991 through the current time. In particular, the chapter will describe how these competitions have evolved through the current time, the standardization of the structure and content of the plans submitted to these competitions, and the changes that have occurred in their structure and content over time. Then it will explain why these changes have occurred. Specifically, that most of the changes that have occurred in these various areas is a direct or indirect result of pressures on the competitions from the major judges used in them — namely U.S. venture capitalists. Appendices A and B will describe the evaluation criteria used in two of the major competitions — Moot Corp/Venture Labs® and the Georgia Bowl® — in more detail, while Appendices C and D will provide information on the Term Sheets and decision-making processes used by such venture capitalists. Appendix E contains four Exhibits that provide

Models of Start-up Thinking and Action: Theoretical, Empirical and Pedagogical Approaches
Advances in Entrepreneurship, Firm Emergence and Growth, Volume 18, 145−211
Copyright © 2016 by Emerald Group Publishing Limited
ISSN: 1074-7540/doi:10.1108/S1074-754020160000018005

additional insights into U.S. venture capitalists' thought processes. The chapter will conclude with a discussion of the additional changes that are likely to happen in the future.

Keywords: Business plans; venture capital; competitions; valuation; decision-making; venture finance

INTRODUCTION

This chapter will describe and analyze the evolution of the basic structure, content, and other key parameters of business plans in international business plan competitions from the beginnings of such competitions in 1991 through the current time. In particular, the chapter will describe the basic purpose and structure of business plans; the evolution of business plan competitions through the current time; and the standardization of the structure and content of the business plans submitted to these competitions, together with the changes that have occurred in their structure and content over time. Then, it will explain why these changes have occurred, and conclude with a discussion of the changes that are likely to occur in the future. The focus will be on business plan competitions at the graduate or MBA level.

THE PURPOSE AND STRUCTURE OF BUSINESS PLANS

The Two Basic Purposes of All Business Plans

All business plans have just two basic purposes: (1) to formalize their author's thoughts about the business that they plan to start and (2) to provide potential investors the information that they require before they will invest any money in the proposed venture.

The Basic Structure of Business Plans

All business plans have three basic components: (1) An executive summary that highlights the most important aspects of the plan in one or at most two pages; (2) The body of the plan that describes for the venture's first

5 years of operations, specifically its (a) goals and objectives, (b) products and/or services, (c) customers and competitors, (d) marketing and sales strategies, (e) operating plans, (f) management and key advisors, (g) pro-forma financials, investment needs, and financials returns, and (h) key risks and contingency plans; and (3) a future growth section that summarizes the venture's most likely growth options for years 6 through 10.

THE EVOLUTION OF INTERNATIONAL BUSINESS PLAN COMPETITIONS

Moot Corp: The First International Business Plan Competition

The first international business plan competition in the world was the *International Challenge of Moot Corp*®, which had originally been created as an internal competition among student teams from the University of Texas, Austin, in the early 1984. In 1991, under the leadership of Dr. Gary Cadenhead, Texas invited 14 other graduate teams from leading U.S. business schools to Austin to compete for a "World Championship" – even though it involved only U.S. schools at the time. In part, the new Moot Corp® Competition was also intended to increase the reputation of Texas as a leading graduate school of Entrepreneurship in both the United States and internationally. By the late 1990s, Moot Corp® had expanded to 24 teams chosen from leading universities around the world as well as from the winners of various "feeder" competitions, which included almost all of the new competitions described below. The venture evaluation packet from Moot Corp® is included in Appendix A. In addition, Moot Corp® established qualifying competitions for teams from Africa, Australia, Europe, Central and South America, and Southeast Asia. In the early 2000s, it also invited the winner from the Idea-2-Product Competition, another University of Texas-Austin based competition that typically involved engineering students from leading universities around the world. In the mid-2000s, Moot Corp® expanded to 40 teams, and in the late 2000s changed its name to Venture Labs® in order to emphasize the fact that most of the competing teams were now actually successfully launching their proposed ventures after their team members had graduated. However, in November of 2015, Venture Labs announced that from 2016 forward it would revert to its original format and be open solely to teams from the University of Texas, Austin.

The Initial Follow-on Competitions

In 1992, San Diego State University (SDSU) created the second national, and later international, business plan competition; which was followed by the Georgia Bowl® Competition in 1993, and the University of Nebraska's National Venture Challenge in 1994. In its initial years, the *SDSU Venture Challenge* solicited plans from graduate schools throughout the United States, but only invited the Top 5 teams to San Diego to compete for the Final Prize. In 1993, the SDSU Venture Challenge was held the second week of May, and its winner defeated the Moot Corp® winner of that year, the first and only time this has ever happened. As a result, Moot Corp® moved its date so that it would always be the last competition of each competition season. In the mid-1990s, the SDSU Venture Challenge expanded, invited 20 U.S. teams to compete, and changed its date to late March of every year. Until then, no team from SDSU ever made the competition finals. However, the SDSU Venture Challenge was discontinued in 2013, although it was subsequently replaced by a California-team only business model competition.

As a result of the Texas and SDSU decisions, the *Georgia Bowl®* is now the oldest continuously held competition in the United States and the world. The Georgia Bowl® is held the first full weekend of February each year, making it the first U.S. competition, of each competition season. In its first few years, it was a competition among teams from the leading graduate schools in the state of Georgia, but it has since expanded its focus and is now open to graduate teams from throughout the United States and Canada. The Georgia Bowl® is also unique in three ways: (1) it had its own set of evaluation criteria that focused on the real-world start-up feasibility of the ventures involved (detailed in Appendix B), and (2) it provided all participating teams a half hour (or more) feedback from its judges, the most feedback of any competition in the world; and (3) through 2016, it was the only major competition that provided no cash prizes to the participating teams. The *Nebraska World Competition* typically invited 10–12 teams from throughout the United States. It was held as part of the state of Nebraska's "Entrepreneurship" week, which is held in late March of every year, and also included an undergraduate competition, plus awards to Nebraska's Top 10 high school entrepreneurs who were chosen from the Top high school entrepreneur from each of the state's 93 counties. During this week, awards were also given to Nebraska's leading real-world entrepreneurs.

The Explosion (and Implosion) of Competitions between the Late 1990s & Late 2000s

As the study of entrepreneurship increased among U.S. graduate schools of business, the number of national business plan competitions exploded between the late 1990s and mid-2000s so that there was quite literally a competition held every weekend from mid-February through mid-April somewhere in the United States. However, holding such competitions is typically quite expensive, and since the winners of most competitions were not usually teams from the host school, many schools that had started such competitions began to discontinue them in the late 2000s and reallocate their money to events, including internal competitions, that focused on the entrepreneurial efforts of their own students. The new competitions that are still in existence today included (1) The *Cardinal Challenge*, which typically invites 12—15 teams, is held the third weekend of February each year, and is hosted by the University of Louisville; (2) The *Historically Black Colleges & Universities Business Plan Competition*, which invites one team from each of the eight historically black U.S. colleges and universities to compete in Atlanta, GA, the third week of April each year; (3) The *Oregon New Venture Challenge*, which usually invites 16 teams, is held the first week of April each year, and is held in Portland, OR; (4) The *Rice Business Plan Competition*, which invites 42 technology-based teams, is held the second week of April each year, and is hosted by and at Rice University; (5) The *Stu Clark Venture Challenge*, which typically invites 12—16 teams each year, is held the last weekend of March each year, and is hosted by the University of Manitoba; and (6) The *WBT IC²* *Technology Commercialization Challenge*, which usually invites about 15 teams and, is held in late March of every year in conjunction with the annual meeting of the Directors of U.S. Collegiate Technology Commercialization Centers.

The new national or international competitions which have now been discontinued include (1) The *Boise Competition*, which was typically held in mid-March of each year, and was hosted by Boise State University; (2) The *McGinnis Competitions*, which was held the first weekend of March every year and was hosted by Carnegie-Mellon University; (3) The *Spirit of Enterprise Competition*, which was held the last week of February every year, and was hosted by the University of Cincinnati; and (4) The *San Francisco State Competition*, which was held in mid-March of every year, was hosted by San Francisco State University.

In addition, two major competitions have "changed their stripes." They are (1) The *Elevator Competition*, which was usually held in late March of every year and was hosted by Wake Forest University; and (2) The *Tulane Business Plan Competition*, which typically invited about 15 teams, was held in late April of every year and was hosted by Tulane University. The Elevator Competition was unique in that the participating teams had to qualify for the Finals by making two 90 second "elevator pitches" to two real-world angels or venture capitalists (VCs) during a real-world elevator ride from the first to the top floor of the tallest building in Winston-Salem. The two sets of judges would then rank all of the teams and choose five Finalists. These five finalists would then get to make full presentations to all the competition judges in the afternoon, during which period the other teams would get feedback from a separate set of reviewers. Initially, the Elevator Competition focused on technology ventures, more specifically ventures with technologies of interest to the competitions' sponsors. In 2013, Wake Forest lost this sponsor, and changed its competition to emphasize health care retailing from 2013 to the current time because of its new sponsorship by CVS Pharmacies. Its date was also changed from late March to to mid-November. About 2012, the Tulane Business Plan Competition changed its focus from new business ventures to new business ventures that addressed "social" and/or health care issues and challenges. Now challengers from around the world may submit executive summaries of their ideas. Then about 21 semi-finalists are invited to submit complete business plans, and the top 3 of these are invited to Tulane to compete in the finals.

Finally, at least two other regional graduate business plan competitions were established, but have since changed. First, the *Camino Real Venture Competition* at the University of Texas El Paso was held in mid-March of each year. It has changed its name to the Paso de Norde Venture Competition and is now open to both graduate and undergraduate teams. Second, the *Big 12 Venture Championship* which was hosted by the Big 12 Center for Economic Development, Innovation and Commercialization, lost its initial sponsor and has now been discontinued.

The Changing Character of Business Plan Competitions over Time

In the 25 years since the first Moot Corp® Competition in May of 1991, there have been about 175 major U.S. or Canadian-based national and international business plan competitions that have involved over 2,500 teams from colleges and universities around the world. During this period, there have been a number of changes in the character and composition of these competitions and the teams that have participated in them. Perhaps the most important of these changes has been the increasing "real-world" character of these competitions. In the early years, most competitions had an "academic" flavor. Specifically, most of the competing teams were presenting plans that they had developed in the business plan classes that they had taken for academic credit. Now, most of the teams are presenting plans for ventures that the team members actually plan to launch after they graduate from school. Dr. Gary Cadenhead captured and described this change in his 2002 book *No Longer MOOT: The Premier New Venture Competition from Idea to Global Impact* (Cadenhead, 2002). Several other related changes have occurred as well. Initially, the ideas around which the business plans were based involved ideas that the students involved "dreamed up" after they joined the business plan class that they were taking. Now, most plans are built around either (1) technologies developed at a major U.S. or Canadian university that were developed using government grants, but which no existing companies are seeking to license and bring to market, and/or (2) ideas for real-world businesses that the team's lead student has been planning to start for several years. Likewise, initially the teams involved were composed of young, primarily MBA students with limited real-world experience who were interested in learning more about Entrepreneurship. Today, most ventures are led by well-balanced teams composed of older students from different schools (MBA, Law, Science, and even Medicine) across the venture's home university with significant years of prior experience in the market and/or industry in which the new venture will compete.

Before discussing the impact of these changes on the structure and character of the business plans written for these competitions, it is necessary to discuss briefly the various sets of materials that all teams were required to submit to these competitions and some of the rules and regulations passed by the competition directors regarding these materials.

THE STANDARDIZATION OF BUSINESS PLAN PARAMETERS ACROSS COMPETITIONS

What was Standardized and What was not Standardized

Initially, each major competition established its own rules and regulations regarding the parameters for selecting teams and for the materials that participating teams would need to submit in order to complete in that com-petition. However, it soon became clear that differences in these rules and regulations imposed a major hardship on any teams that wanted to com-pete in more than one such competition. So, the various competition direc-tors got together at Moot Corp® to develop some commonality of these rules and regulations across all competitions. Rules and regulations were examined in five different areas in this process with standardization across competitions achieved on four of the five. These five sets of regulations involved (1) the composition of the presenting teams; (2) the executive sum-maries that each team was required to submit in order to try to qualify for a competition; (3) the criteria that the judges would use to evaluate all of the teams that participated in the competition; (4) the presentations that each team was required to make during the competition; and (5) the busi-ness plans that each team would submit to the competition.

Team Composition Requirements
From the beginning, all of the competitions involved teams of graduate stu-dents from the various colleges and universities involved. Moreover, since a large number of the participating teams planned to commercialize technol-ogies developed by faculty members at their universities, many of the ventures would include these faculty members as part of their launch teams. Nonetheless, the presentations themselves were restricted to the student members of the launch teams. However, in the early 2000s, one of the stronger ventures involved a team that had only one student who was to be the attorney for the venture involved − all other members of the launch team were either faculty members of real-world entrepreneurs. As a result, the next year, the team composition rules were revised to specify that the students had to (a) occupy the majority of the senior management positions on the venture's launch team and (b) "own" over 50% of the stock that was allocated to the venture's launch team. These team composition rules still hold today.

Executive Summary Requirements
In general, executive summaries are used for two major reasons in national and international business plan competitions. The first and most important use is to select some or most of the teams that will be chosen to compete in these competitions, which include Louisville, Nebraska, Oregon, Rice, Stu Clark (Manitoba), and the WBT IC^2 Technology Commercialization Challenge. Almost all of these competitions require four-to-five page executive summaries that cover the following topics: (1) Venture Overview,

(2) Customer Problem, (3) Products/Services, (4) Industry Size, Growth, and Segmentation, (5) Target Market, (6) Potential Customers, (7) Current and Future Competitors, (8) Key Competitive Advantages, (9) Sales/ Marketing Strategy, (10) Operations Strategy, (11) Management, (12) Business Model, (13) Capital Sought, (14) Pro-Forma Financials, and (15) Investor Returns. However, the Georgia Bowl® and Venture Labs® use executive summaries mostly to provide overviews of the various participating teams to the judges and members of the audience. Both require only two-page executive summaries, although both require that they cover the same 15 topics listed above, although clearly in a much more abbreviated fashion. In short, while there is agreement on the topics to be covered in all executive summaries, each competition has chosen different length and spacing parameters that these Summaries must meet in order to fit its own particular needs.

Evaluation Criteria
Initially, each competition had its own evaluation criteria. However, these were changed in the first competition directors meeting in 1996, so that most competitions adopted the Moot Corp®/Venture Labs® Evaluation criteria. Basically, these Evaluation Criteria, which are described more fully in Appendix A to this chapter, involved assessments of three areas: (1) the quality and effectiveness of the team's written plans (40%), (2) the quality and effectiveness of the team's verbal presentation and ability to answer questions well (20%), and (3) the overall viability of the team's venture (40%). The judges would submit their ratings of the plans before any presentations started and then submit their scores for criteria 2 and 3 immediately after the team's presentation. Moot Corp®/Venture Labs® would then have these computed on its computers and give the judges the scores for all teams before they began their deliberations. However, the judges were also instructed that they should use these evaluations only as rough guidelines and that in the end, they should use their own judgments about which of the ventures they would actually invest in to make their final decisions. With two exceptions, most of the "feeder" competitions would use these criteria even though they did not have the ability to summarize the scores for the judges as Moot Corp®/Venture Labs® did. The exceptions were the Georgia Bowl® and Rice competitions. From the beginning, the Georgia Bowl® had emphasized the "real-world" viability of the ventures involved. Its criteria, which are summarized in Appendix B, focused on (1) the progress that the venture team had made in developing the "real-world" products or services that it would sell, with having a final product to sell being

required to get the highest score. (2) The degree to which the team had determined the attractiveness of its products to potential customers, with having actual customer orders and potential reorders being needed in order to secure the highest score. (3) The completeness and quality of the venture's founding management team and key advisers, with having prior successful launch experience being required to get the highest score. (4) The attractiveness of the venture to real-world investors, with having an actual funding offer in hand being required to get the highest score here. (5) The overall quality and effectiveness of the teams plan and verbal presentation. The score sheets rated each of these five criteria equally, so that 80% of a team's score was placed on the "real-world" viability of its venture and only 20% on the quality and effectiveness of its plan and presentation. Also, as with Moot Corp®/Venture Labs®, the judges were told to use their "real-world" experience to make all final decisions. The Rice competition used different criteria because of one of its most unique characteristics: namely, the number of judges that it used. All other competitions would have between three and five judges evaluating the participating teams in every round of the competition. By contrast, Rice would have between 20 and 25 real-world angels, VCs, and other new venture experts as judges in each and every round of its competition. As a result, trying to summarize score sheets for this many judges would be "problematic" at best. So, Rice simply had each judge rank all of the ventures that they saw from 1 (for the best) to 6 (for the worst). It would then summarize these scores across all judges in order to determine the teams that would advance, and eventually win. Initially, Rice advanced the top two teams from each of its seven brackets to two 7-team semi-finals brackets, with the top two teams from each of these brackets advancing to the four team Finals. Later, Rice added the best third place team from the initial seven brackets and created three five team semi-finals, with the top two teams from each advancing to a six team finals.

Presentation and Question & Answer Requirements
Since all competitions are for students, all competitions restricted the teams' presentations of their plans to the student members of the venture team. However, originally each competition had its own parameters for the lengths of these presentations and the question and answer sessions that followed. For instance, in its first few years, the SDSU competition had 10 minute presentations and 15 minutes for Q&A, while Moot Corp® had 15 minutes for presentations and 15 minutes for Q&A. At the very first competition directors meeting, these parameters were "standardized" – with the standards selected being the Moot Corp®/Venture Labs® parameters of 15 minutes for Presentations and 15 minutes for Q&A. With two

exceptions, these parameters have been followed ever since. The first exception is the Georgia Bowl®. Since it is the first competition of the year, and teams are just developing both plans and presentations, the Georgia Bowl® gives teams a total of 40 minutes for both their presentations and Q&A with no cut-offs. However, all teams are informed of the time that they have used from 10 minutes onward to help them make sure that they leave enough time for Questions. The other exception is the Venture Labs® finals where each team has 45 minutes to complete its Presentation and Q&A with the Judging panel.

Business Plan Requirements
At the first competition director's meeting in 1996, it was decided that all business plans should have the following sections: First, a Cover Page and a Table of Contents. The next sections were: (1) An Executive Summary, (2) A Company Overview, (3) A Section on The Industry & Markets Involved, (4) A Section on Current & Future Competitors, (5) A Section on Sales & Marketing Strategies, (6) A Section on Operations, (7) A Section on the Founding Management Team & Key Advisers, (8) A Section on the Venture's Pro-Forma Financials, Investment Needs and Investor Returns, (9) A Section on Its Key Risks & Contingency Plans, and (10) A Section on Its Future Growth. All Plans also had to contain a Set of Exhibits that included (a) Pro-Forma Income Statements for a period of 5 years, (b) Pro-Forma Cash Flows by year for 5 years, (c) Pro-Forma Cash Flows by Month until the Venture reached Break-even, and (d) Pro-Forma Balance Sheet by year for 5 years. In addition, it was decided that the text of the business plan should be typed in 12 point font and have one inch margins all around. The exhibits were also to have one inch margins all around, but could be typed in smaller font. The materials in sections 1–9 were to cover the first 5 years of the venture's existence, while the Future Growth Section was to cover years 6 through 10. Moreover, these business plan topical content requirements have not changed in any significant ways since they were created. The other changes that have occurred in the length and content of Business Plans will be discussed in the next section.

THE EVOLUTION OF BUSINESS PLAN PARAMETERS OVER TIME: PART 1

Changes in the Length of Business Plans over Time

From 1991 to 2005, the length specified for all business plans was 40 pages, with up to 20 pages of text, with the remaining pages allocated to Exhibits.

The cover page and table of contents page were excluded from these limits. In 2006, these length restrictions were changed to a maximum length of 30 pages with a maximum of 15 pages of text with the remaining pages allocated to exhibits. Again, the cover page and table of contents page were excluded from these limits. Finally, in 2010 the page limits were changed one more time to the current limits of one page for the plan's cover and table of contents, 10 pages for its text, and up to seven pages for its Exhibits.

Changes in the Realism of Business Plans over Time

There have been other major changes in the content of most of the business plans submitted to the major U.S. and Canadian business plan competitions over the past 25 years. The more recent plans have made increasing use of "real-world" data in the teams' plans, in particular, the increasing use of "primary" versus "secondary" data in these plans. In addition more recent plans have reflected an increasing "reality" of the venture valuations contained in the plan, and have also shown an increasing degree to which the teams involved have made progress toward making their plan "real."

Changes in the Character of Business Plan Teams over Time

In the early years of graduate level business plan competitions, most teams were composed of MBA students who were developing such plans to satisfy the requirements of the courses that they were taking. Typically, most of the members of such teams were acquainted or even friends before the team was formed, and if any other selection criteria were used, they were to get team members majoring in the different functional areas of business, for example, a marketing major, an operations major, an accounting major, and a finance major. However, as the prospects for actually creating a potentially successful new business became clearer, the character of such teams changed in at least two major ways. First, far greater emphasis was placed on the real-world experience of potential team members; and second team members were recruited from throughout the entire university – not just the business school. For example, Georgia Tech would team up MBA students in marketing and finance with PhD students in majoring in the area of the team's venture technology and then add third year law students from the Emory University Law School since Georgia Tech did not have a law school. Moreover, by the early to mid-2000s, many universities were following the same or similar practices, including Arkansas, Georgia, Johns Hopkins, Louisville, Rice, MIT, Stanford, and Texas.

Changes in the Types of Judges Used in
Competitions over Time

The increasing reality of the technologies, teams, and business plans, also led to changes in the types of judges used in most of the major graduate level business plan competitions. In the early years, local business men and women and sometimes even faculty members were used as judges. By the mid-to-late 1990s, though, most of the judges for the major competitions were individuals with significant real-world new venture experience, that is, they were successful entrepreneurs, professional advisors to new ventures, such as accountants, lawyers, and technical specialists, and angels and VCs. And by the early to mid-2000s, VCs made up the majority of the members of such judging panels.

Most graduate competitions use panels of judges for each round of the competition, with most of these panels containing four or more typically five judges. Usually judges are allowed to participate in only one round of the competition; and almost all competitions use their most experienced judges in the finals. There are a few exceptions, though. Because the Final round judges have far less time to read the various teams plans, the Georgia Bowl® adds one judge from each first round bracket to its final round judging panel, which usually consists of six judges. Each team in the finals is thus seen and evaluated by five new judges and one old judge. The old judge is given a very specific role, however. If any of the other finals judges mis-read or mis-understands any aspect of a team's plan, it is the explicit duty of the "old" judge to correct this error whether or not that team was his or her first choice. Rice is the other major exception. Rice uses primarily Houston-area VCs in each round of its competition, but because of the number of these individuals in the Houston-area, Rice typically has panels of 20–25 judges in each first round bracket, and a final round panel of 60 to 75 VCs.

This change to judging panels made up mostly of VCs is one of the major driving forces behind the changing structure of the business plans submitted to these competitions as will be more fully explained in the next two sections of this chapter – the first of which will examine how VCs make investment decisions.

Why have these Changes Occurred

These changes have occurred for several basic reasons, including (1) the increasing importance of entrepreneurship in college curricula; (2) the changing character of teams over time; and (3) the types of judges used in most such competitions.

The Increasing Importance of Entrepreneurship in College Curricula
During the late 1980s and early 1990s, several forces combined to significantly increase the importance of entrepreneurship in the MBA curricula of many colleges and universities including the leading MBA programs in the United States. These forces included (a) the 1988 Porter and McKibbin Report on *Management Education and Development: Drift or Thrust into the 21st Century* (Porter & McKibbin, 1988); (b) the development of various entrepreneurship program, course, and teaching methods awards by the two major U.S.-based professional academic organizations of the time – The Academy of Management and the United States Association for Entrepreneurship and Small Business (USASBE); (c) the activities of various major foundations in support of innovations in entrepreneurship education; and (d) changes in U.S. law that gave universities and their faculty and students an incentive to try to commercialize faculty research innovations that had been supported by federal grant money. Each of these forces will be discussed briefly in turn.

The 1988 Porter and McKibbin Report was a three-year study commissioned by the American Assembly of Collegiate Schools of Business (AACSB). It offered seven major conclusions concerning (a) the need for strategic planning in business education (supply/demand patterns, societal expectations); (b) business school missions and niches; (c) curriculum (breadth, external environment, international dimension, information/service society, etc.); (d) faculty preparation and development; (e) AACSB accreditation; (f) managerial lifelong learning; and (g) the future. In particular, it defined seven key thrusts that the authors felt were essential to effective business education in the 21st century. These were: (a) more emphasis on entrepreneurship, (b) more emphasis on the social, political, and legal external environments, (c) more emphasis on the international dimensions of business, (d) more emphasis on communication skills, (e) more emphasis on managing people, (f) more emphasis on ethics, and (g) less emphasis on quantitative methods. One of the major results of this report was that increasing numbers of graduate schools of business in the United States began offering one or more courses in different aspects of entrepreneurship.

This increase in entrepreneurship courses was supported by the development of a variety of national awards for entrepreneurship courses, curricula, and teaching methods by the Academy of Management and USASBE. Most of the Academy's Entrepreneurship Awards were given by its Entrepreneurship Division to entrepreneurship faculty. These included an Award for Lifetime Contributions to the Field of Entrepreneurship and the Coleman Entrepreneurship Mentor Award. In addition, the Academy gave two Awards for Outstanding Doctoral Dissertations in entrepreneurship-related fields, both developed by the author. The first was the Heizer Award for Outstanding Research in New Enterprise Development, which was established in 1976, and the second was the National Federation of Independent Business (NFIB) Award for Outstanding Research in Small and Family Business, which was established in 1993. In about 2011 both Awards were taken over by the Academy's Entrepreneurship Division. USASBE was even more active in setting up Awards to recognize excellence in entrepreneurship education. In 1991, it created two curricular awards – one for Outstanding Undergraduate Programs in Entrepreneurship and the second for Outstanding MBA Programs in Entrepreneurship, both of which have been given annually ever since. In 1997, USASBE added an Award for Outstanding PhD. Programs in Entrepreneurship, and in the early 2000s added an Award for Outstanding Specialty Programs ion Entrepreneurship. USASBE complimented these four Program upwards with an Outstanding Entrepreneurship Educator of the Year Award. These myriad entrepreneurship awards had two major effects: (1) They encouraged schools with entrepreneurship courses and curricula to improve them, and (2) They provided schools without entrepreneurship courses and curricula models to develop them.

The third force driving changes in collegiate entrepreneurship courses and curricula involved the activities of various foundations, such as the Kauffman and Coleman Foundations. The Kauffman Foundation was established by Ewing Marion Kauffman, a highly successful entrepreneur, with over $2.0 billion in funding. Initially, two of the major activities of the Kauffman foundation involved major grants to selected colleges and universities to create innovative entrepreneurship courses and curricula and the identification and training of potential entrepreneurship PhD students to prepare them for academic careers in the area. For a variety of reasons, the Kauffman Foundation has since discontinued both of these activities. Now, it spends most of its "educational" resources on supporting activities in the greater-Kansas City area. Unfortunately, none of these activities has had an impact on the structure and content of major graduate level business plan competitions. The Coleman Foundation, which was established in 1951, has created 10 professorships of entrepreneurship, mostly located in the Midwest, as well as an entrepreneurship center at DePaul University in additional to other activities. In fact, for a time, it also supported the USASBE national program. Most, though not all, of Coleman's activities have been focused at the undergraduate level, so it has also had little influence on the structure and content of the major graduate level business plan competitions.

The fourth and perhaps most important force driving changes in collegiate entrepreneurship courses and curricula were the changes in U.S. law regarding the licensing of technologies developed by college and university faculty members using federal grant monies. More specifically, in the early 1980, the U.S. Bayh-Dole Act made it possible for colleges and universities to license the various technologies developed by their faculty under federal grants to others in order to commercialize these technologies. In many cases, these technologies were licensed to established companies. But given the number of grants and technologies involved, there were many that did not fit the scope of activities of most existing companies. This meant that graduate student teams could seek to license these technologies in order to start new ventures. Moreover, given the technologies involved, many of these efforts involved high potential new ventures.

Moreover, some states passed laws to further stimulate this process. Georgia, for example, passed a law that required that in the licensing of any such technologies that were developed by faculty members at state-supported colleges and universities, absolute priority had to be given first to Georgia-based companies, second to companies with which the inventor of the technology was affiliated, and third to startups. The result was that beginning in the early 1990s, many of the teams participating in the leading graduate level business plan competitions were basing their venture plans on cutting-edge technologies that were superior to those used by existing companies in the field. Moreover, in most cases such technologies were protected by patents or pending patents filed by and paid for by the colleges and universities involved.

The net result is that by the mid-1990s, the leading teams in these graduate level business plan competitions were pitching plans for commercializing breakthrough technologies that had the potential not only to create ventures worth hundreds of millions or even billions of dollars, but in some cases the potential to totally restructure entire industries. Two examples of this are (1) Auditude, a video management company which helps owners grow their video revenues, and (2) the University of Texas' uShip venture, which is a brokerage service connecting individuals with shipping needs to professional transportation services. Auditude was started by a Los Angeles-based MBA team that won the 2005 Rice Competition. Six years later, it was sold to Adobe for $120 million. uShip was started by MBA students at UT-Austin in 2004, was a semi-finalist in the 2004 Moot Corp competition, and received its first round of venture funding in 2005 (Texas Venture Labs, 2015). Currently, it operates in 19 countries and has generated over $500 million in transactions. In sum, this change in the basic character of the plans and the technologies on which they were based has had corresponding impacts on the character of the graduate teams that were put together to develop these plans and on the judges who were used to evaluate them.

HOW VCS MAKE INVESTMENT DECISIONS

This section will discuss how VCs have historically made investment decisions. More specifically, it will describe the five major activities they engage in as they identify, evaluate, and select the ventures in which they will invest, as well as the ways that they then manage these investments. These five steps are (1) Reading the plans they receive; (2) Meeting and interviewing the prospective entrepreneurs; (3) Analyzing and evaluating the proposed venture investment further; (4) Determining the venture valuation and negotiating the deal; and (5) Managing their investment fund over time, in which the primary activity is the investment of the funds that they have committed to the ventures they have selected over time. An important part of this process will be an analysis of how they allocate their time among these various activities. The section will begin with a macro-discussion of how VCs manage the investment process in order to provide some perspective for the other steps in the process. It will conclude with a micro-discussion of how VCs manage the investment process and a discussion of how these investors have begun to change these five sub-processes and the time allocated to them in order to improve their investment performance. This section builds on works such as Joyner (1995), Zider (1998), Gompers and Lerner (1999, 2004), Gladstone and Gladstone (2004), and materials developed by the author.

Managing the Venture Investment Process: A Macro-Discussion

The most important reality of venture fund investing is the realization that no one can predict the future perfectly, so mistakes will be made.

Therefore, it is absolutely essential to invest in more than one venture. However, VCs, like everyone else, have only 24 hours in the day. More specifically, most VCs have about 2,500 hours a year (10 hours a day × 5days a week × 50 weeks a year) to identify, evaluate, select, invest in, and then manage their investments. Also, they cannot invest in too many ventures because they could not manage them effectively. The result is that the vast majority of VCs invest in about 20 ventures in a single fund. But this is just the beginning of the story. Venture funds come in a variety of sizes, ranging from a low of about $50 million to a high of $1 billion to $2 billion. Given a typical fund size of about $200 million, this implies that they would typically invest an average of $10 million per venture. In almost all instances, the ventures involved − at least those that are successful − will need more than a single round of funding before they will be able to go public or self-fund their own growth. So, the VC involved will invest about 30−35% of the funds they have committed to a specific venture initially, while holding back about 65−70% of the money's allocated to a specific venture to fund its future growth. Also, almost all VC funds invest in two ways: (a) actively and (b) passively. Typically most VCs will invest about 70% of a fund actively, which means that they will be the lead investor, that is, the primary investor and decision-maker, and that they will manage future investments in the venture after the initial investment is made. However, to spread their risks, they will invest about 30% of their funds passively, that is, into ventures in which another VC is the lead investor. Finally, since almost all venture funds have a 10-year life, they need to choose the ventures in which they will invest their funds, both actively and passively, in the first 5 years of the fund's life.

In addition, if VCs invest in about 20 ventures per fund, they need to look at the most likely results for that fund as a whole. For a $200 million fund that invests in 20 ventures, this mean an average investment of about $10 million per venture, or an initial investment of about $3 million per venture, that is, about $60 million in total for all 20 initial investments. In addition, over the 10 years life of the fund, the VC will use about $5 million of this money to run their own operations, leaving about $135 million for follow-on investments in the ventures that do not fail. On average, the usual results are that about 10 of the ventures (≈50%) will lose most or all of the money invested in them. Thus, the net investment in these 10 ventures is about a $25 million loss. (Assuming half lose all of the money invested in them and half lose about 67% of that money.) However, since none of these ventures get any follow-on investments, this also means that the $70 million in follow-on investment money initially assigned to them can now be invested in the remaining 10 ventures – essentially doubling the follow-on investments that can be made in them.

Another six of the ventures ($\approx 30\%$) will become modestly profitable. These ventures will get most of their original follow-on investment ($\approx \$7$ million each), so the total dollars invested in them will be about $60 million on which the VC will receive only a small gain, say about 10% each or $6 million in total. However, they will not get any of the follow-on money from the 10 ventures that failed, leaving these funds for the last four ventures, which means that the VC will have about $80 million left to invest in these four ventures. Another three ventures ($\approx 15\%$) will make their expected future projections of doubling, or even tripling, the total funds invested in them. Since these three ventures will have performed success-fully, the VC involved will have made substantial follow-on growth invest-ments of about $20 million in each of them, bringing their total investment in these three ventures to almost $70 M. In total, these 3 ventures will pro-duce a gain between $140 million and $210 million (about $175 million on average), over and above returning the $\approx \$70$ million invested in them.

While this is enough to offset the $\approx \$25$ million in losses in the 10 ven-tures that did not make it and the only modest returns ($\approx \$6$ M) on the 6 ventures that had only marginal performance, the fund as a whole will be up only about $150 M, which is a return of only about 6.0% compounded over 10 years – not nearly adequate for the risks incurred in these invest-ments. So how can VCs deliver the significantly above stock market rates of return ($\approx 10\%$ annually) that they seek? The answer is simple: The 20th venture needs to be a "superstar" – namely a venture that will return at least 20 times the $\approx \$23$ million in total funds that were invested in it, that is, it will produce returns of $\approx \$435$ M, which will increase the earnings of the fund as a whole by $\approx \$585$ million at exit. Increasing the value of a fund in 10 years by about 300% is roughly equivalent to earning about 15% annually, significantly more than the long-term 10% increase in stock market values. In short, the success or failure of a fund is dependent on having at least one "superstar" in it.

Step 1: Reading the Plan – What VCs are Looking for

The ultimate objective of all VCs as they read business plans is to identify new venture opportunities in which they will invest in order to meet the goals of their funds and thus make money for their investors and them-selves. As they begin this process, the most important reality that they face is the need to select ventures that have the potential to become "super-stars," that is, venture selection is their most important task.

So, what kinds of ventures do VCs seek to invest in? There are two important parameters that characterize almost all VC investing. They are (1) venture size and (2) potential future venture value. Since VCs plan to invest millions of dollars in the ventures that they select, and since they know that the majority of these investments will fail, it is absolutely essential that their winners be very large in order to compensate both for their loses and for the fact that it will take years to recover the investments that they make in their winners. In simple terms, VCs need to invest in whales, not minnows, that is, in ventures that will be valued in the hundreds of millions if not billions of dollars when an exit is made. Potential future venture value is the second absolutely essential investment criterion for VCs. As noted, it will usually take over five years for VC investors to recover their investments in their winners. They must, therefore, be assured that the ventures that they invest in will have a high future valuation. In general, there are two ways that this result can be achieved; namely by investing in ventures that (a) operate in markets with high value-to-sales ratios, and (b) will not be displaced by later entrants in the markets involved. VCs try to assure the latter result by investing in ventures that have strong patent protection and/or that operate in oligopolistic markets, that is, in markets in which there will be only a few large, dominant players over the long term. Also, most VCs prefer patents over long-term market structure since the latter can never be guaranteed. The bottom line, then, is that most VCs seek to invest in ventures that have very large sales and profit potential and have very strong patent protection.

So, how do they do this? Most VCs will look for at least 1,500 potential venture investment candidates in a year. They begin this process by reading their business plans. How do they do this and how much time do they spend doing it? Hall (1989) examined this process in his PhD dissertation. He found that the average amount of time that a VC spent reading a business plan was about 3 minutes a plan. In total, they spent about 4,500 minutes ($\approx$75 hours) a year reading business plans. Most VCs read the plan's Executive Summary, management team description, and financial summary, after which they dropped about 1,350 (90%) of the 1,500 plans from further consideration. They then re-read the remaining 150 plans for about an hour each in order to decide which entrepreneurial teams they will interview. In total, then, the typical VC spends about 225 hours ($\approx$9% of their time) reading business plans in order to help decide which five ventures they would ultimately invest in.

Step 2: Meeting and Interviewing the Entrepreneur

After they have read these 150 plans and decided which ventures they might consider investing in, VCs will schedule meetings with the entrepreneurial teams of the ventures in which they are most interested. The exact number will depend on both the VC and the prospective ventures involved, but typically ranges from a low of 15 to a high of 30, that is, between 120 and 135 additional ventures will have been eliminated through the process of re-reading the venture business plans.

VCs have three major goals as they meet with and interview the teams of these 15–30 ventures. These are to: (1) assess the team's capabilities for successfully launching the venture involved, including its strengths, its weaknesses, and holes that may need to be filled during the launch process; (2) assess their own ability to successfully work with the team from the time of initial investment through exit either through an IPO (Initial Public Offering) or sale of the venture – an effort that could take up to seven or eight years; and (3) gather more information about the venture and the key challenges that it will need to face and successfully overcome during the launch process.

And, how long does this take? Most VCs spend at least an hour preparing for these interviews and another hour in the interview itself, so the total process typically consumes between 30 and 60 hours for all of the 15–30 ventures involved, that is, only about 1–2% of their total time, which is why they as so flexible on the number of teams to be interviewed. Put differently, since the long-term success of the venture fund will depend on finding and investing in the one venture that will turn out to be a "superstar," it would make no sense to skimp on one of the least time consuming aspect of the venture selection process. At the end of each interview, the VC involved will almost always tell the team involved that they need to do some more analysis and that they will get back to the team after they have completed their evaluation – a statement that is in fact true.

Step 3: Analyzing and Evaluating the Project Further

The venture team interviews may eliminate a few of these 15–30 ventures from further consideration either because the VC has decided that the venture team is too difficult to work with or because they have found one or more glaring errors in the team's plan. However, for most of the 15–30 ventures involved, the VC will have generated a list of additional issues and questions that they will need to resolve before they make their final "Go/No-Go" investment decision. In almost all instances, these issues and questions will involve some aspect of the team's plan or the team's background, since the VC involved will have already decided whether they think/believe that they can work with the venture's team over time.

In most cases, VCs will hire a consultant with deep experience in the industry in which the venture will be involved to investigate and report back to them on the key issues or questions involved. They do this for two main reasons. First, even though almost all VCs only invest in a limited number of industries, they still will not possess the required deep knowledge of each of these industries that is required to answer many of the additional questions and issues that have been raised during their meeting with the venture's launch team. Second and equally important is the fact that they will need these answers quickly. Why? Because by the time that they have interviewed the venture team, they will have signed an agreement with that team that prohibits the team from seeking potential investment funds from anyone else – usually for a period of 60 days. And, in most cases, the VC will not have the time needed to gather the required information that quickly.

And, how long does this take? Most VCs spend about an hour discussing the information needed on each venture with the consultant that they hire and at least another hour discussing the consultant's findings. So, this step in the venture investment process typically consumes about 2 hours for each of the 12–24 ventures that they have decided to pursue further, that is, about 24–48 hours, or only about 0.5–1% of their total time.

Step 4: Determine Venture Value and Negotiating the "Deal"

Once a VC has decided that they will invest in a particular venture, they need to determine the value they will place on the venture as well as the initial investment they will make in it. While many entrepreneurs believe that VCs undervalue their ventures, VCs base their valuations on the realities of their fund as a whole, as described above. More specifically, they base their valuations on the fact that 80% of the ventures in which they invest will produce essentially no significant returns for the VC fund. Because of this reality, VCs must be careful not to significantly overvalue any new venture. In this context, according to Timmons (1994, p. 513), most VCs use the following formula to determine the value that they will place on a venture.

$$\text{Final Ownership Required} = \left(\frac{\text{Required Future Value of the Investment}}{\text{Total Terminal Value of the Venture}} \right)$$

or

$$\text{Final Ownership Required} = \left(\frac{(1 + \text{IRR})^{\text{Years}}(\text{Investment})}{(\text{P/E Ratio})(\text{Total Net Income})} \right)$$

Nonetheless, the final valuation is determined through negotiations with the entrepreneurial team involved. Moreover, most VCs will accept the entrepreneur's valuation if it is reasonable both to get the "deal" done and because they realize that the valuation of any specific venture is not a "deal-breaker" because it will not affect the overall success of their fund. Why is this so? Let us examine the various options. If the venture involved turns out to be one of the 10 losers, valuation would not matter because the VC will either lose all or most of their investment in the venture. Put differently, in these 10 cases there will not be any returns to split. What if the venture is one of the six break-even candidates? In this case, valuation is also essentially irrelevant because the returns are so low that the VC could never make their goals even if they got 100% of the returns involved. And, what if the venture involved was one of the three successes? Here again, valuation is essentially irrelevant because, while these ventures are highly successful, there are not enough of them to enable the VC to achieve the fund's goals if the valuation terms were changed significantly. Finally, what if the venture involved is a "superstar?" Once again, valuation is not an important variable because, in this case, the VC will make more than enough to achieve the goals of their venture fund regardless of the exact valuation terms. However, even though all VCs know this, they are also prepared to walk away from a possible deal if the entrepreneur has a "wildly overinflated" assessment of what their venture is worth. Why? Primarily because it is a strong indication that (1) the entrepreneur involved has not done their homework on a very important aspect of their venture, and (2) they will probably be difficult to work with on other key issues in the future.

Along the way, the VC works up the specifics of the term sheet that will be offered to the entrepreneur. See Appendix C for an example of a "typical" VC Term Sheet Template. As this template illustrates, several different sections of the template contain a number of different options from which the VC may choose. These include, but are not limited to: (a) Anti-Dilution Provisions; (b) Dividend Provisions; and (c) Liquidity Event Preferences.

However, the management of the venture involved can request modifications in these various options as part of their negotiations with their prospective VC fund. The template in Appendix C is a combination of the templates of two major VC firms who wish to remain anonymous. Readers may also visit the National Venture Capital Association website, which contains a different sample term sheet template as well as eight other sample documents associated with VC investing. Other sample term sheets are available at these locations: (1) https://www.ycombinator.com/documents/; (2) https://www.cooleygo.com/documents/y-combinator-safe-financing-document-generator/; and (3) http://www.businessinsider.com/founder-friendly-term-sheet-2013-6; among others.

And how much time does this take? Given the length and complexity of typical VC term sheets, it may take the venture's team a day or two to review the entire proposal, after which they will frequently request a few changes in various terms. From the VC's perspective, it may take about 2–4 hours to decide on the set of various terms that they will propose to the venture's management team. An additional 2–4 hours may be spent responding to the venture teams' various questions about the term sheet. Finally, at least 2 hours will be spent in the investment signing meeting. So, the VC will typically spend 6–10 hours on each of the five new venture investment decisions that they will make each year for the first 4–5 years of the fund's life. In sum, most VCs will spend between 30 and 50 hours a year in the process of negotiating and signing the deal.

Step 5: Managing Their Investment Fund over Time

In total, the four steps above will consume about 270 hours of the 2,500 hours that most VCs spend on the management of their funds in a typical year, that is, about 11% of their time. This means that most VCs will spend most of their time ($\approx$ 89%) managing their Investment Fund over time. This consists of two activities (1) raising the funds that they will invest and manage, and (2) managing their investments in the 20 ventures that they will have chosen for their fund.

Raising Money for the Venture Fund
One could argue that the raising of money for their Investment Fund had to occur before any of the activities described above, and this is technically true. However, almost all successful VCs are involved with more than one fund. So, while they are still managing Fund X, they will need to be raising

money for Fund X + 1. The time required to do this will depend primarily on two factors: (1) the successes of their previous funds, and (2) the overall state of the economy at the time. In general the most important of these is their success with previous finds. Nonetheless, the state of the nation's economy does play a part. Thus in the "boom" of the late 1990s, literally hundreds of funds were created by individuals with "good" resumes. Most of these funds later went bust in the late 2000s; while in the late 2000s it was quite difficult even for experienced VCs with good track records to raise new funds quickly.

Where do most VCs get the monies they need to start their various funds? The very first U.S. venture fund was created by General Georges Doriot, a lecturer at the Harvard Business School, in the late 1946, just after the Second World War (Ante, 2008). He raised the money for his fund from very wealthy private individuals in the greater Boston area. Edgar F. Heizer, Jr. began his venture capital career by running the VC fund of Sears' Allstate subsidiary whose funds came from Allstate and Sears. He then created the first Heizer Fund in Chicago in 1969 by securing funds to do so from a small number of wealthy Chicago-area individuals whom he knew, which was necessary because it was five years before the passage of the Employment Retirement Income Security Act (ERISA) Act of 1974, which allowed financial institutions to invest up to 2% of their funds in venture capital. After the act was passed, however, Heizer used these institutions as a primary source of money for his subsequent Heizer Funds. Why did Heizer and most other U.S. VCs turn to such institutions as a source of funds? Because this sourcing significantly reduced the time it takes to create a new fund because these institutional funds had far more money available than most wealthy private individuals. The result is that it currently takes about 4–6 months to create a new fund. And why did most pension funds seek to invest some of their funds in venture capital? Because the returns that they generated were significantly greater than those pensions funds could make by investing in bonds and/or the stock market.

In summary, most of this time commitment comes in the second 5 years of a typical fund's life. Averaged on the life of the fund, this would total just over 200 hours per year, or about 8% of the VC's time, leaving over 80% of their time for managing the 20 investments that they have made.

Managing the Investments that They have Made
Once they have made an investment in a particular venture, most VCs will try to visit it at least once a month to discuss its progress with its management team. Interestingly, while the venture teams come to the VC's office

to make their pitch, the reverse is true once the investment has been made — in part because that's where most of the information that the VCs will want to ask about is located, and in part because the VC will get a sense of the venture's progress by the "bizziness" of its facilities. Typically, these trips will take between a half day and a day, depending on the location of the venture involved. This is also why almost all venture funds are regional, not national or even semi-national, in character. Whenever possible, the VC will try to schedule visits to two ventures in the same or nearby locations on the same day. Nonetheless, venture visits will normally consume about 15 days of their time every month, that is, about 150 hours a month, or 1,800 hours, a year. Table 1 summarizes a typical VC's time commitments over a year with a normal fund, although one must remember that these totals will vary over the 10-year life of the fund.

The Changing Character of VC Decision-Making over Time

So, how have these various steps of the VC investment decision-making process changed over time? Basically, there have been four major changes. They are to: (1) Get a macro-view of more plans more quickly to sift out the most likely winners; (2) Spend less time valuing plans; (3) Spend less time monitoring the launch processes of your losers; and (4) Spend more time reviewing the team's implementation plan. Each of these changes will now be explored in greater detail.

Table 1.   Annual VCs Time Commitments.

VC Activity	Minimum Time	Maximum Time
1. Reading business plans	150	150
2. Meeting venture teams	30	60
3. Further venture analysis	24	48
4. Venture valuation	30	50
5. Meeting funded teams	1,800	1,800
Raising $ for new funds	200	200
Summary	2,234	2,308
Free time for extras	266	192
Total annual time available	2,500	2,500

Getting a Macro-View of more Plans Quickly
Initially venture business plans were 40 pages long with 20 pages of text and 20 pages of exhibits. So, even though most VCs read only the Executive Summary, Management Team section, and Venture Finance section, they were reading about six pages of text and possibly one or two pages of financial exhibits in the three-and-a-half minutes they spent reading these plans. The reduction of plan length first to 30 pages (15 pages of text and 15 pages of exhibits); and later to 17 pages (10 pages of text and 7 pages of exhibits) has meant that they can now read more of the venture's business plan in the same time. In particular, it has given them the time needed to read more about the venture's products, markets, technologies, and competitive advantages – factors that could influence their decisions on whether to drop the venture from further consideration or move it forward for a more careful evaluation. Put differently, this change has meant that VCs are less likely to drop a potential real winner or superstar, and also less likely to spend their valuable time on plans with hidden flaws that need to be caught later in the venture evaluation process.

Spend Less Time in Valuing Plans
VCs do not spend significant amounts of time in valuing the plans they read for potential investment, as noted above. Nonetheless, they have made a key change in their venture valuation process both to reduce the time required for such valuations and improve the accuracy of the valuation processes itself. Specifically, they have changed the formula that they use to make such valuations to the one shown below.

$$\text{Final Ownership Required} = \frac{(\text{Required Future Value of the Investment})}{(\text{Total Terminal Value of the Venture})}$$

or

$$\text{Final Ownership Required} = \frac{(10)(\text{Investment})}{(\text{Total Net Sales})(\text{Value-to-Sales Ratio for the Industry Involved})}$$

This VC developed formula is detailed in Appendix D. The two key changes are (1) the simple requirement of a $10\times$ return on the investment involved; and (2) the use of sales rather than net profits as the financial parameter used to estimate future venture value. These two changes simplify the valuation process while increasing its accuracy. More specifically, a 10× return on one's investment in 5 years corresponds to an Internal Rate of Return (IRR) of about 60% compounded — a substitution that clearly simplifies the valuation calculation. Likewise, calculating the venture's total value after 5 years by using the venture's projected net sales and the value-to-sales ratio for its industry is both easier and more accurate than trying to use net profits after tax times a price earnings ratio, especially since many new ventures may not have yet earned any significant profits at the five year point in their launch process.

Spend Less Time Monitoring the Launch Processes of Your Losers
Monitoring the launch processes of all of the ventures in one's portfolio is a key to successful venture investing. In this context, Guler's (2003) dissertation has shown that one of the main factors that discriminates between highly successful and less successful VCs is their handling of the losers in their portfolio. More specifically, the more successful VCs terminate their less successful venture investments much sooner and more effectively than the less successful VCs. Among other things, this gives them both more time and more money to invest in their potential future successes.

Spend more Time Reviewing the Team's Implementation Plans
Once they have decided to invest in a venture, the VC involved will provide the team involved the first tranche of their initial investment in that venture after which they will meet with the team to discuss their progress and plans for future growth. Tranches reflect the ideas that even though the VC may have signed a contract to invest $3.0 million in a specific venture, they will not give that venture the entire $3.0 million immediately. Instead, they will provide, say $750,000, with which they expect the venture team to achieve certain milestones, after which additional funds will be provided, with each set of funds called a tranche. Since no one can predict the future perfectly, there will always be some flexibility in this process because of unexpected opportunities or roadblocks. However, VCs have changed their approach to this aspect of managing the venture launch process over the past 20+ years.

   Initially, the team's business plan was the document that would be used to "guide" this process. Why? Because these initial 40-page plans really consisted of two parts. They were: (1) a description of the venture's market opportunity and its macro-strategy for capitalizing on that market opportunity, and (2) some details of the initial decisions and actions that would be needed to capitalize on this market opportunity. The latter materials were frequently not as detailed and carefully thought out as they could have been, though. The newer 17-page business plans focus mostly on the information described in part 1 above. And, to improve the likelihood of overall venture success, most VCs now ask for a very detailed 100-day launch plan that spells out precisely how the venture team will use the initial investment money that it receives, because such 100-day launch plans were one of the tools that the more successful VCs used to limit the total capital that they committed to their losers. In particular, such 100-day implementation plans are much more thorough about how the venture team will begin the launch process, that is, they describe far more completely the various actions and decisions that the team will make during this 100-day period and the results that should be achieved as a result of these actions and decisions. See Block and MacMillan, 1985.

THE EVOLUTION OF BUSINESS PLAN
PARAMETERS OVER TIME: PART 2

This section will examine in depth the various changes that have occurred since 1991 in the structure of the business plans submitted to major national and international business plan competitions as well as the changes that are likely to occur in the future because of the pressure from the VCs that serve as the primary judges for most of these competitions.

The Initial BP Structure was a Combination of Several Elements

As noted above, the 40-page business plans that were used in the initial business plan competitions combined five elements. These were: (1) a description of the proposed venture; (2) a description of that venture's strategy for successfully entering its chosen market; (3) a description of the venture's management team; (4) a description of the venture's growth plan for the next 5 years; and (5) descriptions of the venture's key risk contingency plans and grown plans for years 6–10.

The major problems with these plans were (1) the combination of the market entry strategy and 5 year growth plan sections, which essentially almost doubled the length of these plans versus current plans; (2) the use of secondary data sources for the various statistics and other information contained in the plan; (3) unrealistic venture valuations; and (4) very limited progress toward making any aspects of the proposed venture real.

Since, as noted above, most VCs spend only about three (3) minutes reviewing the myriad plans that are recommended to them during which they read primarily the Executive Summary, the Management Team section, the Finance section, and perhaps a few Financial Exhibits, this means that they examined only about six pages of text and say two pages of Exhibits, or about one fifth of the plan's content.

If they read so little of these plans, how could they be as successful as they were? From what we know today, there are several answers. Most VCs acknowledge that from 80% to 90% of the information contained in most of these business plans was wrong. So by not reading it, one is not mislead. But let us dig a little deeper. What is it that they did not read? Specifically, it was venture strategy and growth plan sections plus the key risks and future growth sections. Today, VCs want to see a 100-day launch plan, not a 5 year launch plan, because the most relevant research (Amram & Kulatilaka, 1998, Guler, 2003) shows that the VCs who are winners are those who cut their losses quickly. Put differently, cutting one's losses in the third, fourth, or fifth year after launch is not doing so quickly, which means that most of the data in these original business plans that covered the various descriptions of the venture's growth plans was wrong. And this information is a major part of what was deleted when the move was made in 2010 to the current 17-page business plans.

Current BP Structure and Content

Today's business plans contain 10 pages of text and 7 pages of exhibits, that is, a total of 17 pages plus a cover page. Assuming that VCs still spend only about three minutes scanning all of the plans that they receive, this means that they will be able to read about six pages of text ($\approx 60\%$) and two or three of the seven pages of exhibits. Since the Executive Summary, the Management Team section, and the Finance section are now each only about one page long, this means that they can read about half of the rest of the plan's text — clearly an improvement if the information contained therein is useful and relevant. And much of it is because increasingly these plans are using real-world primary data rather than secondary data. They also have significantly improved valuations. In fact, most plans now include tables of the valuations of venture purchases and/or IPOs done in their space over the past 5 years. In addition, most teams have also made greater progress toward the actual real-world launch of their proposed venture.

Nonetheless, the common wisdom in entrepreneurship and strategic planning classes is that most successful ventures do not change their product-market strategies often. Put differently, over 90% of all successful ventures either follow their initial; product-market strategy or make only a single change in their product-market strategy after launch. Consequently, one would think that VCs might do even better if they would be able to read the entirety of a venture's product-market launch strategy during the initial three minute review process.

Is there any evidence of the changes that might make sense to achieve such goals? Yes there is. It involves the executive summary requirements for most of the major business plan competitions. Except for the Georgia Bowl® and Venture Labs®, both of which use two-page executive summaries, all of the other major competitions require five-page executive summaries from all of the participating teams. If one added a three-page set of Financial exhibits to these Summaries, one would have a document that is essentially short enough that the typical VC could read all of it in their initial 3 minute scan of the materials submitted for review.

The Probable Structure of Future BPs

So, what will happen in the future? My prediction is that all major competitions will move toward the use of five or six page executive summaries that cover the following eleven (11) topics: (1) a venture summary, (2) a statement of the problem or need the venture solves, (3) a description of the venture's product, including its current development status, (4) a synopsis of its patents, licenses, and other intellectual property, (5) an analysis of its customers and markets, (6) an analysis of its potential market size and market share, (7) a description of its key competitive advantages, (8) a discussion of its management team, including the members' relevant experience, (9) an overview of its financials, including 3–5 year projections of its revenues, profits, and cash flows, (10) its investment needs and the use of these funds, and (11) a summary of the key risks it faces and its contingency plans for dealing with these risks.

Another way to look at this issue is to ask what parts of todays' current 10 pages of text business plans get seriously cut back or deleted altogether. Basically, four parts get cut back or deleted, which account for four to five pages of text, thus producing a five to six page executive summary. The three sections that get cut altogether are (1) the sales and marketing section, (2) the operations section, and (3) the future growth section. The section that gets cut back is the executive summary section because its various parts are now covered in the 11 parts of the full executive summary described above.

Basically, these changes are likely to happen so that VCs can improve the ways that they evaluate the various business plans to leverage that major difference between highly successful VCs and their less successful colleagues, namely cutting their losses in their losers as quickly as possible, through the improved identification of those losers in the review process of the coming new generation of business plans. Appendix D provides four ways VCs think about the specifics of investing in their everyday work.

This is likely because one of the keys to even marginally successful new venture investing is to make sure that you have at least one "superstar" venture in your fund. In short, if changes in VC's decision-making processes enable them to find and include two "superstars" in their venture fund this would almost guarantee that firm being among the most successful VC firms on the planet.

SUMMARY AND CONCLUSIONS

This primary purpose of this chapter was to describe and analyze the evolution of the basic purpose, structure, content, and other key parameters of business plans in international business plan competitions from the beginnings of such competitions in 1991 through the current time; to explain why these changes have occurred; and then to describe the changes that are likely to occur in the future.

The primary conclusion is that while the basic purpose of business plans has remained essentially constant over the past 25 years, their structure, content, and selected key parameters have changed over this period and that the primary reasons for these changes in structure, content, and other key parameters has been the increasing use of VCs as the primary judges in these competitions coupled with the changing nature of what these VCs are seeking in the myriad real-world business plans that they gather and evaluate during the process of investing the funds that have been entrusted to them by the pension funds and wealthy individuals who are their primary clients.

The primary key to success as a VC today is to cut one's losers as quickly as possible, as noted earlier. In fact, this is the primary reason for the now almost universal use of 100-day implementation plans by U.S. VCs. These implementation plans contain much of the information on a prospective ventures' sales, marketing, and operations strategies that were previously covered for a period of 5 years in traditional business plans. A key point here is that it makes far more sense to try it, and then to quickly fix it if it is not working than it does to spend substantial time to make 5 year projections – most of which will be wrong.

However, all VCs are really in the business of trying to find "superstars." Given the fact that 80–90% of the information contained in most traditional business plans will prove to be inaccurate and that 100-day implementation plans are now used to cut one's losers, one of the potentially best ways to try to find more "superstars" is to use shorter plans – even just long executive summaries – so that one can use the additional information to better screen the myriad ventures that one sees during the first five years of one's venture fund, which is when almost all of one's successful investments will be made.

REFERENCES

Amram, M., & Kulatilaka, N. (1998). *Real options: Managing strategic investment in an uncertain world*. Oxford: Oxford University Press.
Ante, S. E. (2008). *Creative capital: Georges Doriot and the birth of venture capital*. Boston, MA: Harvard Business Review Press.
Block, Z., & MacMillan, I. C. (1985). Milestones in successful venture planning. *Harvard Business Review, September/October*, 184–188.
Cadenhead, G. (2002). *No longer MOOT: The premier new venture competition from idea to global impact*. Austin, TX: Remoir Press.
Gladstone, D., & Gladstone, L. (2004). *Venture capital investing: The complete handbook for investing in private businesses for outstanding profits*. Englewood Cliffs, NJ: Prentice Hall Financial Times.
Gompers, P., & Lerner, J. (2004). *The venture capital cycle*. Cambridge, MA: MIT Press.
Gompers, P. A., & Lerner, J. (1999/2004). *The venture capital cycle*. Cambridge, MA: MIT Press. The second edition was published in 2004 with the following ISBN number 9780262072557.
Guler, I. (2003). A study of decision making capabilities and performance in the venture capital industry. Unpublished doctoral dissertation, University of Pennsylvania, Philadelphia, PA.
Hall, H. J. (1989). Venture capitalists decision making and the entrepreneur: An exploratory investigation. Unpublished doctoral dissertation, University of Georgia, Athens, GA.
Joyner, B. (1995). Key tasks and behaviors of founding entrepreneurs during successful new venture creation and development – An exploratory study. Unpublished doctoral dissertation, University of Georgia, Athens, GA.

Porter, L. W., & McKibbin, L. E. (1988). *Management education and development: Drift or thrust into the 21st century?* New York, NY: McGraw Hill. ISBN: 0070505217.

Texas Venture Labs. (2015, April 7). *uShip | Mccombs business school*. Retrieved from https://www.mccombs.utexas.edu/Centers/Texas-Venture-Labs/Investment-Competition/Success-Stories/uShip. Accessed on April 2, 2016.

Timmons, J. A. (1994). *New venture creation: Entrepreneurship for the 21st century* (4th ed., pp. 511–515). Boston, MA: Irwin.

Zider, B. (1998). How venture capital works. *Harvard Business Review, November/December*, 131–139.

APPENDIX A: MOOT CORP®/VENTURE LABS® EVALUATION CRITERIA

The Evolution of Business Plans in International Business Plan Competitions

Global Venture Labs Competition – Judge's Evaluation

Company: _____

Judge's Number_____

I Written Business Plan (40%)

Please evaluate the written business plan on the following aspects
(Using this scoring system: 1 = very poor, 2 = poor, 3 = fair, 4 = adequate, 5 = good, 6 = very good, 7 = excellent)

1. Executive Summary (5%)

(Clear, exciting and effective as a   1   2   3   4   5   6   7
stand-alone overview of the plan)

Comments/Questions _____

_____

2. Company Overview (5%)

(Business purpose, history, genesis of   1   2   3   4   5   6   7
concept current status, overall strategy
and objectives)

Comments/Questions _____

_____

3. Products or Services (10%)

(Description, features and benefits, pricing,   1   2   3   4   5   6   7
current stage of development,
proprietary position)

Comments/Questions _____

_____

4. Market and Marketing Strategy (10%)

(Description of market, competitive   1   2   3   4   5   6   7
analysis, needs identification, market
acceptance, unique capabilities,
sales/promotion)

Comments/Questions _____

_____

5. Operations (15%)

    (Plan for production/delivery of product   1   2   3   4   5   6   7
    or services, product cost, margins,
    operating complexity, resources required)
    Comments/Questions _____

_____

6. Management (10%)

    (Backgrounds of hey individuals, ability to   1   2   3   4   5   6   7
    execute strategy, personnel needs,
    organization structure, role of any
    non-student executive, which students
    will execute plan)
    Comments/Questions _____

_____

In rating each of the above, please consider the following questions

- Is this area covered in adequate detail?
- Does the plan show a clear understanding of the elements that should be addressed?
- Are the assumptions realistic and reasonable?
- Are the risks identified and the ability to manage those risks conveyed?

Company: _____ **Judge's Number**_____

I Written Business Plan (40%)

Please evaluate the written business plan on the following aspects

(Using this scoring system: 1 = very poor, 2 = poor, 3 = fair, 4 = adequate, 5 = good, 6 = very good, 7 = excellent)

7. Summary Financials (10%)

    (Presented in summary form and easy to read and understand Consistent with plan and effective in capturing financial performance: Monthly for year 1, Quarterly for years 2 and 3, annually for years 4 and 5)

(a) Cash Flow Statement	1	2	3	4	5	6	7
(b) Income Statement	1	2	3	4	5	6	7
(c) Balance Sheet	1	2	3	4	5	6	7
(d) Funds Required/Uses	1	2	3	4	5	6	7
(e) Assumptions/Trends/Comparatives	1	2	3	4	5	6	7

    Comments/Questions _____

_____

8. Offering (10%)

(Proposal/terms to investors – indicates   1   2   3   4   5   6   7
how much needed, the ROI, the structure
of the deal, and possible exit strategies)
Comments/Questions _____

9. Viability (20%)

(Market opportunity, distinctive   1   2   3   4   5   6   7
competence, Management understanding,
investment potential)
Comments/Questions _____

10. Brevity and Clarity (5%)

(Is the plan approximately 17 pages with   1   2   3   4   5   6   7
minimum redundancy)
Comments/Questions _____

Additional Comments

Global Venture Labs Competition – Judge's Evaluation

Company: _____ Judge's Number_____

II Presentation (20%)

Please evaluate the verbal presentation on the following aspects

(Using this scoring system: 1 = very poor, 2 = poor, 3 = fair, 4 = adequate, 5 = good, 6 = very good, 7 = excellent)

1. **Formal Presentation (50%)**

   (a) Materials presented in a clear, logical   1   2   3   4   5   6   7
   and/or sequential form

   (b) Ability to relate need for the company   1   2   3   4   5   6   7
   with meaningful examples, and
   practical applications

   (c) Ability to maintain judges' interest   1   2   3   4   5   6   7

   (d) Quality of Visual Aids   1   2   3   4   5   6   7

2. **Questions and Answers (50%)**

   (a) Ability to understand judges' inquiries   1   2   3   4   5   6   7

   (b) Appropriately respond to judges   1   2   3   4   5   6   7
   inquires with substantive answers

   (c) Use of time allocated   1   2   3   4   5   6   7
   (minimum redundancy)

   (d) Poise and confidence (think effectively   1   2   3   4   5   6   7
   on their feet)

Strength of Presentation

Weaknesses of Presentation

Global Venture Labs Competition – Judge's Evaluation

Company: _____ Judge's Number_____

III Viability of Company (40%)							
	Definitely				Definitely		
	No				Yes		
1. Market Opportunity (20%)							
(There is a clear market need presented as well as a way to take advantage of that need)	1	2	3	4	5	6	7
2. Distinctive Competence (20%)							
(The company provides something novel/ unique/special that gives it a competitive advantage in its market)	1	2	3	4	5	6	7
3. Management Capability (20%)							
(This team can effectively develop this company and handle the risks associated with the venture)	1	2	3	4	5	6	7
4. Financial Understanding (20%)							
(The team has a solid understanding of the financial requirements of the business)	1	2	3	4	5	6	7
5. Investment Potential (20%)							
(The business represents a real investment opportunity in which you would consider investing)	1	2	3	4	5	6	7

Company Strengths

Company weaknesses

Additional Comments

APPENDIX B: THE GEORGIA BOWL®
EVALUATION CRITERIA

The Evolution of Business Plans in International Business Plan Competitions

GEORGIA BOWL® NEW VENTURE BUSINESS PLAN EVALUATION CHECKLIST

Copyright © 1991 by Charles W. Hofer

VENTURE NAME _____ REVIEWER _____

	Possible	Actual
I. SHORT-TERM STARTUP FEASIBILITY	100	
(A) Product/Service Feasibility	25	
(B) Market/Customer Feasibility	25	
(C) Operations Feasibility	25	
(D) Financial Feasibility	25	
II. LONG-TERM PROFIT POTENTIAL	100	
(A) Size of (Potential) Market/Customer Base	25	
(B) Number & Strength of Competitors	25	
(C) Number & Size of Your Competitive Advantages	25	
(D) Sustainability of Your Competitive Advantages	25	
III. MANAGEMENT CAPABILITIES	100	
(A) Completeness of Founding Venture Team	25	
(B) Team = Prior Startup & Industry Experience	25	
(C) Ability of Team to Start & Build the Business	30	
(D) Quality & Completeness of Advisory Board	20	
IV. INVESTOR RISK/REWARD TRADEOFFS	100	
(A) Magnitude of Risks Involved (High Risks = High Score)	(75)	( )
(B) Effectiveness of Contingency Plans	75	
(C) Effectiveness of Exit Strategy	40	
(D) Risk/Reward Ratio Attractiveness	60	
V. PLAN AND PRESENTATION EFFECTIVENESS	100	
(A) Organization & Completeness of the Written Plan	25	
(B) Clarity & Professionalism of the Oral Presentation	25	
(C) Effectiveness of Question & Answer Responses	25	
(D) Overall Persuasiveness of the Plan & Presentation	25	
TOTAL SCORE	500	

SHORT-TERM STARTUP FEASIBILITY

Copyright © 1991 by Charles W. Hofer

Venture _____

Reviewer _____ **Date** _____

SHORT-TERM STARTUP FEASIBILITY RATINGS

I. PRODUCT/SERVICE FEASIBILITY (Pick one)	Score
1. Product/Service Idea Conceived	5
2. Product/Service Design Finalized	10
3. Product/Service Prototype Completed	15
4. Product/Service Final Product Available	20
5. Product/Service In Use & Reliability Checked	25

II. MARKET/CUSTOMER FEASIBILITY (Pick one)	Score
1. Market/Customer Demand Assumed	5
2. Survey of Customers Market Completed	10
3. Some Customers Have Made (Offered to Make) Purchases	15
4. Substantial Numbers of Customers Have Made Initial Purchases	20
5. Substantial Numbers of Customers Have Made Repurchases	25

III. MANUFACTURING/DISTRIBUTION FEASIBILITY (Pick one)	Score
1. Manufacturing/Distribution Capability Assumed	5
2. Manufacturing/Distribution Options & Costs Thoroughly Analyzed	10
3. Manufacturing/Distribution Methods Finalized	15
4. Actual Production/Distribution of a Few Products/Services Has Occurred	20
5. Long-Term Manufacturing/Distribution Systems in Place	25

IV. FINANCIAL FEASIBILITY (Pick one)	Score
1. Rough Estimates of Financial Needs & Sources	5
2. Financial Needs & Sources Analyzed Thoroughly	10
3. Startup Capital Partially Secured	15
4. Startup Capital Fully Secured	20
5. Startup Capital + Working Capital Fully Secured	25

V. OVERALL SHORT-TERM STARTUP FEASIBILITY (Pick one)	$\sum$ Score
1. Little or No Chance of Successful Startup	20
2. Moderate Chance of Successful Startup	40
3. Good Chance of Successful Startup	60
4. Very Good Chance of Successful Startup	70
5. Excellent Chance of Successful Startup	80
6. Has Started & Is Close to Breakeven	90
7. Has Started & Is Substantially Past Breakeven	100

LONG-TERM PROFIT POTENTIAL
Copyright © 1991 by Charles W. Hofer

Venture _____

Reviewer _____   **Date**_____

LONG TERM PROFIT POTENTIAL RATINGS

I. SIZE OF (POTENTIAL) CUSTOMER BASE (Pick one)   **Score**

   1. Limited Appeal Market (Niche Market)   5

   2. Moderate Appeal Market (Small Segment)   10

   3. Intermediate Appeal Market (Medium Segment)   20

   4. Mass Appeal Market (Large & Very Large Segments)   25

II. ANNUAL SALES REVENUES PER CUSTOMER (Pick one)   **Score**

   1. $1 to $100/year   5

   2. $100 to $1,000/year   10

   3. $1,000 to $10,000/year   20

   4. ∃ $10,000/year   25

III. NUMBER & STRENGTH OF COMPETITORS (Pick one)   **Score**

   1. A Few Weak Competitors   25

   2. Many Weak Competitors, or a Few Competent Competitors 20

   3. Several Competent Competitors   15

   4. Many Competent Competitors, or a Few Strong Competitors 10

   5. Several Strong Competitors   5

IV. YOUR COMPETITIVE ADVANTAGES   **Score**

   1. Several Minor Advantages, or a Few Moderate Advantages 5

   2. Many Moderate Advantages, or a Few Strong Advantages 15

   3. Many Strong Advantages   25

V. SUSTAINABILITY OF ADVANTAGES (Pick one)   **Score**

   1. Advantages Primarily Short-Term in Duration   5

   2. Advantages of Intermediate Duration   15

   3. Advantages of Long Duration   25

VI. OVERALL LONG-TERM PROFIT POTENTIAL (Pick one) $\sum$ **Score**

   1. Relatively Small Long-Term Profit Potential   25

   2. Moderate Long-Term Profit Potential   50

   3. Large Long-Term Profit Potential   75

   4. Very Large, Long-Term Profit Potential   90

   5. Has Fortune 1000 Potential   100

ENTREPRENEURIAL TEAM CAPABILITIES

Copyright © 1991 by Charles W. Hofer

Venture _____

Reviewer _____ Date _____

ENTREPRENEURIAL TEAM CAPABILITIES	POINTS POSSIBLE	RATING
I. TEAM COMPLETENESS (Rate Each Factor)		Score
1. Founding Entrepreneur Identified & Fully Committed	10	
2. Marketing Executive(s) Identified & Fully Committed	5	
3. Production Executive(s) Identified & Fully Committed	5	
4. Financial Executive(s) Identified & Fully Committed	5	
Total Score	25	
II. TEAM EXPERIENCE (Rate Each Factor)		Score
1. Prior Work Experience of the Team in General	10	
2. Prior Work Experience of the Team in the Industry Involved	10	
3. Prior Work Experience of the Team in Business Startups	5	
Total Score	25	
III. TEAM CAPABILITIES & COMPETENCE (Pick one)		Score
1. Little or No Evidence of Outstanding Job Performance	0	
2. Some Evidence of Outstanding Job Performance	10	
3. Strong Evidence of Outstanding Job Performance	20	
4. Overwhelming Evidence of Outstanding Job Performance	30	
IV. TEAM ADVISORS & ALLIANCES (Rate each factor)		Score
1. Key Advisors Identified & Fully Committed	5	
2. Completeness of Advisory Board@	5	
3. Strategic Partners Explicitly Identified	5	
4. Strategic Partners Fully Committed	5	
Total Score	20	

V. GRAND TOTAL ($\sum$ I + II + III + IV)_____

VI. OVERALL TEAM CAPABILITY ASSESSMENT (Pick one)		Score
1. Team is incomplete & has limited skills and experience	0	
2. Team is partially complete & has some capabilities & experience	25	
3. Team is mostly complete & has strong capabilities & experience	50	
4. Team is complete & committed & has very strong capabilities & experience	75	
5. Team is complete, fully committed, & has exceptional skills & experience	100	

VII. FINAL TEAM CAPABILITY ASSESSMENT
(Compare V vs. VI & Decide)* _____

INVESTOR RISK-REWARD TRADEOFFS

Copyright © 1991 by Charles W. Hofer

Venture _____

Reviewer_____   Date _____

INVESTOR RISK-REWARD TRADEOFFS	POINTS POSSIBLE	RATING
I. MAGNITUDE OF RISKS INVOLVED		**Score**
(Rate Each Factor)		
1. Product Liability Risks	1—15	
2. Customer Acceptance Risks	1—15	
3. Competitive Response Risks	1—15	
4. Supplier Vulnerabilities	1—15	
5. Technological Obsolescence Risks	1—15	
6. Political and/or Legal Risks	1—15	
7. Other Risks	1—15	
Total Riskiness of Venture	(Maximum Score = 75)	
II. EFFECTIVENESS OF CONTINGENCY PLANS (Pick one)		**Score**
1. Have No Explicit Contingency Plans	0	
2. Have Contingency Plans for Some Key Risks	15	
3. Have Contingency Plans for Most Key Risks	30	
4. Have Effective Contingency Plans for Some Key Risks	45	
5. Have Effective Contingency Plans for Most Key Risks	60	
6. Have *Very Effective* Contingency Plans for Most/All Key Risks	75	
III. EFFECTIVENESS OF EXIT STRATEGY (Pick one)		**Score**
1. Have No Explicit/Formal Exit Strategy	0	
2. Exit Strategy Explicitly Described	10	
3. Have a Few Reasonable Exit Strategies	20	
4. Have Several Reasonable Exit Strategies	30	
5. Have Several Very Effective Exit Strategies	40	
IV. TOTAL RISK MANAGEMENT SCORE ($\sum$II + III)		
V. RISK-REWARD RATIO ATTRACTIVENESS (Pick one)		**Score**
1. Probable Venture Risks Exceed Probable Venture Returns	(15)	
2. Low Risks — Low Rewards	0	
3. Medium Risks — Medium Rewards	5	
4. Low Risks — Medium Rewards	10	
5. High Risks — High Rewards	20	
6. Medium Risks — High Rewards	30	
7. Low Risks — High Rewards	40	
8. Medium Risks — Very High Rewards	50	
9. Low Risks — Very High Rewards	60	

VI. TOTAL ADJUSTED RISK MANAGEMENT SCORE (IV vs. V Comparison) _____

QUALITY OF PLAN & PRESENTATION

Copyright © 1991 by Charles W. Hofer

Venture _____

Reviewer _____   **Date** _____

PLAN & PRESENTATION EVALUATION CRITERIA	POOR	FAIR	GOOD	VERY GOOD	EXCELLENT
01. Customer Analysis					
02. Market & Industry Analysis					
03. Competitor Analysis					
04. Supplier Analysis					
05. Macro-Environmental Analysis					
06. Venture Startup & Growth Strategies					
07. Marketing Strategy & Tactics					
08. Manufacturing Systems & Plans					
09. New Product Development Plans					
10. Organization & Management Systems					
11. Financial Plans & Projections					
12. Deal Structure & Investor Returns					
13. Risk Mitigation Analysis					
14. Presentation Organization					
15. Ability to Gain & Hold Your Attention					
16. Effective Use of Time					
17. Quality of Slides & Other Visual Aids					
OVERALL EFFECTIVENESS					

Note: Use your judgment and experience to choose a score that best captures the ability of this team to successfully launch the venture involved.
Note: Transfer your scores from the following pages to this summary sheet.
Other Observations on the Verbal Presentation

APPENDIX C: A TYPICAL VENTURE CAPITAL TERM SHEET

The Evolution of Business Plans in International Business Plan Competitions

ABC, L.L.P.

LETTER OF INTENT

This LETTER OF INTENT summarizes the principal terms with respect to a private placement of equity securities of _____ (the "Company") by ABC, L.L.P. ("ABC") and _____ (hereinafter referred to, collectively, as the "Investors"). Hereinafter, ABC, Investors and any other holder of Preferred Stock of the Company are sometimes referred to, collectively, as "Holders" and, individually, as a "Holder."

PROPOSED PRIVATE PLACEMENT

GENERAL TERMS:

(1) AMOUNT: $ _____

(2) TYPE OF SECURITY: Series A Convertible Preferred Stock ("Preferred")

(3) PRICE PER SHARE:

$1.00 per share ("Original Purchase Price") for _____ shares, for an aggregate purchase price of $_____ ("Original Total Purchase Price"). The Original Total Purchase Price has been computed based on an assumed purchase of ___% of the Company's common stock (the "Common Stock") on a Fully Diluted Basis, representing a post money valuation of $_____.

For purposes of this Letter of Intent, "Fully Diluted Basis" means computation of outstanding Common Stock after giving effect to the exercise of all outstanding options and warrants, conversion of all securities convertible into shares of Common Stock (including the Preferred) and payment for any stock appreciation rights or phantom stock rights.

---

(4) CAPITALIZATION POST-CLOSING:

The following capitalization chart reflects all classes of Company securities to be outstanding post-closing on a Fully Diluted Basis:

Number	Type	Percentage
_____	Common Stock	_____ %
_____	Preferred Stock	_____ %
_____	Reserved Employee Shares	_____ %
_____	Options and warrants	_____ %
	Total	100%

The Company shall provide to ABC, within 7 days after the date of this Letter of Intent, a capitalization table showing the number of shares by shareholder of all classes of securities that will be outstanding following the closing of the investment contemplated by this Letter of Intent, and the percentage ownership represented by each such class of securities.

The Company and ABC propose a private placement of shares of Preferred Stock on the following terms:

RIGHTS, PREFERENCES, PRIVILEGES AND RESTRICTIONS ON PREFERRED:

(1) DIVIDEND PROVISIONS:

Alternative 1: Discretionary
The Holders owning Preferred shall be entitled to receive dividends only when, as and if declared by the Board of Directors. No dividends shall be paid on the Common Stock unless the Preferred shall participate with the Common Stock on an as-converted basis.

Alternative 2: Scheduled Payment
The Holders owning Preferred will be entitled to receive quarterly cumulative cash dividends commencing _____, _____, at the rate of _____% per annum of the Original Total Purchase Price prior to any distribution with respect to Common Stock. For any other dividends or distributions, Preferred shall participate with Common Stock on an as-converted basis.

In the event the Company shall fail to make a dividend payment when due, then, at option of Holders owning the Requisite Percentage of Preferred, the Company shall issue to the Holders that number of shares of Preferred determined by dividing the dollar amount of the dividend to have been paid by the Original Total Purchase Price.

Alternative 3: Deferral Until Liquidity Event
The Holders owning Preferred will be entitled to receive quarterly cumulative cash dividends commencing _____, _____, at the rate of _____% per annum of the Original Total Purchase Price, plus all accrued but unpaid dividends, prior to any distribution with respect to Common Stock. Payment of these dividends shall be deferred until the occurrence of a Liquidity Event (as hereinafter defined). For any

other dividends or distributions, Preferred shall participate with Common Stock on an as-converted basis.

(2) LIQUIDITY EVENT PREFERENCE:
Alternative 1: Participating Preferred
Upon the occurrence of a Liquidity Event, the Company shall first pay to the Holders owning Preferred an amount equal to the Original Total Purchase Price plus all accrued but unpaid dividends, plus a preferred return equal to _____ percent (___%) of the Original Total Purchase Price; thereafter, Preferred and Common Stock shall share any remaining assets pro rata on an as-converted basis.

Alternative 2: Fixed Return as Multiple of Original Purchase Price
Upon the occurrence of a Liquidity Event, the Company shall pay to the Holders owning Preferred, first, an amount equal to any accrued but unpaid dividends, and then an amount equal to _____ (___) times the Original Total Purchase Price; thereafter, Preferred and Common Stock shall share any remaining assets pro rata on an as-converted basis.

Alternative 3: Pro Rata
Upon the occurrence of a Liquidity Event, the Company shall pay to the Holders owning Preferred, first, an amount equal to any accrued but unpaid dividends, and then an amount equal to the greater of (i) the percentage of the fair market value of the remaining assets of the Company represented by the Preferred percentage ownership of the Company on a Fully Diluted Basis, or (ii) the Original Total Purchase Price.

Required:
"Liquidity Event" shall include (i) a liquidation, dissolution or winding up of the Corporation involving the assets which constitute substantially all of the assets of the business of the Corporation; (ii) a merger, reorganization or consolidation of the Company; (iii) any other transaction in which control of the Company is transferred; or (iv) the sale, transfer, or lease (but not including a transfer or lease by pledge or mortgage to a bona fide lender), of all or substantially all the assets of the Corporation.

(3) CONVERSION:
Optional: Subject to anti-dilution adjustments, a Holder of Preferred will have the right, at its option, to convert its shares of Preferred at

any time into shares of Common Stock at a conversion price of $1.00 per share (the "Conversion Price"), resulting in an initial conversion ratio of one share of Common for each share of Preferred. The amount of Common Stock into which the Preferred shares may be converted will be initially the number necessary to equal ____% of the Common Stock on a Fully Diluted Basis.

Automatic: Upon the closing of a Qualified Public Offering, the Preferred will be automatically converted into Common Stock, at the then applicable Conversion Price.

For purposes of this Letter of Intent, "Qualified Public Offering" means a firmly underwritten public offering of Common Stock yielding gross proceeds of at least $ _____ at a public offering price per share (prior to underwriter commissions and expenses) that is not less than $_____.

(4) ANTI-DILUTION PROVISIONS: Stock Issuances at less than Original Price Per Share:
Alternative 1: Full Ratchet
In the event that the Company shall issue shares of its capital stock or debt at a price per share that is less than or equal to the Original Purchase Price, then the Conversion Price shall be reduced to equal the price per share of the stock in such issuance.

Alternative 2: Weighted Average Dilution (Favorable to Current Shareholders)
In the event the Company shall issue shares of its capital stock (a "New Issuance") at a price per share that is less than or equal to the Original Purchase Price, then the Conversion Price shall be reduced to a price (calculated to the nearest cent) determined by the following formula:

$$\frac{(N+C)}{(CP' = CP*N + AS)}$$

where:

CP' = the new Conversion Price resulting from the antidilution adjustment;

CP = the Conversion Price before the dilutive issuance;

N = the number of shares of Common Stock outstanding immediately prior to such issuance (or deemed issuance) assuming exercise or conversion of all outstanding securities exercisable for or convertible into Common Stock;

C = the number of shares of Common Stock that would have been purchased with the aggregate consideration received (or deemed to be received) by the Corporation in the dilutive issuance if the purchase price per share had been equal to the Conversion Price before the dilutive issuance;

AS = the number of shares of Common Stock so issued or deemed to be issued in the dilutive issuance.

Alternative 3: Weighted Average Dilution (Favorable to Investors)
In the event the Company shall issue shares of its capital stock (a "New Issuance") at a price per share that is less than or equal to the Original Purchase Price, then the Conversion Price shall be reduced to a price (calculated to the nearest cent) determined by the following formula:

$$\frac{(N + C)}{(CP' = CP * N + AS)}$$

where:

CP' = the new Conversion Price resulting from the antidilution adjustment;

CP = the Conversion Price before the dilutive issuance;

N = the number of shares of Common Stock into which the Preferred outstanding immediately prior to the dilutive issuance can be converted;

C = the number of shares of Common Stock that would have been purchased with the aggregate consideration received (or deemed to be received) by the Corporation in the dilutive issuance if the purchase price per share had been equal to the Conversion Price before the dilutive issuance;

AS = the number of shares of Common Stock so issued or deemed to be issued in the dilutive issuance.

Stock Issuances related to Performance Warrants:
In the even the Company shall issue shares of its capital stock pursuant to any option or warrant pursuant to the terms of which the number of shares of capital stock that can be purchased is either increased or

decreased based on the Company achieving or failing to achieve certain performance goals or milestones (A "Performance Warrant"), then the Conversion Price shall be adjusted in an equitable manner to insure that the Holders' ownership of capital stock of the Company is not diluted or reduced in any manner as the result of the exercise of any such Performance Warrant.

Stock Issuances at more than Original Price Per Share
  (Preemptive Rights):
In the event the Company desires to issue shares of its capital stock at a price per share that is greater than the Original Purchase Price, then Holders owning Preferred shall have a preemptive right to purchase up to $_____ of the offering(s) and thereafter, each Holder of Preferred shall have a preemptive right to purchase that amount of the shares to be issued that will result in such Holder's maintaining its then percentage ownership of the Company, calculated on a Fully Diluted Basis. If a Holder does not exercise their preemptive right, then that right is assignable to ABC.

(5) VOTING RIGHTS:
Holders owning Preferred shall have voting rights on an as-converted to Common Stock basis. In addition, the consent of the Holders owning the Requisite Percentage of Preferred shall be required to approve any of the following: (i) the creation or issuance of any debt or equity securities of the Company, or any rights convertible into any debt or equity securities of the Company (other than the Reserved Employee Shares and shares issuable upon conversion of the Preferred); (ii) any vote which could materially or adversely alter or change the rights, preferences or privileges of the Preferred, or increase the authorized number of shares of Preferred (other than increases occurring as a result of a stock split or stock dividend), (iii) any vote involving the sale, lease or other transfer of the Company or of a substantial portion of its assets, any merger of the Company with another entity, or any liquidation or transfer of control of the Company; (iv) any amendment of the Company's Articles of Incorporation or Bylaws; (v) any transaction constituting a deemed dividend under U.S. tax law or any payment of dividends (other than dividends required to be paid to Holders owning Preferred); (vi) any re-purchase of Company stock or securities (other than repurchases of Preferred pursuant to exercises by Holders owning Preferred of put rights); (vii) the Company incurring debt,

including obligations in all forms, whether direct or contingent, exceeding amounts to be determined prior to closing, (viii) any proposed change in the principal line of business of the Company; (ix) payment or accrual for payment of increases in executive compensation (including without limitation salary, wages, bonuses and stock rights) in excess of amounts to be determined prior to closing; (x) re-payment of Company debt to stockholders except as determined prior to closing and agreed to in writing; and (xi) Company transactions with or creation of affiliates.

As used herein, "Requisite Percentage of Preferred" shall mean _____ % of the outstanding Preferred.

(6) PUT OPTION:

The Holders shall have the right to require the Company to purchase any or all of their shares of stock, whether Preferred or Common Stock, at any time or times after the fifth (5th) anniversary of the closing (the "Put"). The price of such shares shall be the greater of cost plus a 20% annual return or fair market value (not discounted for minority interests), as agreed upon by the Company and Holders owning the Requisite Percentage of the Preferred, or if no agreement between the two parties has been reached, then as determined by a third party mutually selected by the Company and Holders owning the Requisite Percentage of the Preferred. Such third party shall be instructed to value the Company based on its enterprise value without regard to discounts for minority interests and any lack of liquidity. Holders will provide notice of their intent to exercise a put at least 120 days prior to exercise date. The Holders' right to payment for any stock as to which the Put shall have been exercised shall, in all events, be prior to any other obligation of the Company to redeem shares of its stock or any other securities.

INFORMATION RIGHTS:

So long each Holder owns any of the Company's outstanding stock, the Company will deliver to such Holder standard financial reports including without limitation monthly and year-to-date income, balance sheet and cash flow statements as compared to budget and comparable period in prior year, a rolling 12-month forecast, and a written summary of operations each month by the 20th of each month. No later than 30 days prior to the end of each fiscal year, the Company shall provide a budget for the next fiscal year. An annual audit of the Company's financial statements shall be performed by an accounting firm as approved by the Board of Directors. The Holders shall also have standard and statutory inspection rights. The rights outlined in this section (other than statutory inspection rights) shall terminate upon a Qualified Public Offering.

Registration Rights

(1) DEMAND:
   Beginning at the earlier of two (2) years after closing, or three (3) months after the filing of a registration statement for a public offering, Holders may, so long as they then hold at least 20% of the Preferred or 20% of the Common Stock issued or issuable upon conversion of Preferred ("Holders' Stock"), demand that the Company file a registration statement covering the public sale of stock owned by the Investors. Upon any such demand, the Company will use its best efforts to cause such shares to be registered. The Company will not be obligated to effect more than three (3) registrations under these demand registration provisions.

(2) FORM S-3:
   The Holders owning the Holders' Stock will have the right to require the Company to file an unlimited number of registration statements on Form S-3 (or any equivalent successor form) provided the anticipated aggregate offering price is at least $750,000 and that not more than two Form S-3 registration statements are filed within any 12-month period.

(3) PIGGYBACK RIGHTS:
   The Holders owning the Holders' Stock will be entitled to unlimited "piggyback" registrations (i.e., inclusion in a registration undertaken by the Company), subject to a pro rata cut-back at the underwriter's discretion.

(4) REGISTRATION EXPENSES:
   Registration expenses (exclusive of underwriting discounts and special counsel fees of a selling shareholder) arising out of or in connection with any demand, Form S-3 or piggyback registration will be borne by the Company, and all expenses of any other registered offering shall be borne pro rata among the selling shareholders and, if it participates, the Company.

(5) OTHER:

The Company shall not engage or enter into any agreement with any underwriter in connection with any public offering of shares of the Company's stock unless such underwriter, and the terms of such agreement, shall have been approved in advance and in writing by Holders of the Requisite Percentage of Preferred, which approval shall not be unreasonably withheld or delayed.

Board Representation and Company Meetings

(1) BOARD AND COMMITTEES:

The Bylaws of the Company and any other appropriate corporate documents of the Company (including without limitation the Shareholders' Agreement and the Articles of Incorporation to the extent deemed appropriate by ABC) shall provide that (i) the number of directors shall be _____; (ii) that the Board and its standing committees shall meet no less frequently than quarterly; and (iii) the Board shall have a standing compensation committee and a standing audit committee, each of which shall have at least one member who is Independent. For purposes of this Letter of Intent, "Independent" shall refer to an individual who is not an employee, founder or controlling shareholder of the Company.

(2) BOARD REPRESENTATION:

ABC shall have the right to elect one (1) member of the Board of Directors and the current shareholders of the Common Stock shall have the right to elect _____ members of the Board of Directors. The _____ member shall be mutually agreed upon by Holders of the Requisite Percentage of Preferred and the current shareholders and shall be Independent.

(3) OBSERVATION RIGHTS:

Each Investor (including without limitation ABC) shall have the right to have a representative present at all meetings of the Board of Directors of the Company and all meeting of the standing committees thereof (the "Observation Rights"), and there shall be no meeting of the Board of Directors or a standing committee of the Company unless (i) a representative of each Investor shall be present or (ii) an Investor shall have waived, in writing, its Observation Rights with respect to such meeting. In addition, each Investor shall have the right to review any consent resolutions of the Board of Directors prior to signing. Exercise of the Observation Rights shall not be, and shall not be construed as being, participation by such Investor on the Board of Directors of the Company.

(4) BOARD VOTES:

The following shall require approval of a majority of the Board of Directors (including the director appointed by ABC):

(i) A change in executive management including those positions commonly referred to as the Chief Executive Officer, Chief Operating Officer and Chief Financial Officer (the "Executive Officers"); (ii) any change in compensation of any Executive Officer; (iii) amendment of any agreement with any Executive Officer; and (iv) a change in the accounting or legal firms currently employed by the Company.

(5) EVENT OF CHANGE:

Holders' of the Requisite Percentage of Preferred shall be entitled to elect a majority of the Board of Directors (which shall include the Director appointed by ABC) upon the occurrence an "Event of Change," which will be defined to include (i) a breach by the Company or the controlling shareholders of any representation, warranty, covenant or other provision set forth in any of the documents contemplated hereby; (ii) a breach of any material agreement entered into by the Company not cured within the time allowed by that agreement; (iii) an event of bankruptcy (as such term shall be defined in the Shareholders' Agreement); (iv) failure to redeem the Preferred upon exercise of the Put rights; (v) the death or long term disability of _____ or _____; and (vi) such other events as shall be agreed upon by the parties.

(6) TERMINATION:

The rights granted to the Investors with respect to Board of Directors meetings shall terminate upon a Qualified Public Offering.

(7) EXPENSES:

The Company shall reimburse each Investor for all out-of-pocket expenses incurred (i) by its representative for attending meetings of the Board of Directors or Board committees; (ii) by its representative for attending any other meetings, conferences, trade shows or other sale and marketing events if such Investor's attendance thereat shall have been approved in advance by the President of the Company, which approval shall not be unreasonably withheld; and (iii) by such Investor for other on-going legal fees and expenses arising out of or in connection with its investment in the Company.

(8) INSURANCE:
The Company shall use its best efforts to obtain and maintain directors' and officers' liability insurance underwritten by such company, and in such amount, as shall be approved by ABC, which approval shall not be unreasonably withheld.

USE OF PROCEEDS:

The proceeds from the sale of the Preferred, subject to the specific approval of Cordova, will be used for the purposes set forth on Exhibit A attached to and made a part of this Letter of Intent.

CONDITIONS TO CLOSING AND OTHER PROVISIONS

The closing of this proposed Private Placement shall be subject to certain conditions precedent including, without limitation, the following:

EMPLOYEE AGREEMENTS:

The Company has or will have an agreement, satisfactory to ABC, with each of the following individuals and other future employees hired to fill the positions referred to in the following provision:

_____

_____

Each such agreement shall contain (i) confidentiality, non-disclosure, non-competition, non-solicitation and non-inducement covenants acceptable to Cordova and (ii) covenants providing that any inventions or other proprietary information or trade secrets developed by the employee during the term of employment shall be the sole and exclusive property of the Company.

CORPORATE OFFICERS:

The Company will elect persons acceptable to ABC to the following positions:

President and/or Chairman
Chief Executive Officer

Chief Operating Officer
Chief Financial Officer
Chief Technical Officer
VP – Sales and Marketing
VP – Business Development

KEY PERSON INSURANCE:
The Company shall obtain prior to closing and shall maintain key person life insurance on each of and in the amount of at least $_____ per individual, with the Company named as the sole beneficiary of the proceeds. The proceeds of any such policy shall be used solely for general corporate purposes and working capital, and not to redeem the stock owned by any employee, founder or controlling shareholder.

SHAREHOLDERS' AGREEMENT:
All shareholders of the Company, including ABC, the controlling shareholders and any minority shareholders, shall enter into a Shareholders' Agreement which shall, among other things, provide that (i) no holder of Common Stock shall sell, pledge or encumber in any way any of his Common Stock except for up to five percent (5%) of the amount of stock owned as of the Closing which may be transferred for estate planning purposes; (ii) the Company shall have the option, upon the death or long-term disability of a controlling shareholder, to purchase such shareholder's stock at its then fair market value; (iii) the Company shall have the option to purchase all of the shares of Common Stock held by an employee shareholder (including without limitation a controlling shareholder) upon termination of employment for any reason; (iv) first the Company and then the Holders shall have a right of first refusal to purchase any shares which a shareholder (other than a Holder) desires to sell; and (v) each holder of Holder's Stock shall have a co-sale right to participate in any sale of Common Stock of the Company on a pro rata basis. The purchase price for any stock purchased by the Company shall be paid in five (5) annual installments commencing on that date _____ days after the closing of the purchase. Entering into the Shareholders' Agreement shall be a condition precedent to the issuance of stock to any new shareholders.

RESERVED EMPLOYEE SHARES:
The Company may reserve up to shares of the Company's Common Stock (the "Reserved Employee Shares") for issuance to employees. The Reserved Employee Shares will be issued from time to time under such

arrangements, contracts or plans as are recommended by management and unanimously approved by the Board. The price of such shares shall be set by the Board and in no event shall be less than a price per share of $. Holders of Reserved Employees Shares will be required to execute agreements that, among other things, restrict their right to transfer their stock.

STOCK PURCHASE AGREEMENT:

The purchase of the Preferred will be made pursuant to a Stock Purchase Agreement and such other agreements as may be necessary, in each case to be drafted by counsel to ABC and reasonably acceptable to the Company and the Investors. The Stock Purchase Agreement will contain, among other things, appropriate representations and warranties of the Company and the controlling shareholders to be made on a joint and several basis; covenants of the Company reflecting the provisions set forth herein; indemnification provisions from the Company and the controlling shareholders, on a joint and several basis, to indemnify the Investors for a breach of any representation, warranty or covenant in the Stock Purchase Agreement; appropriate conditions including qualification of the shares under applicable Blue Sky laws; a requirement to file the Certificate of Amendment to the Company's Articles of Incorporation to authorize the Preferred; and an obligation to deliver an opinion of independent legal counsel for the Company and the controlling shareholders.

DUE DILIGENCE REVIEW:

ABC and the other Investors shall have completed their due diligence review and shall be satisfied with the results thereof, and there shall be no material adverse changes in the Company's financial condition, business or business prospects as determined by ABC.

EXPENSES:

The Company will pay to ABC at closing _____ Dollars ($_____) to cover all legal, due diligence and other fees, costs and expenses incurred by Cordova arising out of or in connection with this transaction. Such obligation of the Company is not conditioned upon closing the transaction contemplated herein and in the event such transaction shall not close, such expenses shall be payable on demand from ABC.

FINDERS:
The parties acknowledge that no finder's fee is due with respect to this transaction.

CLOSING:
The closing of the transaction is expected to occur on or before _____ (the "Closing").

EXCLUSIVITY:
For a period of forty-five (45) days after the date of this Letter of Intent, the Company, and its officers, agents, representatives and directors agree that they will terminate discussions with all other parties relating to financing arrangements that are, in any material respect, competitive with the private placement proposed in this Letter of Intent. During that time, and hereafter, so long as Cordova in good faith is working toward closing, the Company and its agents, representatives, officers and directors will not consummate or solicit proposals or offers from any parties and will not discuss unsolicited proposals or offers from third parties for financing competing with this private placement or any merger, acquisition or consolidation involving the Company or any sale, lease, license or other transfer of a substantial portion of the assets of the Company

NON-BINDING AGREEMENT:
The parties acknowledge that this Letter of Intent outlines the current understanding between the parties as to the proposed investment, but that neither party shall be bound to the other by this Letter of Intent for damages, expenses, failure to agree on a formal and final contract or in any way except as to the Company's obligations as set forth in the paragraphs headed Expenses and Exclusivity.

EXPIRATION:
The terms and conditions of this Letter of Intent shall expire, and any offer set forth herein shall be deemed to be revoked by Cordova, in the event this Letter of Intent shall not be signed by the Company and returned to Cordova by 5:00 p.m. on _____, ____.

DATED this _____ day of _____, _____.

ACCEPTED

_____, Inc.   ABC Partners, L.L.P.

By: _____   By: _____

Name Printed: _____   Name Printed: _____

Title _____   Title: ABC & Company, LLC General Partner

APPENDIX D: THE NEW VENTURE VALUATION PROCESS

The Evolution of Business Plans in International Business Plan Competitions

Some Definitions

vpm = Pre-money Valuation of the New Venture
VPM = Post-money Valuation of the new Venture
M = The Amount of Money secured from the Angel or VC
α = The VC's percentage Ownership of the New Venture

Some Basic Formulas

$$M = \alpha \times VPM \tag{1}$$

or

$$VPM = M/\alpha \tag{2}$$

In most situations, you will know how much Money (M) you want to raise from the VC. So, you can calculate the Post-money Value of the Venture by dividing M by the percentage of Ownership you will need to give up to get the Money (M).

Let's look at ABC venture's A-round of funding in which it is seeking

α	50%	40%	33%	25%	20%
VPM	$4.0 M	$5.0 M	$6.0 M	$8.0 M	$10.0 M

$2.0 million. By looking at different Values for **α**, you can calculate the different possible Post-money Valuations of ABC as shown below.
Also,

$$vpm + M = VPM \tag{3}$$

or

$$vpm = VPM - M \tag{4}$$

And once you calculate the Post-money Valuation, you can then quickly calculate the Pre-money Valuation using the formulas above. Remembering that the amount of money that you're seeking M is $2.0 million, the Pre-money Valuations for each different **α** are as follows.

α	50%	40%	33%	25%	20%
VPM	$4.0 M	$5.0 M	$6.0 M	$8.0 M	$10.0 M
M	$2.0M	$2.0M	$2.0M	$2.0M	$2.0M
vpm	$2.0M	$3.0M	$4.0M	$6.0M	$8.0M

Also, remember that from a VC's perspective, very few ventures have ever been worth more than $10.0 M pre-revenue. Moreover, in today's markets the maximum Pre-revenue Pre-money valuations are much lower, frequently less than half of that. However, as you move into B and C rounds, all of these Valuations go up.

APPENDIX E: FOUR EXHIBITS ON VENTURE CAPITAL INVESTOR THOUGHT PROCESSES

The Evolution of Business Plans in International Business Plan Competitions

A different but useful way of looking at these changes to the structure of business plans is to compare the 11 topics in this new executive summary with the major criteria used for most venture capital investing. Exhibit 1 and Exhibit 2, which were developed by the author, summarize the various criteria used by most VCs when they invest in new ventures. Exhibit 1 summarizes these seven investment criteria, while Exhibit 2 presents them in a different way using key questions and desired answers from several successful VCs in the 2010 period.

Exhibit 1: The Seven P's of Venture Capital Investing.

1. POTENTIAL

What is the long-term size of the market in which this venture will compete? It should be large enough so the venture could become an institutional growth stock since the primary way VCs make money is to sell the stock of the ventures they've funded. Also if the market is large enough, the venture does not have to be #1 in its industry to have sufficient upside potential to justify investing in it. Put differently, VCs do NOT invest in small opportunities.

2. PAIN and/or PASSION

How much PAIN do the venture's primary target customers feel? Is it enough to change their existing buying behavior? In most instances, a venture's target customers are already doing something to meet their current needs. Changing buying behavior is one of the most difficult things to do in business. So VCs want strong evidence that the venture's potential customers really will start to behave in new ways once the venture's products are brought to market. Put differently, the target customer's PAIN with existing products should be immediate, obvious, and significant. Best of all is strong evidence of passionate customer acceptance of the venture's products, such as some initial (or even better repeat) sales to significant customers.

3. PROPRIETARY POSITION

What are the venture's significant long-term competitive advantages? Even if a venture can start successfully, it will usually take several years for it to grow large enough to go public. During this time, new competitors will seek to enter the market if it has any upside potential whatsoever. In order for a venture to be able to withstand such competitive entry, it must have some significant and enduring competitive advantages.

4. BUSINESS MODEL/PLAN and PROFITS

How will the venture make money? From whom will the venture receive revenues, and for what? What are the key elements of its cost structure, and how realistic are these costs? Does its chosen business model offer an attractive value proposition to its target customers, while capturing a significant portion of the value in this space for the venture itself? What returns will the venture's business model generate for its investors? How quickly will these returns be generated? Are they commensurate with the magnitude of the risks involved?

5. PEOPLE

Does the founding entrepreneurial team have the managerial and technical skills needed to successfully start and grow this venture? In almost every startup, the development and growth of the venture deviates in significant ways from the initial plans. So, VCs seek assurances that the team has the skills needed to respond effectively to such uncertainties. Prior startup and/or industry experience is most desirable of such evidence.

6. PROGRESS TO DATE

What has the founding team accomplished to date? Another indicator of the founding team's abilities is the progress that it has made in getting the venture started with the resources it has been able to attract. From a VC's perspective, the more significant these achievements by the time venture capital is sought, the more attractive the investment opportunity.

7. PARTICULARS

Are the details of the venture's plan accurate? Are they consistent with the particulars of the industry involved? If NOT, one must ask, What else is wrong here? No plan is ever perfect. However, excessive errors in the details suggest that a second look is needed.

Exhibit 2:   Current VC Investment Criteria.

Next "Big Thing" Criteria	
1. Strong Proof of Concept	
Product or Service	
Need Fulfilled	
Current Sales	
Evidence of Sales	
2. Large Potential Market [> $500 Million] & High Sales [> $20 Million Year 3]	
U.S. Potential	
Worldwide Potential	
Sales @ 3 Years	
3&4. Rapid Expected Growth Rate (after Funding) [> 25% /Year] & Scalability	
Annual Growth Rate	
Scalability	
4&5. Strong Sustainable Competitive Advantage(s) & Barriers to Entry	
Product Advantages	
Patents	
Years to Catch Up	
6. Effective Commercialization Strategy	
1st Target Customers	
Breakeven Sales	
7. Realistic Business Model	
Initial "Burn" Rate	
Initial Funding Needs	
Follow-on Funding	
8. Experienced Management (& Advisory) Team	
Prior Industry Experience	
Prior Startup Experience	

These various VC investment criteria can be classified and summarized into two major categories: market criteria and company criteria. The primary market criteria are (1) large market size, that is, the magnitude of the market's long-term (5–10 years) sales potential and (2) major customer pain, which translates into rapid customer acceptance and market growth rates. The primary company criteria are: (1) the ventures' key people and their relevant experience(s), (2) the venture's strategy and intellectual property together with the competitive advantages that these factors will provide to the venture, and (3) the venture's business model and progress to date, which also provide evidence of the capabilities of the venture's management team to make it happen. The key risks that the venture faces affect both of these sets of criteria.

A third way of summarizing these points is the set of "10 Commandments" for new venture success provided that was also created by the author. These "10 Commandments" are presented in Exhibit 3.

The author's set of "10 Commandments" for new venture success and Denton's revised view of the VC's primary investment criteria which focuses on their primary goal of earning a 10 return on the funds that they invest are both shown below.

Exhibit 3:   The 10 Commandments of Venture Capital Investing.

1	The Lead Entrepreneur MUST be a generalist, not a specialist, and must know the Keys to New Venture Failure
2	You MUST BE RIGHT the FIRST TIME because the #1 Option is always significantly larger than the #2 Option
3	The ONLY PRIORITY is the SEGMENT with the GREATEST PAIN
4	One MUST get the FIRST ADOPTER ASAP
5	One MUST have a 100-Day Plan to achieve the Goals above and have Maximum Organizational Impact
6	One MUST REACH KEY VALUATION MILESTONES in order to produce Results with Significant Organizational Impact
7	To reach such Milestones, one must craft a Successful Growth Strategy
8	A key part of such Strategies will be to Minimize Fixed Costs while Maintaining Adequate Quality
9	In all such Decision-Making, one MUST ACT QUICKLY which means that one should always do Order of Magnitude Evaluations of All Possible Options
10	Finally, for all new ventures, one MUST REMEMBER that CASH IS KING!

Finally, an additional way to summarize VC's current processes for investing the funds that have been entrusted to them is shown in Exhibit 4 which summarizes the various criteria used in VCs' decision-making in a slightly different way. More specifically, Exhibit 4 emphasizes the fact that the primary goal of almost all VC's is to secure a 10 return from the various ventures in which they invest. Exhibit 4 was developed by Dr. F. Russell Denton, one of my MBA students, in a class on VC decision-making.

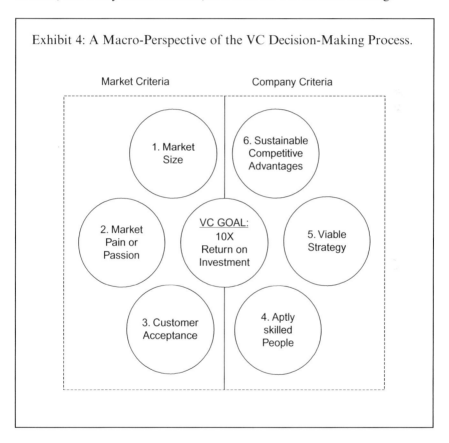

Exhibit 4: A Macro-Perspective of the VC Decision-Making Process.

Market Criteria   Company Criteria

1. Market Size

6. Sustainable Competitive Advantages

2. Market Pain or Passion

VC GOAL: 10X Return on Investment

5. Viable Strategy

3. Customer Acceptance

4. Aptly skilled People

Almost all of the changes described above have been made by U.S. VCs as part of the real-world process that they go through to invest the funds that have been entrusted to them by their primary clients. Overall, from a macro-perspective, these changes provide VCs the opportunity to review more of the information that prospective entrepreneurs provide to them about the ventures that these entrepreneurs are seeking to get funded.

CHAPTER 6

AN EXPLORATION OF THE PHENOMENON OF BUSINESS PLANNING IN NASCENT AND YOUNG FIRMS

Christophe Garonne and Per Davidsson

ABSTRACT

Whether or not nascent entrepreneurs should spend time developing a business plan is still an issue of debate for both scholars and practitioners. This chapter contributes to a better understanding on the uses and expectations of planning among business start-ups by taking a deeper and more granular approach than previous research. The chapter examines not only if *planning is used but also* how *it is used and how this changes over time. Contrary to current thinking, the research suggests that for most firms the issue of planning may be a question of choice more than a request from institutional pressure. The insights developed in this chapter provide a foundation for future theorizing about the antecedents and effects of business planning for start-ups.*

Keywords: Business planning; formal; nascent; use of planning

Models of Start-up Thinking and Action: Theoretical, Empirical and Pedagogical Approaches
Advances in Entrepreneurship, Firm Emergence and Growth, Volume 18, 213–236
Copyright © 2016 by Emerald Group Publishing Limited
All rights of reproduction in any form reserved
ISSN: 1074-7540/doi:10.1108/S1074-754020160000018006

INTRODUCTION

The creation of a business plan has been considered by academia, policy makers, advisors, and funding bodies as a more or less compulsory step toward the successful emergence of a venture (Brinckmann, Grichnik, & Kapsa, 2010; Shane & Delmar, 2004). However, some have questioned the value of business planning (Honig & Karlsson, 2004; Karlsson, 2005; Karlsson & Honig, 2009) and stressed that major companies such as Calvin Klein and Microsoft were launched successfully without a business plan (Bhidé, 2000).

Many previous studies focused on comparing the mere presence versus absence of business plans in new ventures to measure its impact on performance in terms of growth, sales, or survival rates (Delmar & Shane, 2003; Frese, 2007). However, no consensus on the benefits of planning has emerged (Brinckmann et al., 2010) and the debate about its effects on performance is still active (Delmar, 2015; Honig & Samuelsson, 2014). One of the reasons for the inconsistent results in previous literature may be that a too coarse grained view of business planning was applied. Therefore, this chapter takes a step back and leaves the performance effects of business planning aside. Instead, it examines not only *if* planning is used but also *how* it is used and how this *changes over time*. Descriptive knowledge of these issues may help future theorizing about the antecedents and effects of business planning for start-ups.

Specifically, this chapter looks at three elements, namely *degree of formalization*, *revision*, and *types of use* of planning. The degree of formalization of business plans has barely been mentioned in previous research, recent exceptions being Brinckmann and Kim (2015) and Hechavarria, Renko, and Matthews (2012). This chapter examines the prevalence and changes of planning formalization over the course of development of new ventures by studying both nascent and young firms over three years.

In a qualitative study with six nascent firms, Karlsson and Honig (2009) found that business plans are rarely updated after their completion. However, the question of revision of the plan has not been investigated on a large longitudinal random sample of emerging firms. Therefore, this chapter addresses the prevalence and frequency of business plan revision among start-ups.

Finally, while previous research stressed the various types of potential value business planning can have during the early stages of venture creation (Frese, 2007), we know very little about how start-ups *actually* use business plans. We examine actual and intended use of the plan for the following four purposes suggested in prior literature:

• As an action plan to be followed step by step (Armstrong, 1982; Brinckmann et al., 2010)
• As a means to obtain funding or other benefits from external sources (Karlsson & Honig, 2009)
• As an analytic tool to seize opportunities or avoid mistakes (Delmar & Shane, 2004)
• As an internal communication tool to disseminate strategic action (Delmar & Shane, 2003)

By exploring the phenomenon of business planning our main contribution is to provide an essential input for theorizing and testing in future research. In addition, our empirical description may help entrepreneurship educators and others stakeholders involved in new venture development avoid taking incorrect assumptions as their vantage point.

In the next section, we describe the methods and the dataset used to investigate the phenomenon of business planning. We then report the results before discussing our results and their implications for future research.

METHOD

Sample and Data Collection

We use the random samples of nascent and young firms from the Comprehensive Australian Study of Entrepreneurial Emergence (CAUSEE). The sampling methodology used in CAUSEE was previously developed for the Panel Study of Entrepreneurial Dynamics II (PSED II) in the United States and is specifically designed to capture random samples of nascent ventures (Reynolds & Curtin, 2008). CAUSEE expanded the sampling to include also a separate sample of young, operational ventures. For an elaborate method description see Davidsson, Steffens, and Gordon (2011) and the CAUSEE Handbook at http://eprints.qut.edu.au/49327/.

From July 2007 to March 2008, adults in 28,383 randomly sampled Australian households were screened for eligibility through telephone interviews. The screening identified 977 nascent firms (3.4%) and 1,011 young firms (3.6%). The full Wave 1 interview was completed by 591 nascent firms and 514 young firms.[1] The questionnaire is composed of 13 sections for a total of 210 questions, and the interviews lasted for 40−60 minutes.

All eligible (i.e., not yet terminated) cases were contacted for follow-up interviews after 12 and 24 months. Random digit dialing (RDD) was used for the initial screening, and Computer-aided telephone interviewing (CATI) was employed for all data collection.

As with any longitudinal survey, attrition is an issue that needs to be considered and addressed. Attrition happens because cases terminate or because they choose not to continue their participation in the survey. Planning behavior may be correlated with either of these factors. Since the objective of this chapter is not to explain the continuation of ventures nor the relationships between business planning and the performance of new firms, the most relevant analysis strategy is to focus mainly on the surviving cohort over the three waves. The cohort of surviving firms that continued to participate in the study through Wave 3 (24 months after the initial interview) consists of 252 nascent and 309 young firms. While we consider this – or the part thereof that uses a plan – our main sample we use a larger (all available cases) or a smaller sub-sample (only planners) in some analyses. The most restrictive analyses are limited to cases that reported using a business plan in each wave. Such analyses include 98 nascent and 99 young firms (regular planners). For analyses where alternative sample definition logics could be applied we comment as needed on any apparent divergence in results.

Business Planning Variables

Presence or absence of a business plan was assessed in Wave 1 by an affirmative answer to the following question: "A business plan usually outlines the markets to be served, the products or services to be provided, the resources required and the expected growth and profit for the new business. Have you ever prepared a business plan for this business?" In subsequent waves the question was adapted to reflect presence/absence in the previous wave.

In each wave, firms that reported having a plan were asked whether the plan was "unwritten or in your head, informally written, or formally prepared." From this information we computed two variables. *Formal Plan* and *Informal Plan*, each coded 1/0. After deliberations supported by preliminary analyses we decided to regard those reporting an "unwritten plan" as non-planners.

Revision of the plan: This variable assesses if firms with an informal or formal plan report having revised their plan since first writing it (Wave 1) or during the last 12 months (Waves 2 and 3). This variable is also coded 1/0.

Two questions were asked to assess uses of the business plan. The first asks planners (only) about *Actual Use* of the plan over the past twelve months. The second asks all respondents about *Intended Use* over the coming 12 months. Answers were obtained for four separate types of use on 5-point Likert scales ranging from "1 = not important at all" to "5 = very important." The below is the exact wording for actual use.

"How important or unimportant has your business plan been for the following uses:

- As an action plan? (*Action Plan*)
- As a means to obtain external finance or benefits from others? (*Obtain Funding*)
- As a means of thinking things through in order to seize opportunities or avoid mistakes? (*Analytic Tool*)
- As a tool for communicating strategic actions within the business?" (*Communication*)

RESULTS

Existence and Formalization of Business Plans

Fig. 1 displays an all-available-cases analysis of the existence or non-existence of a business plan over time. As the importance of having a business plan during the early stages of the venture creation process is emphasized by academic programs, practitioners and institutional bodies, it is not entirely surprising to discover that almost 60% of nascent firms report having a business plan at the time of the first interview. Among young firms there is a majority of non-planners in all waves (more than 55%).

Over time, the percentage of nascent firms with a business plan decreases, especially from Wave 1 to Wave 2. Further, the gap between nascent and young firms persists in Wave 3. All in all, this suggests that:

- Roughly half of all start-ups have a business plan at any given time.
- The prevalence of business planning decreases over time.

This pattern holds up also in analyses of the cohort that survives all three waves.

Institutional pressures may explain the difference between nascent and young firms. Ventures in a very early stage of development may face more

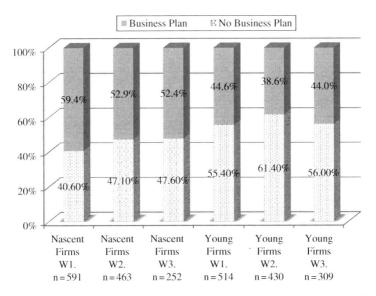

Fig. 1. Existence of Business Plans among Nascent and Young Firms for the Three Waves (in %).

institutional pressure to produce a business plan to increase their legitimacy with potential partners or to obtain external funding. Young firms that are by definition already operating ventures may have developed some business legitimacy through their operations and relationships with customers and other parties, rendering the presence of a business plan less important or less relevant. If their activities have become routinized they may also feel less need for a business plan.

Formalization of the Business Plan

Figs. 2 and 3 depict the distribution and evolution of business plan formalization. Fig. 2 uses all available cases in each wave while Fig. 3 only includes "regular planners," that is, cases reporting having a business plan in every wave as described in the section "Sample and data collection."

The overall shape of the distributions in Figs. 2 and 3 is similar:

— There is a roughly equal split between formal and informal planners.
— Regular planners are more likely to have a formal plan (Fig. 3).
— For young firms, the proportion of formal planners decreases over time.

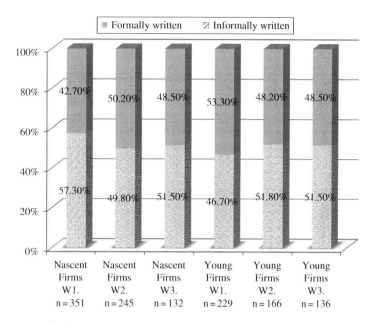

Fig. 2. Distribution among Planners in the Population of Nascent and Young Firms (in %).

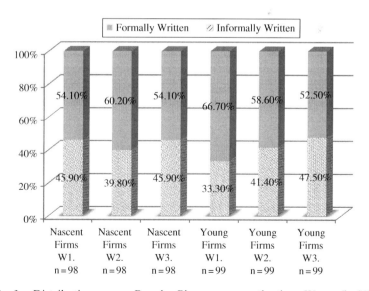

Fig. 3. Distribution among Regular Planners across the three Waves (in %).

Fig. 4 displays how the formalization of plans evolves over time. The results indicate that both upgrades and downgrades of the plans occur. That is, some move from no plan to a plan or from an informally written plan to a more elaborated form, whereas others move from a higher to a lower formalization or even to no plan. Further, the statistical tests suggest the transition patterns are not random occurrences.[2]

Fig. 4 also reveals that it is not common for a non-planner to move to a formal plan. Among both nascent and young firms less than 10% of Wave 1 non-planners have a written plan in Wave 3, and the shift from non-planner to informal planner is only slightly higher. This suggests that:

— Planners and non-planners to a great extent represent different categories of entrepreneurs (or possibly different types of ventures).

Changes in the start-up's situation over time do not to seem to be the major determinant of the planning versus non-planning choice. The stability of the non-planner group appears somewhat more pronounced among the young firms.

Those with an informally written plan are the most prone to change, with less than half remaining informal planners by Wave 3. This may be a natural consequence of them being an intermediate group which can change in two directions. The proportion downgrading is higher than the proportion upgrading, and this pattern is similar for nascent and young firms. This is in line with a general trend in our results, namely that the "planning intensity" of start-ups seems to decrease over time.

More surprising is perhaps that only half the Wave 1 formal planners remain formal planners by Wave 3. That is, the proportion keeping their former status is only slightly higher than what we found for informal planners. Again, the pattern is similar for nascent and young firms.

Revision of the Business Plan

Revision or updating of the plan may also be an important aspect to consider. Previous research drawing on institutional theory (DiMaggio & Powell, 1983) suggested that business plans are used to fulfill external requirements and/or are developed for legitimization purposes (Delmar & Shane, 2004) but are not actually used in practice (Karlsson & Honig, 2009). Consequently, it is argued that the plan is rarely updated after having served its legitimization purpose (Karlsson & Honig, 2009).

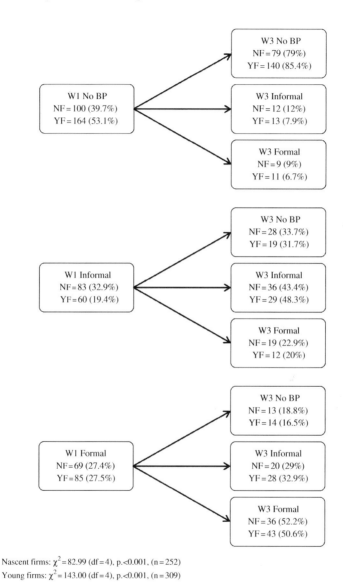

Nascent firms: $\chi^2 = 82.99$ (df = 4), p.<0.001, (n = 252)
Young firms: $\chi^2 = 143.00$ (df = 4), p.<0.001, (n = 309)

Fig. 4. Changes in Planning Formalization for Nascent and Young Firms between Wave 1 and Wave 3.

This section examines revision of the plan by contrasting nascent and young firms over three waves to observe the prevalence and frequency of plan revision, and how this varies by plan formalization.

Both nascent and young firms revise their plan, with around 60% or more updating their plan in any wave (Fig. 5). In an analysis including all available (planning) cases in each wave the prevalence of revision remains at the 56–63% level. The data suggest only a slight (if any) tendency toward reduced use of revision over time.

Hence, contrary to some suggestions in prior literature our results suggest that:

— Among the start-ups who plan, revision is the norm, not the exception.

This holds up for both nascent and young firms across the different samples. However, the results for business plan revision by the form of plan follows different patterns for nascent versus young firms. For nascent firms, revision is more prevalent for those with a formally written plan. In Wave 1 the difference between formally written and informally written plans is statistically significant for Wave 1 ($\chi^2 = 3.17$ [$df = 1$], $p < .01$). In contrast,

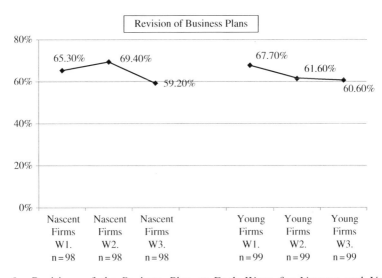

Fig. 5. Revisions of the Business Plan at Each Wave for Nascent and Young Firms for Regular Planners.

among young firms there is no statistically significant difference in revision by form of plan.

Our analysis reveals that recurring revisions of the plan is a common feature in both nascent and young firms (Fig. 6). Depending on whether all planners or only regular planners are included in the analysis, 30–40% of planners report revising the plan at least once every year (i.e., they report having revised the plan since the last interview). This figure is much higher than the proportion reporting never revising the plan. Again, our data clearly shows that among those who have a business plan, revision is the norm rather than the exception. This suggests that many planners use their plan and find value in doing so. As a result, they dedicate some time to updating their plan on a regular basis. Importantly, this is not limited to nascent firms but it is also prevalent among established young firms.

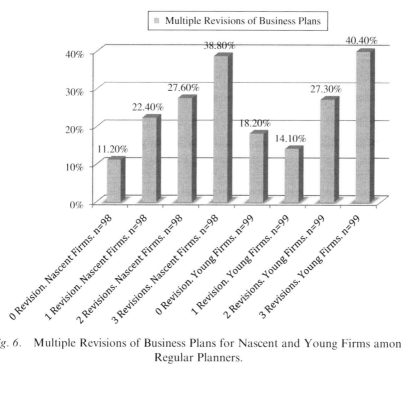

Fig. 6.   Multiple Revisions of Business Plans for Nascent and Young Firms among Regular Planners.

Different Uses of the Business Plan

In this section we will investigate the importance nascent and young ventures attribute to the business plan for the following four purposes:

— As an action plan to guide the development of the firm step by step,
— As a means to obtain external sources of finance,
— As an analytic tool to reflect, detect opportunities, and avoid mistakes,
— As an internal communication tool.

Moreover, these uses and their emphasis may change over time and may be different according to the maturity of the firm. This section reports on the actual uses (i.e., how important the business plan has been for the four aforementioned uses in the last 12 months?) as well as the intended uses (i.e., how important the business plan is expected to be for these four uses in the next 12 months). By doing so over three years we can compare expected use with actual, subsequent use. For example, the period covered by the intended use of the business plan in Wave 1 (Wave 1 + 12 months) is the same period as the actual uses of the business plan in Wave 2 (uses in the last 12 months).

All the analyses in this section were conducted both for all the available cases with a business plan and for the subsets of "regular planners." As similar results were found we only display one set of analyses.

What do Start-ups Use the Business Plan for?
To understand how the uses of business plan may change over time, actual and intended uses of the plan are compared for both nascent and young firms across the three waves using paired t-tests. The mean score for each use of business plan is based on a 5-point Likert scale that ranges from "1 = Not important at all" to " = Very important."

The analysis in Fig. 7 uncovers the following four main findings:

— Nascent firms use their plan more and expect more use of it than young firms.
— Both nascent and young firms expect more use of their plan in the next 12 months than they have actually used it in the last 12 months for all of the four uses.[3] Similarly, the reported actual use is almost always lower than the expected use reported 12 months earlier.
— Both nascent and young firms experience a decrease in the actual and expected uses of plan over time. The only exception is the actual use of a business plan as a communication tool for young firms, which remains

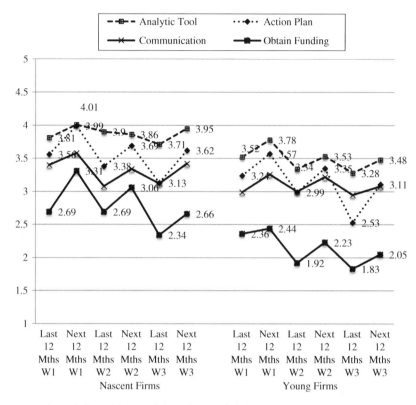

Fig. 7. Actual (Last 12 Months) and Intended (Next 12 Months) Uses of Business Plan for Regular Planners in Nascent and Young Firms (NF, *n* = 98; YF, *n* = 99).

steady over the three waves. This is likely due to some firms expanding their staff, thus increasing the need for a plan for internal communication.

– Using the plan to obtain external finance is always considered the least important use.

These findings are consistent across the different samples (i.e., planners only and regular planners). Overall, more than three-quarters of the nascent firms consider three uses of business plan as important, namely (in order of importance) using the plan as an analytic tool, as an action plan, and for internal communication. This ranking in the importance of the uses of business plan remains identical over the three years for both nascent and young firms. Consistently, the rated importance of the plan for obtaining funding and other resources is markedly lower.

The finding that few nascent firms consider a business plan important for obtaining external finance may come as a surprise considering the importance often attributed to business plans for attracting or convincing investors. Several factors may explain this result. First, the CAUSEE sample was randomly selected across all industries and thus the majority of ventures included in the dataset are mundane compared to the outlier cases highlighted by general media or research on "gazelles." As such, most of them are not in search of large amount of capital. Second, in this group of firms external funding − if used at all − may be obtained through personal loans and credit card debt which does not require a business plan. The results suggest that business plans are mostly used as an internal management tool rather than for external purposes. Hence, a business plan may not necessarily be considered as the most appropriate means of legitimization.

The paradox of decreasing use of the business plan over time in combination with expectations that the plan will be more important in the next 12 months is interesting. As mentioned previously, popular media, institutional bodies and academia have emphasized the necessity and usefulness of having a business plan. However, while planners appear to use their plan and to consider its potential uses as important, they may also realize that either the plan has already delivered its potential or that it has not been as useful as expected. The higher expected use of plan may be linked to an overly optimistic belief (cf. Cassar, 2010) that more is going to be initiated and achieved in the coming 12 months than what actually turns out to be the case.

Actual and Intended Uses of the Plan among Nascent Firms by Plan Formalization

Fig. 8 depicts the actual uses of the plan among formal and informal planners in nascent firms over time.

Three main results stand out:

- Nascent firms with a formal plan always consider the plan to be more important for any of the four actual uses than informal planners.
- The gap between formal and informal planners regarding how they use the plan increases over time.

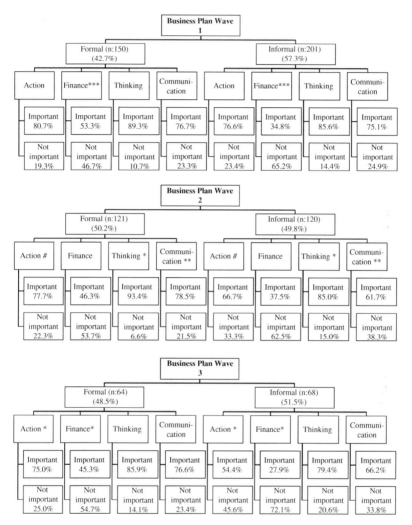

Wave 1: Finance: $(\chi^2 = 12,02\ (df=1),\ p<.001)(n=351)$
Wave 2: Action: $(\chi^2 = 3,64\ (df=1),\ p<.1)\ (n=241)$
Wave 2: Thinking: $(\chi^2 = 4,40\ (df=1),\ p<.05)$
Wave 2: Communication: $(\chi^2 = 8,16\ (df=1),\ p<.01)$
Wave 3: Action: $(\chi^2 = 6,09\ (df=1),\ p<.05)\ (n=132)$
Wave 3: Finance: $(\chi^2 = 4,29\ (df=1),\ p<.05)$

Fig. 8. Forms and Actual Uses of Business Plan for Nascent Firms for the Three Waves. $^{\#}p < .1;\ ^{*}p < .05;\ ^{**}p < .01;\ ^{***}p < .001.$

- Both informal and formal planners rank the actual uses of the plan in a similar order, ranking the use as analytic tool highest and obtaining finance lowest.
- For intended uses of the plan, the pattern is not as clear. Informal planners may at times consider the uses of the plan more important than formal planners.

Our analyses cannot determine if formal planners develop a formal plan because they attribute more importance to planning, or if it is the formal nature of the plan that makes them attribute more importance to it. Future research could investigate this aspect further.

The difference between formal and informal planners in their actual use of a business plan to obtain finance is striking, with only a third of informal planners considering it as important. This difference was expected as a formal plan is necessary to apply for funding to institutional bodies. Hence, for a subgroup there may be support for this "textbook" understanding of the role of the plan. The decrease over time of the importance given to the plan to obtain external funding may indicate that the financing has been solved in many cases. Alternatively, confrontation of the venture with the market may have led to more realistic expectations or to finding alternative solutions such as credit card debt or bootstrapping (Winborg & Landstrom, 2001).

Actual and Intended Uses of the Plan Among Young Firms
In contrast to nascent firms, there is among the young firms no clear-cut difference in how important formal and informal planners consider the different uses of plan. Use as an analytic tool is the most important actual use for formal and even more so for informal planners (Fig. 9).

Surprisingly, informal planners consistently rank expected uses of the plan as more important than formal planners. Young firms with an informal plan seem to expect more importance of the plan as an analytic tool. This might suggest that more mature firms have increased their planning efficiency over time and are able to extract the most of their business planning activity without developing a formal plan.

We have also performed analyses contrasting revisers and non-revisers. The results of these analyses were similar across nascent and young firms and did not reveal any fundamentally new patterns. For the most part, the contrasts highlighted differences of the same kind as in the comparison between formal and informal planners.

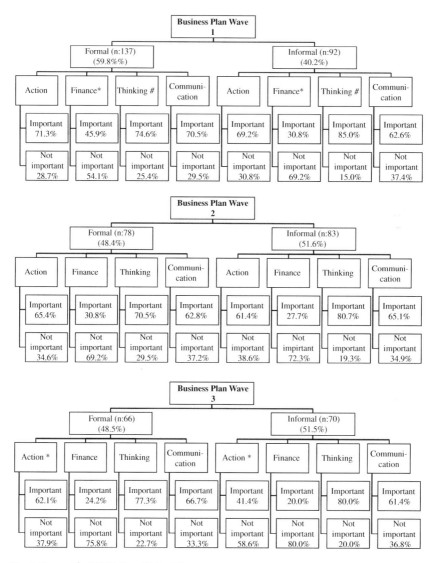

Wave 1: Finance: ($\chi^2 = 5,44$ (df=1), p<.05) (n=229)
Wave 1: Thinking: ($\chi^2 = 3,82$ (df=1), p<.1)
Wave 2: (n=161)
Wave 3: Action: ($\chi^2 = 5,82$ (df=1), p<.05) (n=136)

Fig. 9. Forms and Actual Uses of Business Plan for Young Firms for the Three Waves. $^{\#}p < .1$; $^{*}p < .05$; $^{**}p < .01$; $^{***}p < .001$.

DISCUSSION

Our descriptive analyses of business planning over time in random samples of nascent and young firms yield the following stylized facts:

1. *Roughly half of all start-ups report having a business plan at any given time.*

    This means business planning is prevalent, but also that many start-ups move forward without any type of written business plan. Although "half and half" may serve as a useful rule-of-thumb, these proportions could obviously vary across time and place. This said, data on random samples in Sweden and the United States indicate the same type of ball-park figure (Delmar & Shane, 2003; Reynolds, 2007).

2. *Only about half of those who report having a (written) business plan have prepared a formal document suitable for external use.*

    This reminds us that it is important to have the right mental image of what it is respondents have in mind when they report having a business plan. In many cases it is evidently something far less ambitious than the formal document business students or venture capital hopefuls are asked to present. This is important not least in the light of results indicating marked performance differences related to degree of plan formalization (Garonne, 2014).

3. *There seems to exist a sizeable group of "dedicated non-planners."*

    Some 75–80% of those who do not report a plan when first contacted still have no plan 24 months later. By contrast, there is more oscillation between formal and informal forms of planning, and even movement from having to not having a written business plan. Importantly, analyses reported elsewhere indicate no strong relationship between type of founder (prior experience) or type of venture (level of innovativeness) on the one hand, and mere presence of a plan on the other. Neither is there a strong relationship between presence of a plan and business performance (Garonne, 2014). Hence, there is still a lot to explain about how different types of founders and ventures find ways to their goals with or without a business plan.

4. *The "planning intensity" of individual start-ups often decreases over time.*

    This tendency shines through in most of our analyses. The presence of a business plan decreases somewhat over time among nascent firms and is lower still among established young firms (Fig. 1). Among young firms, the proportion of informal (compared to formal) plans increases over time (Fig. 3). More cases downgrade their "level" of planning over time compared to those who upgrade it (Fig. 4). The importance attributed to the plan as an analytic tool, action plan, or funding attractor also decreases over time (Fig. 7). There even appears to be some tendency towards decrease in planning revision over time (Fig. 5).

This tendency towards less (intense) planning is somewhat ironic in the light of the argument that planning makes relatively more sense in a less uncertain environment. If this were true, there should be more planning when the start-up has "found its way" and has a better handle on what it wishes to offer, to whom, and how to make profits from this. However, it may be the case that once things have settled and the firm has developed routines there may be less internal need for a (written/formal/revised) plan. Once the firm has regular income that covers running costs, and when it has gained some legitimacy as a regular actor in the market, there may also be less need for a plan as an external legitimacy signal.

5. *"Regular planners" take their planning more seriously.*

It is interesting to note that those who consistently report having some kind of business plan stand out not only in terms of having a plan – which they do by definition – but also on most planning-related criteria. Hence, the regular planners are more likely to have a formal plan; more likely to revise the plan, and rate all uses of the plan as more important. They also seem to have less of a discrepancy between actual and expected use of the plan. Just like there is a group of dedicated non-planners at the other end of the spectrum there appears to exist a rather distinct group of dedicated planners who put some serious thought and effort into the development and use of business plans.

6. *Revision of the plan is the rule, not the exception.*

This finding is clearly an important contrast to claims that the business plan typically is a mere symbol used to gain external legitimacy (and then put aside). Among regular planners, 40% report having revised the plan (again) in every interview. This is to be contrasted with only 10–20% (the higher figure pertaining to young firms) reporting never having revised the plan. In an analysis including all available cases (with a plan) in each wave, the proportion of "regular revisers" falls to 31–36% but remains higher than the proportion that never revised the plan (15–25%). The importance of considering revision is evident also in the light of preliminary findings suggesting a relationship between plan revision and business performance (Garonne, 2014). Future research should capture the extent to which the business plan is revised, and how often.

7. *The most important use of the business plan is as an analytic tool; a help to think things through in order to seize opportunities and avoid mistakes.*

  Although there may exist smaller subgroups or individual cases that see other uses as more important, a fairly consistent pattern in all our analyses of actual and intended use is that the internal, "analytic tool" use is the most important. This holds true for both nascent and young firms. It remains the most important across all covered stages of development, even if the rated importance for this use declines somewhat over time.

8. *Helping to obtain external finance is consistently rated the least important of the four possible uses of the business plan covered in our research.*

  This is another important contrast to received views. It appears that most of the time most start-ups in random samples are not looking for external infusions of capital. Hence, they do not rate this as an important reason for having a business plan. It is worth reminding here that this pertains to the (roughly) half of the sample that has a business plan at all. Therefore, when using this type of representative sample, theorizing antecedents and effects of business planning solely or mainly from the perspective of its instrumentality for obtaining finance is a very dubious practice. At best, the minority that uses the plan predominantly for such purposes will shine through in the form of supportive but diluted results. At worst, researchers will misinterpret the real mechanisms behind supportive results or be forced to reject theoretical ideas that may well be true for much more select samples of business start-ups.

The above set of stylized facts emerges fairly clearly from our analysis. Some of the observations may appear familiar for those who have deep knowledge of what the full population of business start-ups looks like, while others come across as more surprising. Either way, the fact is that very limited information exists in prior literature about formalization, revision, and (importance of) different types of use of business plans. Further, almost no such detailed information previously existed regarding how these things develop over time. This should make our set of stylized facts a useful input into future research with theory-testing or theory-developing ambitions.

Our results highlight the need for a better and more accurate operationalization of business planning in future research. They also suggest that the dichotomy between planners and non-planners is not the best approach to explain the phenomenon of business planning, even if a subgroup of dedicated non-planners indeed seems to exist. Instead, we recommend the following.

First, researchers should introduce a greater granularity in the operatio-nalization of business planning. This would allow capturing the degrees of formalization of planning and the various uses of business planning. Contrasting the effects of the different degrees of planning formalization on the venture emergence may help disentangling the previous inconclu-sive results.

Second, instead of focusing on whether or not emerging ventures craft a plan, future research should look at for what the plan is used. This, too, may help disentangle previous inconsistent findings. In the same vein, pre-vious research may have confused presence and uses of the plan assuming that when a plan was crafted, it was used. In addition, the differences between the intended versus the actual uses of the plan caution against using one as a proxy for the other and encourages further investigation into the cognitions at play during the planning process.

Third, the prevalence of business planning revision among planners is a strong call for a better consideration of this aspect in future research. Critics have portrayed planning as a hindrance to flexibility (Mintzberg, 1990) and as a document with a short life span due to the uncertainty and dynamism of the market (Brews & Hunt, 1999). Revision of the plan sig-nals awareness of and counter-action against such perils. Our results reveal that regular business planning revision is a common feature among nascent and young firms. This suggests that founders differentiate the process of business planning (the revision) and the outcome (the plan itself). In this way, revision of planning serves also as a proxy for use of the plan. So far, revision has barely been looked at in business planning research. We sug-gest including revision of planning as an important variable to better understand the planning phenomenon.

Finally, this chapter provides an important contribution to a better understanding on the uses and expectations of planning among the "mod-est majority" (Davidsson & Gordon, 2012) of business start-ups. In a ran-dom sample like CAUSEE few respondents are actually looking for external finance. This suggests that for the "average" firm, engaging into planning may be a question of choice (Chwolka & Raith, 2012) more than a request from institutional pressure (Honig & Karlsson, 2004). Complementary analyses were conducted on the same dataset to investigate the relationships between the different variables of business planning and the context in which the ventures were developed (Burke, Fraser, & Greene, 2010; Gruber, 2007) such as the type and the degrees of innovation of the firms (Dahlqvist & Wiklund, 2012). In analyses reported elsewhere we found no significant differences in planning prevalence or planning uses between firms low versus high in innovation. Similarly, no significant differences were found for firms with low or high levels of entrepreneurial, managerial, or industrial experience (Garonne, 2014). This suggests that even though our results are colored by the "modest majority" their validity is not restricted solely to novice founders of imitative start-ups.

In all, much remains to be learned about business planning among business start-ups. We believe our portrayal of business planning in nascent and young firms can serve as an important input to future theory-development and theory testing.

NOTES

1. Numbers of households screened and eligible cases identified are somewhat lower than in some other CAUSEE-based reports because our sample does not include a pilot sample otherwise integrated in the main data. This is because of design changes to the business planning section between pilot and main study.
2. These results were also confirmed by analyses that compared changes between each wave N and $N + 1$.
3. This difference is statistically significant for all uses and the three waves for nascent firms (except "analytical tool" in Wave 2). For young firms, the difference is also statistically significant except the use to obtain finance in Wave 1, and communications in Wave 3.

REFERENCES

Armstrong, J. S. (1982). The value of formal planning for strategic decisions: Review of empirical research. *Strategic Management Journal, 3*, 197–221.

Bhidé, A. V. (2000). *The origin and evolution of new businesses.* New York, NY: Oxford University Press.

Brews, P. J., & Hunt, M. R. (1999). Learning to plan and planning to learn: Resolving the planning school/learning school debate. *Strategic Management Journal, 20*(10), 889–913.

Brinckmann, J., Grichnik, D., & Kapsa, D. (2010). Should entrepreneurs plan or just storm the castle? A meta-analysis on contextual factors impacting the business planning–performance relationship in small firms. *Journal of Business Venturing, 25*(1), 24–40.

Brinckmann, J., & Kim, S. M. (2015). Why we plan: The impact of nascent entrepreneurs' cognitive characteristics and human capital on business planning. *Strategic Entrepreneurship Journal, 9*(2), 153–166.

Burke, A., Fraser, S., & Greene, F. J. (2010). The multiple effects of business planning on new venture performance. *Journal of Management Studies, 47*(3), 391–415.

Cassar, G. (2010). Are individuals entering self-employment overly optimistic? An empirical test of plans and projections on nascent entrepreneur expectations. *Strategic Management Journal, 31*(8), 822–840.

Chwolka, A., & Raith, A. G. (2012). The value of business planning before start-up: A decision-theoretical perspective. *Journal of Business Venturing, 27*, 385–399.

Dahlqvist, J., & Wiklund, J. (2012). Measuring the market newness of new ventures. *Journal of Business Venturing, 27*(2), 185–196.

Davidsson, P., & Gordon, S. R. (2012). Panel studies of new venture creation: A methods-focused review and suggestions for future research. *Small Business Economics, 39*(4), 853–876.

Davidsson, P., Steffens, P., & Gordon, S. R. (2011). Comprehensive Australian Study of Entrepreneurial Emergence (CAUSEE): Design, data collection and descriptive results. In K. Hindle & K. Klyver (Eds.), *Handbook of research on new venture creation* (pp. 216–250). Cheltenham: Edward Elgar.

Delmar, F. (2015). A response to Honig and Samuelsson (2014). *Journal of Business Venturing Insights, 3*, 1–4.

Delmar, F., & Shane, S. (2003). Does business planning facilitate the development of new ventures? *Strategic Management Journal, 24*(1), 165–1185.

Delmar, F., & Shane, S. (2004). Legitimating first: Organizing activities and the survival of new ventures. *Journal of Business Venturing, 19*, 385–410.

DiMaggio, P., & Powell, W. (1983). The iron cage revisited: Institutional isomorphism and collective rationality in organizational fields. *American Sociological Review, 48*, 147–160.

Frese, M. (2007). The psychological actions and entrepreneurial success: An action theory approach. In J. R. Baum, M. Frese, & R. A. Baron (Eds.), *The psychology of entrepreneurship* (pp. 151–188). Mahwah, NJ: Lawrence Erlbaum Associations.

Garonne, C. (2014). *Business planning in emerging firms: Uses and effects.* Ph.D. thesis, Australian Centre for Entrepreneurship Research, Queensland University of Technology, Australia. Retrieved from http://eprints.qut.edu.au/72949/

Gruber, M. (2007). Uncovering the value of planning in new venture creation: A process and contingency perspective. *Journal of Business Venturing, 22*, 782–807.

Hechavarria, D. M., Renko, M., & Matthews, C. H. (2012). The nascent entrepreneurship hub: Goals, entrepreneurial self-efficacy and start-up outcomes. *Small Business Economics, 39*(3), 685–701.

Honig, B., & Karlsson, T. (2004). Institutional forces and the written business plan. *Journal of Management, 30*(1), 29–48.

Honig, B., & Samuelsson, M. (2014). Data replication and extension: A study of business planning and venture-level performance. *Journal of Business Venturing Insights, 1–2*(0), 18–25.

Karlsson, T. (2005). *Business plans in new ventures. An institutional perspective.* JIBS Dissertation Series, 30.

Karlsson, T., & Honig, B. (2009). Judging a business by its cover: An institutional perspective on new ventures and the business plan. *Journal of Business Venturing, 24*, 27–45.

Mintzberg, H. (1990). The design school: Reconsidering the basic premises of strategic management. *Strategic Management Journal, 11*(3), 171–195.

Reynolds, P. D. (2007). New firm creation in the US: A PSED overview. *Foundations and Trends in Entrepreneurship, 3*(1), 1–151.

Reynolds, P. D., & Curtin, R. T. (2008). Business creation in the United States: Panel study of entrepreneurial dynamics II initial assessment. *Foundations and Trends in Entrepreneurship, 4*, 3.

Shane, S., & Delmar, F. (2004). Planning for the market: Business planning before marketing and the continuation of organizing efforts. *Journal of Business Venturing, 19*, 767–785.

Winborg, J., & Landstrom, H. (2001). Financial bootstrapping in small businesses: Examining small business managers' resource acquisition behaviors. *Journal of Business Venturing, 16*(3), 235–254.

CHAPTER 7

HOW SHOULD ENTREPRENEURSHIP BE TAUGHT TO STUDENTS WITH DIVERSE EXPERIENCE? A SET OF CONCEPTUAL MODELS OF ENTREPRENEURSHIP EDUCATION

Zhaocheng (Elly) Zeng and Benson Honig

ABSTRACT

Entrepreneurship education has been largely treated as a pedagogical "black box." Despite the emergence of popular entrepreneurship models such as business planning, the lean startup, or business model canvas, neither theoretical nor pedagogical foundations are typically evident. This limits the accumulation of useful evidence that could inform better teaching practices. In this chapter, we develop a set of conceptual models anchored in learning theory regarding how entrepreneurship education should be taught to students. These conceptual models are built on the techniques of entrepreneurship pedagogy such as experiential education. They are developed for three groups of students: students without any

Models of Start-up Thinking and Action: Theoretical, Empirical and Pedagogical Approaches
Advances in Entrepreneurship, Firm Emergence and Growth, Volume 18, 237–282
Copyright © 2016 by Emerald Group Publishing Limited
ISSN: 1074-7540/doi:10.1108/S1074-754020160000018007

*entrepreneurship experience, students with previous entrepreneurship
experience, and students who are currently running their start-ups. A set
of potential variables that could be used for course evaluation purposes is
also included. The proposed models meet the needs of students with
different levels of entrepreneurship experience. Theoretically, we demonstrate that entrepreneurship students should not be treated as a homogeneous group, as they have different levels of startup experience and
different educational needs. Lecturers of entrepreneurship programs
could choose the suitable model proposed in this chapter in teaching
based on the characteristics of their students. The chapter provides novel
insights with regard to how entrepreneurship programs should be
designed for students with different levels of entrepreneurship experience.*

Keywords: Entrepreneurship education; evidence-based education;
experiential learning; business planning; simulation; human capital

INTRODUCTION

In recent decades, entrepreneurship education and training has grown
rapidly in universities and colleges worldwide (Honig, 2004; Kauffman
Foundation, 2008), with the aim of helping students develop knowledge
and skills to become better entrepreneurs (Katz, 2007; Pittaway & Cope,
2007a). While the contents of entrepreneurship courses may vary depending
on factors such as the lecturers, the students, and the institutional and pro-
grammatic context, writing a business plan is usually one of the important
components in most entrepreneurship classes (Bliemel, 2014; Solomon,
2007). Students are carefully taught how to create a business plan and may
learn how to present their work in business plan competitions and elevator
pitches. The business plan is typically a static document that includes the
illustration of an existing business problem, an opportunity embedded in
the problem, a proposed solution provided by the startup, and typically a
five-year financial projection for potential revenues and profits (Blank,
2013). Advocates of business plan education claim that a plan allows entrepreneurs to show stakeholders the business opportunities they have and the
way they intend to exploit them, while at the same time serving as a road
map for entrepreneurs themselves to follow (Jones & Penaluna, 2013). It is
believed that if entrepreneurs conduct their planning carefully, they

increase their chances to achieve their business goals (Hisrich, Peters, & Shepherd, 2010).

The underlying assumption of writing a business plan is that entrepreneurs are able to predict what is likely to happen in advance, before they carry out their ideas (Blank, 2013). However, opponents of business planning criticize this assumption, suggesting that such activities are "a work of fiction" (Jones & Penaluna, 2013; Mullins & Komisar, 2009). First, they point out that entrepreneurs usually face a lot of uncertainties in their businesses, and therefore, it is impossible to forecast the unknown conditions in order to make a detailed plan to deal with so many contingencies in advance (Blank, 2013). Second, rather than trying to plan the future, entrepreneurs are subjected to institutional forces such as coercion and mimetic pressures to produce written business plans (Honig & Karlsson, 2004). Such plans are often produced to satisfy the demands of external actors. Hence, they may play primarily a symbolic, loosely coupled role for new organizations without positively contributing to successful business outcomes (Karlsson & Honig, 2009). Third and foremost, there is very little empirical evidence supporting the link between prior business planning and increased eventual performance (Honig & Samuelsson, 2012; Jones & Penaluna, 2013). For example, a six-year longitudinal study shows that neither formal planning nor changes in the business plan enhance startup performance. (Honig & Samuelsson, 2012). Of course, it may be the case that individuals who develop a comprehensive plan may discover, through the planning process, that their initial idea lacks potential, and so abandon the effort or radically change their idea. Research in this volume examines this very point (Honig & Hopp, 2016). Measuring this process from a pedagogical angle would be very difficult, however, as it would be virtually impossible to estimate the odds of activities not pursued.

Recognizing the weakness of business planning, a new approach called the lean startup has quickly emerged in recent years, asserted to make the venture creation process less risky and more manageable. In this paradigm, the lean definition of a startup is "a human institution designed to create a new product or service under conditions of extreme uncertainty" (Ries, 2011, p. 8). Rooted in the lean manufacturing principles of Toyota and adapted to the context of entrepreneurship, the lean startup is claimed to provide a new methodology to create innovation and manage new ventures. Instead of focusing on traditional elaborate planning and long-term product development, the lean startup approach favors validated testing, fast customer feedback, and iterative product design (Ries, 2011).

According to Ries, from the moment they start a venture, entrepreneurs tend to build assumptions about their businesses. For example, one important assumption might be that customers need their products. However, from the lean startup perspective, all these assumptions are considered as a series of untested hypotheses. It is a waste of time if entrepreneurs take these statements for granted and develop something that nobody wants. To solve this problem, the lean startup references another adopted framework called the business model canvas (Blank,2013; Osterwalder, 2004; Osterwalder & Pigneur, 2010), published as a diagram that helps entrepreneurs organize their hypotheses within the following nine parameters: key partners, key activities, key resources, value proposition, customer relationship, channels, customer segments, cost structure, and revenue streams (Osterwalder & Pigneur, 2010). Each element in the business model canvas represents a set of hypotheses that need to be tested as early as possible (Blank & Dorf, 2012; Müller & Thoring, 2012). In addition, the lean startup applies a concept called a validated learning experiment to guide the hypothesis-testing process (Ries, 2011), in which entrepreneurs build a minimum viable product (MVP), present it to customers quickly soliciting feedback from them, measuring their response, learning from the results, and deciding whether to preserve the original hypothesis or pivot to a new one. Through this Build-Measure-Learning feedback loop, entrepreneurs are said to engage in an iterative process of continually adding value that customers care about regarding particular products or services. Although the lean startup methodology is still very new, it has rapidly achieved popularity in the startup world. Many business schools have already started to teach the lean startup approach in their entrepreneurship courses (Blank, 2013). Yet, the appeal of the lean startup approach is not just recognized by business schools. Quickly extending its influence outside the university, the lean startup approach has even been adopted by the National Science Foundation (NSF) as the entrepreneurship model for teaching faculties and students in science, technology, engineering and mathematics fields (Blank, 2015; National Science Foundation [NSF], 2016). Notably, Blank and Ries have no formal research or pedagogical experience, and there is no research attesting to their model's success. Their credibility seems to come from the face validity of their approach as well as being entrepreneurs themselves.

Despite the attractive concepts introduced by the lean startup to the market, it seems that this approach is not built on solid theoretical foundations, any more than previous models built on the business planning paradigm. In other words, much like the previous veneration for business planning, where there is a stream of research which largely failed to support the investment in time and energy, there appears to be little clear theoretical or empirical evidence to support the proposed arguments embedded in the lean startup model. Although the core concepts, that is, running tests and learning from customer experience, imply that the lean startup approach may be connected to experiential learning theories to some extent, more rigorous research is required to examine its scope, framework, potential connection to theories, and the contexts where it could be applied.

Despite the plethora of untested models, the view that entrepreneurship education and teaching should become an evidence-based practice continues to grow (Biesta, 2007). The evidence referred to in this perspective includes the strength and pattern of relationships between different variables that impact the processes and outcomes of education (Davies, 1999). Good evidence is based on at least several observations in different studies, and has the power to inform entrepreneurs' actions (Frese, Bausch, Schmidt, Strauch, & Kabst, 2012). Evidence-based education has its pedagogical roots in the field of medicine (Rousseau, 2006). After gaining acceptance in many medical programs, it has gained influence in other health fields such as nursing and dentistry, and even to the more distant fields of professional activity such as management, social work, and education (Biesta, 2007; Cook, Smith, & Tankersley, 2012). While there is some debate as to whether evidence-based practices in medicine can be directly generalized to the field of education, including how it should be properly implemented (Pirrie, 2001; Simons, 2003), the importance and value of the practice has attracted considerably more attention from educational scholars. Many believe that evidence-based practices in education can help create a culture in which evidence is valued over subjective opinion, and progressive and systematic improvement in both research and teaching can be realized (Baba & HakemZadeh, 2012; Slavin, 2002). These advocates suggest that solid evidence could enhance decision making in organizations, and should be at the core of management education and training. They point out that the key to building strong evidence is the alignment of methodological fit, contextualization, replicability, transparency, and scholarly and experts' consensus.

In spite of many benefits, Hargreaves (1996) warns that there are existing problems in the education field that require immediate attention before we can fully take advantage of evidence based practice. First and foremost, there is a lack of agreed upon theory in the entrepreneurship field, and research seldom employs unique theory in entrepreneurship scholarship (Kuratko, 2005; Sorenson & Stuart, 2008). Kuratko (2005) suggests that this is the sign of immaturity in entrepreneurship field. This lack of theoretical foundation may threaten the reliability and generalizability of obtained results, and further prevent the accumulation of useful evidence in the field. It is worthwhile to note that there is a difference of opinion on this matter. Using three key indicators proposed by Dess, Lumpkin, and Eisner (2006) to analyze the maturity level of entrepreneurship field, Katz (2008) shows that entrepreneurship is a fully mature discipline, characterized by academics' ability to handle multiple inconsistencies in research. Explicitly refuting Kuratko (and implicitly Sorenson and Stuart), he further suggests that the entrepreneurship field is capable of embracing different ideas, theories and insights (Katz, 2008). Second, a gap exists between teaching and research communities. Instead of being informed by research evidence and pedagogical theory, the entrepreneurship teaching agenda is usually driven by conventional wisdom, political ideology, personal interests, financial expediency or opportunity, or even parental choice (Biesta, 2007; Honig, 2014, 2016; Oakley, 2002). Further, it appears to be somewhat uncommon for entrepreneurship lecturers to utilize research to inform their everyday teaching practices (Hillage, Pearson, Anderson, & Tamkin, 1998; Honig & Martin, 2014). To overcome these obstacles, evidence should be generated through the guidance of solid theories, and should be relevant and accessible to teaching practice (Atkinson, 2000; Hargreaves, 1996).

In this chapter, we develop a set of conceptual models anchored in learning theory regarding how entrepreneurship education should be taught to students. These models are built on the techniques of entrepreneurship pedagogy such as experiential education. We make two contributions in this chapter. First, we contribute to the advancement of fundamental theory and teaching practice in entrepreneurship education. Second, Collins, Hannon, and Smith (2004) suggest that different students have diverse experience and diverse needs toward entrepreneurship learning. Hence, it is inappropriate to use a one-size-fits-all approach to teach all of them. These scholars call for a change in the entrepreneurship education model in order to meet the different needs of students. Instead of treating all entrepreneurship students as one homogeneous group, we answer this call by dividing them into three groups based on their entrepreneurship experience: students without any entrepreneurship experience, students with previous entrepreneurship experience, and students who are currently running their own businesses. Whether students are qualified to be considered as having previous entrepreneurship experience depends on whether they, alone or with others, previously tried to start a new independent firm and completed at least one gestation activity (see Table A1 in the appendix section for the assessment questions of students' level of entrepreneurship experience). Following these criteria, students who were previously engaged in business activities such as selling products on eBay, offering babysitting services, providing tutoring services, or offering computer repairs may not be considered as having entrepreneurship experience unless they clearly indicate that they tried to build a new firm with the products or services they offered. By this we mean creating a new organization, and planning to hire staff (Aldrich, 1999). The reasons we choose to divide students into these three groups are as follows: First, research has shown that people with previous entrepreneurship experience are more likely to perform better than their counterparts who have no experience, because their previous involvement in new venture creation enables them to develop a better understanding of business and entrepreneurship (Davidsson & Honig, 2003; Jo & Lee, 1996; Stuart & Abetti, 1990). Hence, students with entrepreneurship experience and those without this experience should be in separate classes because they have different levels of relevant knowledge and skills (Vygotsky, 1980). More advanced programs might want to separate those with extensive experience, such as serial entrepreneurs, however we do not make that particular distinction in our models. Second, students who are currently running a business are different than those with previous entrepreneurship experience in the sense that their experience is fresher and more updated, because they keep accumulating new experiences and receiving feedback from their everyday practices. Therefore, we argue that entrepreneurship teaching should also take these characteristics of experience into consideration and put these students into different groups. Based on the above reasons, we generate the three aforementioned student groups. A conceptual model is proposed for each of these three groups, respectively.

CONCEPTUAL MODELS

Model 1: Students without Any Entrepreneurship Experience

Students in Fig. 1 have no previous entrepreneurship experience. Although they may get some influence from their family members or friends who engage in entrepreneurial activities, given the fact that they lack direct experience, they may not have sufficient understanding, knowledge or skills regarding entrepreneurship. Some people may argue that there is heterogeneity within this group, because some students with no entrepreneurship experience may attend the entrepreneurship program with a goal or a strong passion to start a business, while others may just consider the entrepreneurship class as something interesting to explore. These arguments suggest that students with passion should be separated from those who lack it, with different teaching models proposed for each group. However, we argue that this idea has a flaw. There is no guarantee that students with strong enthusiasm while entering a program will continue their passion for entrepreneurship until the end. They may find that there is a poor fit between them and the entrepreneurship career after they take the courses, and then they gradually lose passion for start-up activities. Similarly, a student who lacks passion for entrepreneurship at the beginning may change his/her attitude later. We argue that it is unsuitable to further divide students without entrepreneurship experience into two subgroups based on their passion or goal to start a business. They should be included in the same group because they both face the same big challenge-that of a lack of entrepreneurship experience.

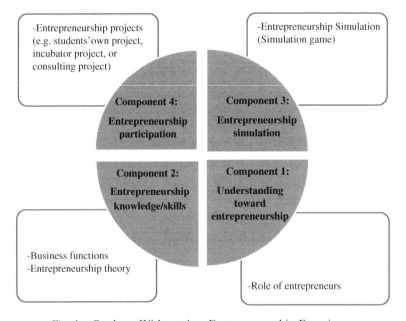

Fig. 1.   Students Without Any Entrepreneurship Experience.

Based on the characteristics of these students, we propose four components in this model: understanding toward entrepreneurship, entrepreneurship knowledge/skills, entrepreneurship simulation, and entrepreneurship participation.

Component 1: Understanding toward Entrepreneurship

Different people have different social roles in their daily lives (e.g. musicians, professors, aircraft pilots). Role theory suggests that each social role is associated with a set of duties, rights, norms, and thinking, which is considered as a cluster of social cues that guide and shape a person's behavior in a given context (Biddle, 1986; Sarbin & Allen, 1954; Thomas & Biddle, 1966). Different roles rarely share the same expectations for role behavior (Biddle, 2013). Hence, without fully understanding a role position, people are unlikely to demonstrate behaviors that meet with the socially defined expectations associated with this role. Education is one way in which we prepare individuals for particular roles and activities.

An entrepreneur is a type of social role, however, one very difficult to define or specify. Depending on the entrepreneurial activity in question, different social roles may be required — there is no "one size fits all" entrepreneurial set of social roles. An entrepreneur may need to satisfy a range of expectations placed on him/her: to exploit market opportunity through technical or organizational innovation (Schumpeter, 1965), be willing to take risks (Drucker, 1970), to build something of recognized values around perceived opportunities (Bolton & Thompson, 2004), to demonstrate initiative and creative thinking, be able to effectively organize resources into practical use (Hisrich, 1990), be able to confront failure (Ucbasaran, Shepherd, Lockett, & Lyon, 2013), and more. Students who have no entrepreneurship experience are unlikely to have sufficient understanding toward the entrepreneurial role. This lack of understanding, if left unhandled, may influence the quality of the entrepreneurship learning because students may find it difficult to fit themselves into the "entrepreneurial context" (Harrison & Leitch, 2005; Kempster & Cope, 2010). We argue that lecturers of entrepreneurship courses should familiarize their students with the entrepreneurial role at the beginning of the class. Students should understand what a self-employed career looks like, what the general characteristics of entrepreneurs are (e.g. workload), and how entrepreneurs usually motivate themselves. Further, it is important to understand how they perceive risks. Risk-taking lies in the heart of entrepreneurship. This is not because entrepreneurs prefer to take more risks than non-entrepreneurs, but because they view risks as a source of new opportunities and new ideas (Palich & Bagby, 1995). In addition, students should know that failures in the process of starting a business are inevitable because of the unpredictable nature of entrepreneurship (Politis & Gabrielsson, 2009). Of course, this does not mean that all entrepreneurs will fail in the end. But it suggests that most entrepreneurs have to experience many failures before they eventually make their way to success. Therefore, it is important to develop a positive attitude toward failures and start to learn how to manage it.

The importance of this component in the model is it not only that it helps students develop sufficient knowledge toward the role of the entrepreneur, but also that it reduces students' positive illusion associated with entrepreneurship (e.g. it is easy to be a boss and make a lot of money!). Positive illusion has been reported to have harmful effects on students' performance (Gresham, Lane, MacMillan, Bocian, & Ward, 2000; Kwan, John, Robins, & Kuang, 2008).

In this component, for example, lecturers could invite students to participate in a simple one-week entrepreneurial experiment in which students are randomly divided into groups, and each group is offered $20 as seed capital. Students are required to use this amount of money to start a small business and try to make a profit out of it in a week. The experiment enables students to play and get familiar with the role of an entrepreneur, as well as to experience some of the challenges of team activity, and possible failures along the way. In addition, lecturers may use entrepreneurs and practitioners (EPs) in the class to help students enhance their educational experience. By sharing their start-up experiences grounded in realities and complexities of the real world, entrepreneurs and practitioners play an important role in facilitating student developing a basic understanding toward entrepreneurship. However, a critique of this approach is that there may be no theoretical framework, and while entertaining, it may fail to increase students' entrepreneurial skills or abilities (Fiet, 2001a, 2001b). Therefore, in this process, lecturers need to learn to work with these EPs, and make their presentations relevant and helpful for students (Katz, 1995).

Component 2: Entrepreneurship Knowledge/Skills

Human capital is defined as skills, knowledge, and the abilities possessed by people (Becker, 2009). According to human capital theory, entrepreneurs' knowledge and skills are positively associated with their performance (Coff, 2002; Davidsson & Honig, 2003). Hence, one of the goals of entrepreneurship courses is to provide students with skills and knowledge related to self-employment (Kourilsky, 1995). Although what should be taught in entrepreneurship courses is under continuous debate (Fiet, 2001a; Ronstadt, 1987; Solomon, 2007), several major themes have emerged and have been widely recognized as the most significant subjects in entrepreneurship education (Kuratko, 2005). Some of these themes are venture financing, entrepreneurial strategies, entrepreneur cognition, entrepreneurship ethics, business strategic management (e.g. innovation management, entrepreneurship networking, internationalization, organizational learning, human resource management, new venture growth, see Ireland, Hitt, Camp, & Sexton, 2001), corporate entrepreneurship, social entrepreneurship, and family business management.

In addition to the aforementioned subjects, it is believed that entrepreneurship lecturers should also teach students entrepreneurship theory. Entrepreneurship theory is defined as "a set of empirical generalizations about the world, economy, and how entrepreneurs should behave that allows for the prediction of true outcomes" (Fiet, 2001b). Fiet (2001a) argues that theory is an essential part of an entrepreneurship course because it offers rules and frameworks which allow students to better anticipate the future and make better entrepreneurial decisions.

Based on the discussions above, we suggest that in component 2, lecturers should teach students important entrepreneurial knowledge/skills, and relevant theories that guide and direct students to properly apply their knowledge/skills to real-world occasions.

Component 3: Entrepreneurship Simulation

Entrepreneurs often need to interact with other stakeholders. These people may be the entrepreneur's start-up team members, customers, investors, suppliers, social contacts or friends. The interactions are usually continuous over the whole start-up process. During these interactions, both the entrepreneurs and the stakeholders need to follow rules and adjust their conduct for the interests of the group. In his education theory, Dewey (2007) defines such interactions as a social control process in which a group of individuals are involved and their actions are governed by the rules that are agreed by members of the group. At the same time, they both share and participate as cooperative and interacting parts of the common experience that benefits the whole group. One example of the social control process is a soccer game. To get good performance in the game, players need to conform to the rules set by the game, and work closely with their coaches and their team members. Dewey (2007) states that "it is not the will or desire of any one person which establishes order but the moving spirit of the whole group. The control is social, but individuals are parts of a community, not outside of it" (p. 52). He further emphasizes that students should participate in activities that allow them to experience the social control process, and he believed that this kind of experience helps students improve their function in the social setting. Moreover, this process enables students to develop their team work skills. Although there are a growing number of solo self-employed entrepreneurs running their own businesses (Van Stel & de Vries, 2015), many start-ups are formed by entrepreneurial teams (e.g. start-ups pursued by public policy advocates) (Cooper & Daily, 1997; Ensley, Carland, & Carland, 2000; Kamm, Shuman, Seeger, & Nurick, 1990). Profit opportunities can be more efficiently discovered and exploited if entrepreneurs share common interest and combine their efforts to pursue the same goal (Harper, 2008). However, forming a team does not guarantee a business success. Hoegl and Gemuenden (2001) show that the teamwork quality is positively associated with the success of joint projects. That is, how members of an entrepreneurial team communicate, coordinate and support each other has an important impact on the outcome of the venture creation process, particularly entrepreneurial activities that are designed around high growth prospects, such as gazelles (Acs & Mueller, 2008; Henrekson & Johansson, 2010). In fact, research findings show that team-founded ventures show better performance than individually founded ventures (Chandler, Honig, & Wiklund, 2005; Cooper & Bruno, 1977; Weinzimmer, 1997). Hence, by participating in activities that allow them to practice and build up their teamwork skills, students are able to develop more confidence and competence in handling team-related issues in the start-up process.

In an entrepreneurship course for students without any experience, it is important that we provide our students with an opportunity to contribute and participate in such social control activities. One of the potential opportunities could be a computer-based entrepreneurship simulation game in the class. A simulation game is defined as a dynamic model of the real entrepreneurial process in which a balanced number of decision variables require strategic integration (Keys & Wolfe, 1990). Entrepreneurship education can benefit from using simulations as an integral component of the educational process because simulations, designed to reflect the realities and complexities of running a business, provide a chance for students to learn through contact with the real world (Bellotti et al., 2012; Hindle, 2002; Katz, 1995; Katz, Gundry, Low, & Starr, 1994). As an advanced pedagogical tool, simulation facilitates student understanding toward the entrepreneurial process as well as developing problem-solving skills (Katz, 1999, 2008). It also helps "inoculate" students against future failure (Sitkin, 1992). Recognizing the value of gamed simulations in entrepreneurship education, an increasing number of entrepreneurship classes have started to incorporate this component in their curricula (Bellotti et al., 2012; Katz, 1999). Usually, students play a game simulation with a group. The game enables students to apply the knowledge/ skills they have learned, to acquire firsthand experience of managing complex business interrelationships and to experience competition in one common marketplace. Students allocate their virtual resources, process the market information, follow the rules set by the virtual business world, communicate and coordinate with their team members, interact with other stakeholders, and make their decisions (Huebscher & Lendner, 2010). The results of the game are usually evaluated in terms of profit, loss, or market share compared to other competitors. This dynamic process mirrors the whole real entrepreneurial process and teaches students how to properly function in a business world and work as a team. Despite many potential benefits brought by the use of simulations in the classroom, lecturers should recognize that simulations are supplementary to the conventional method of instruction, rather than its replacement (Feldman, 1995). Besides, there is no one-size-fits-all simulation content that could satisfy the needs of all entrepreneurship classes (Katz, 1999). When lecturers choose gamed simulations for pedagogical purpose, they need to base their judgment on the objectives of the class and take the following factors into consideration: validity of the simulation, the level of its connection to the reality, the richness of human experience embedded in the simulation, the thought-provoking context, and the reliance on theories to achieve particular outcomes (Chin, Dukes, & Gamson, 2009; Katz, 1999).

Because a simulation component is included in Fig. 1, we suggest that the evaluation of simulations should be conducted after the course by lecturers in order to get a better understanding of how simulations influence student learning. Simulations should connect to reality, provide values for students, and allow them to practice their knowledge and skills (Katz, 1999). Student satisfaction could reflect the quality of the selected simulation (Chin et al., 2009). Here, we suggest the use of a simulation satisfaction scale adapted from Feingold, Calaluce, and Kallen (2004) (Please see Table A2 in the appendix section for the details of the scale). This instrument has three dimensions including realism, transferability, and value. It has 10 items in total. Respondents are asked to indicate to what extent they agree or disagree with each item on a 5-point Likert scale with 1 = strongly disagree and

5 = strongly agree. The scale has been adapted to fit into the entrepreneur-ship context. Some sample items are: "Scenario used with the simulation recreates real-life business situations," "My interaction with the entrepreneur-ship simulator improved my start-up competence," and "Overall, the simula-tion experience enhanced my learning."

Component 4: Entrepreneurship Participation

At this stage, students have learned useful knowledge and skills related to starting a business, and have gained the preliminary experience from the simulation game, thus, it is time for them to participate in real-world entrepreneurial projects. Experiential learning theory suggests that stu-dents learn by doing, and they create knowledge from the combination of grasping and transforming experience they gained in reality (Dewey, 2007; Kolb, 2014; Kolb, Boyatzis, & Mainemelis, 2001; Piaget, 1953; Vygotsky, 1980). The experience itself as well as the feedback and self-reflection on the experience are vital to the experiential learning process (Corbett, 2005; Jennings & Wargnier, 2010; Neck, Greene, & Brush, 2014). Actual experience gained from the real business world plays an important role in entrepreneurship education, and contributes signifi-cantly to sustainable learning (Higgins & Elliott, 2011; Politis, 2005). Teaching entrepreneurship should be seen as a method, which focuses on encouraging students to practice entrepreneurship and to learn through experience (Neck & Greene, 2011). Students learn new venture creation not only by memorizing the relevant knowledge and skills, but also by applying what they have learned and taking real actions (Cooper, Bottomley, & Gordon, 2004). These actions contribute to the develop-ment of experience, and serve as a base for further learning. Hence, lecturers should provide opportunities for students which allow them to fully participate in entrepreneurship practice (Neck et al., 2014). Students could engage in the experiential learning by participating in their own start-up projects or assume a role as a consultant for other people's new ventures to solve real-world problems (e.g. an incubator project). For example, students at Chalmers University of Technology in Sweden build teams around selected intellectual property, and begin developing start-up activities both for academic credit, as well as for eventual emergence.[1] Only a subset of participating students continues with any particular business, but they are all exposed to the challenges. For students who have not obtained their start-up ideas, acting in the role of consultants to help other new ventures can also provide them opportunities to fully experience the start-up process (Fontenot, Haarhues, & Hoffman, 2015; Wolverton & Cook, 2000). For example, entrepreneurship students at the University of Limerick are offered a chance to work with small businesses at the start-up or early growth stages. Students teams provide consulting service to these owners and help them deal with management-related issues such as product development and marketing (O'Dwyer, Birdthistle, Hynes, & Costin, 2011). There are many benefits associated with this entrepreneurship participation process. Studies show that students with experiential learning have improved interpersonal and other non-cognitive skills (Gentry, 1990; Pittaway & Cope, 2007b). Besides, experiential learning enables students to enhance their skills in the areas of problem solving, decision making, planning, oral and written communication, and creativity (Bobbitt, Inks, Kemp, & Mayo, 2000). In addition to skill improvement, students' learning abilities are improved while they involve in the experiential learning process (Morgan, Allen, Moore, Atkinson, & Snow, 1987; Pittaway & Cope, 2007b; Slavin, 1980). As an entrepreneur, both cognitive and non-cognitive skills, as well as the ability to learn, are significant for the survival of the business. Real entrepreneurial projects help students develop their competence in managing a new venture.

To evaluate the effectiveness of the model, there is a need to test the link between the proposed model and the educational outcomes. Although we are not going to empirically test the model in this chapter, we would like to propose a set of potential variables that could be used for course evaluation purposes for our readers. There are four variables that are widely used to evaluate the effectiveness of entrepreneurship education: entrepreneurial self-efficacy, entrepreneurial attitude, entrepreneurial intentions, and learning outcomes (Souitaris, Zerbinati, & Al-Laham, 2007). We will discuss these four variables in the following section. To enable comparisons and detect the true effect of the entrepreneurship model, the four measures below should be tested before and after the entrepreneurship class (i.e. both pre- and post-course). To ameliorate the potential social desirability issues in the survey, students should be allowed to make their responses anonymous (Joinson, 1999).

Entrepreneurial Self-Efficacy

Entrepreneurial self-efficacy refers to an individual's belief in his/her personal capability to accomplish a job or a specific set of tasks related to a new venture creation (Bandura, 1977). We suggest the use of the entrepreneurial self-efficacy (ESE) scale proposed by Chen, Greene, and Crick (1998) (please see Table A3 in the appendix section for the details of the scale). This scale contains 22 items in five dimensions (i.e. marketing, innovation, management, risk-taking, and financial control dimension). Respondents are asked to indicate their degree of certainty in performing each of the roles/tasks on a 5-point Likert scale with 1 = completely unsure and 5 = completely sure. Some sample items are: "set and meet market share goals," "Reduce risk and uncertainty," "New products and services."

However, self-assessment of entrepreneurial capability is often flawed when it is used to reflect a student's objective competence in creating a new venture (Dunning, Heath, & Suls, 2004). Achieving accurate self-evaluation is inherently difficult since people tend to make self-judgments based on opinions and information they favor (Dunning, 2005). This creates a concern for evidence-based education. When self-assessment biases are introduced into the capability evaluation process, the results of the evaluation may fail to reflect the true quality of the entrepreneurship courses and the true learning outcomes of students. If people mistakenly take these results as useful evidence to inform further research or practice, it may deteriorate the quality of evidence-based education. To ameliorate the problem of self-assessment capability, lecturers could supplement the entrepreneurial self-efficacy evaluation with other relatively objective measures. For example, lecturers could use a knowledge test which covers important entrepreneurship topics. We recommend the Entrepreneurship Knowledge Inventory (EKI) developed by Besterfield-Sacre et al. (2013). This is a tool containing 105 items that assesses students' familiarity with fundamental entrepreneurship concepts and terms.

Entrepreneurial Attitude
Students' entrepreneurial attitude influences their chance to become entrepreneurs (Ajzen, 1991; Kolveried, 1996). One important goal of entrepreneurship education is to change people's established attitude to entrepreneurship, hopefully, in a positive way (Garavan & O'Cinneide, 1994; Gorman, Hanlon, & King, 1997). We suggest the use of the attitude to self-employment scale proposed by Kolveried (1996) (please see Table A4 in the appendix section for the details of the scale). This scale contains 33 items. Respondents are asked to indicate to what extent they agree or disagree with each item on a 5-point Likert scale with 1 = strongly disagree and 5 = strongly agree. Some sample items are: "job security," "to keep a large proportion of the result," "to create something."

Entrepreneurial Intentions
Similar to entrepreneurial attitude, entrepreneurial intentions also have an important influence on students' initiation of start-up behaviors (Ajzen, 1991; Krueger, Reilly, & Carsrud, 2000). It is also one of the important outcomes of entrepreneurship education (Souitaris et al., 2007). Here, we suggest the use of the entrepreneurial intentions scale proposed by ASTEE (Assessment Tools and Indicators for Entrepreneurship Education), a common European framework for measuring entrepreneurship education across all formal education levels (Moberg et al., 2014) (please see Table A5 in the appendix section for the details of the scale). This scale contains three items. Respondents are asked to indicate to what extent they agree or disagree with each item on a 5-point Likert scale with 1 = strongly disagree and 7 = strongly agree. A sample item is: "I often think about starting a business."

Learning Outcomes
We suggest the use of the learning outcomes scale proposed by Souitaris et al. (2007) (please see Table A6 in the appendix section for the details of the scale). This scale includes five items. Respondents are asked to indicate to what extent the entrepreneurship program has enhanced their ability listed in each item on a 7-point Likert scale with 1 = Not at all and 7 = To a large extent.[2] A sample item is: "enhance your practical management skills in order to start a business."

Model 2: Students with Entrepreneurship Experience

Compared to students in Fig. 1, students in Fig. 2 have some entrepreneurship experience. As we have pointed out before, students need to satisfy two requirements to be considered as having entrepreneurship experience: (1) they explicitly indicate that they have previously, alone or with others, tried to start a new independent firm; and (2) they have completed at least one start-up activity in their previous start-up effort (see Table A1 in the appendix section for the list of start-up activities). Given these criteria, students who have engaged in business activities such as selling products on Amazon, washing cars for customers may not be considered as having entrepreneurship experience, unless they clearly indicate that they have tried to create a new firm with the products or services they offered. For students who have some entrepreneurship experience, they usually have a clearer understanding of what a self-employment career looks like, and what their strengths and weakness are in pursuing entrepreneurship.

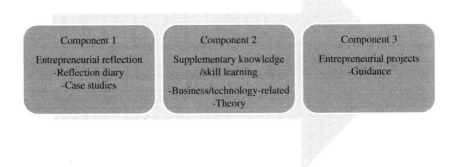

Component 1	Component 2	Component 3
Entrepreneurial reflection -Reflection diary -Case studies	Supplementary knowledge /skill learning -Business/technology-related -Theory	Entrepreneurial projects -Guidance

Fig. 2.   Students with Entrepreneurship Experience.

Based on the characteristics of these students, we propose three components in Fig. 2: Entrepreneurial reflection, supplementary knowledge/skills
learning, and entrepreneurial projects.

Component 1: Entrepreneurial Reflection

Students have accumulated entrepreneurial experience from their previous
start-up activities. However, the quality of the experience is not always
guaranteed. Experience can be good or bad. Good experience refers to
those that enable learners to achieve growth and creativity in their subsequent activities, while bad experience usually prevents or distorts a learner's
further development (Dewey, 2007). Hence, lecturers of entrepreneurship
courses should help students distinguish between different types of experience, and decide what should be kept and what should be abandoned. This
process is called as "reflection" (Dewey, 2007). The importance of reflection
in the learning process has been covered extensively in the literature.
Reflection is a vital process which turns acquired experience into knowledge (Boud, Keogh, & Walker, 2013; Kolb, 2014). During this process,
people think about their previous experience, trying to make sense of what
has happened and why, which usually leads to thoughts or ideas that are
more insightful (Baker, Jensen, & Kolb, 2005; Kolb & Kolb, 2005). The
main goal of reflection is deep learning, in which students develop a

stronger desire and a more proactive attitude to grasp and synthesize information for long-term use (Neck & Greene, 2011). This kind of learning is particularly important for students, because they are now facing a world of ever-increasing turmoil, and the experience acquired from it is usually perplexing (Neck & Greene, 2011; Neck et al., 2014). In fact, students who engage in reflection processes have better course-specific learning outcomes (Bringle & Hatcher, 1999; Moon, 2013). With proper reflection of their study, students can achieve a higher development of their learning skills (Cope, 2003; Main, 1985).

Lecturers of entrepreneurship courses should assist students in conducting reflective activities. For example, lecturers could encourage students to keep a reflection diary of previous experience. The goal of the diary is to provide students' an opportunity to express inner thoughts, record experience of past events, and reflect on what they did by re-experiencing the processes and feelings associated with those events (Atkins & Murphy, 1993; Lindström et al., 2006). Entrepreneurs use professional understanding and knowledge, which are usually theoretic and rooted in technical rationality, to inform their business actions and to solve problems (Schön, 1983). However, such professional awareness has its limitation because it is not always situated in practice. To overcome this weakness, reflection is important since it allows entrepreneurs to develop real-life awareness of the problems, to reframe the knowledge and understanding that accounts for the problems, and to inform new actions and new ideas that are rooted in their own practice (Jarvis, 1992). A reflection diary is considered as an important means of releasing thoughts, feelings and emotions on the experience, through which insight can be gained (Nadin & Cassell, 2006). However, there is a tendency that students may sometimes get stuck in their self-reflection process by focusing too much on discharging unpleasant feelings, which can hamper their effective learning from experience (Burt, 1994). To better make use of this approach, reflection should include self-awareness and self-appraisal (Cardon, Wincent, Singh, & Drnovsek, 2009), the context of the experience (Nadin & Cassell, 2006), and problem-solving linked to the experience (Grant, Franklin, & Langford, 2002). Self-awareness here refers to the question "what am I feeling physically?" and self-appraisals refer to "what is the cause of this feeling?" (Cardon et al., 2009). Answering these two questions allows students to record their thoughts and emotions for the specific experience. The context of the experience should also be examined. The interpretations and understanding of a certain component of experience cannot happen without contexts (Cutcliffe, 2003). When describing their experience, students should clearly document the particular setting under which thoughts and feelings occur (Cutcliffe, 2003). As well, reflection on grief and business loss provides students a chance to examine and learn from their failure (Politis & Gabrielsson, 2009; Shepherd, 2004). However, students should avoid describing their unpleasant feelings or emotions related to the business failure excessively because the purpose of a reflection diary is not just providing an outlet for students to air their grievance (Burt, 1994). To maximize the experience of learning from failure, a problem-solving approach should be incorporated into the reflection process. That is, in addition to show their real feelings regarding the experience, students should be required to provide tentative solutions which address their failure in their diary. Through this, students will be able to increase their level of insight (Grant et al., 2002). The reflection diary strategy has many benefits. Richardson and Maltby (1995) show that a reflective diary increases students' learning performance in a community setting. Also, reflection-on-action is associated with more effective practice (Brockbank & McGill, 2007; Schön, 1983). In the class, lecturers should encourage students to exchange their reflection diaries (p.s. maybe in anonymous form), provide comments, and facilitate the student discussions of the contents in the diaries.

Besides the reflection diary, lecturers could also use case studies in the class to help students conduct reflection activities. Thomas (2010) defines case studies as "analyses of persons, events, decisions, periods, projects, policies, institutions, or other systems that are studied holistically by one or more method." This type of studies usually provides a comprehensive image of the companies under research over time for consideration and discussion by students (Theroux & Kilbane, 2004). By introducing some reality into the classroom and providing a risk-free environment for students, the case study method enables students to broaden their experience and develop their decision making skills (Wolverton & Cook, 2000). Studies show that the case method is effective in enhancing students' ability to analyze and synthesize information as well as improving their communication skills (Andrews & Noel, 1986; McEwen, 1994). Positioning themselves into the context of a case study students use theoretical paradigms to analyze the case to answer critical questions (e.g. What is the main issue faced by the company? What did the company do right? What did it do wrong? What experience helps the company make good decisions? What experience biases the company's understanding toward the market? Why some experiences are not working in some occasions? How to evaluate the quality of the acquired experience?) (McDade, 1995). Through this process, students are presented with opportunities to objectively look at the problems confronted by other companies and to practice their analysis skills (Theroux & Kilbane, 2004). These skills are also useful for students when they conduct reflection on their own experience because an effective reflection cannot happen without good analyses (Neck et al., 2014).

In addition to case studies, lecturers should also encourage students to share and discuss their experience in the class (Solomon, 2007). These in-class discussions may be organized in a structured way (Fiet, 2001b). At the beginning of each class, Fiet recommends that lecturers assign students to lead the discussion of a specific concept and its relevant activities. Students are encouraged to express their thoughts toward the selected topic, but the points they make should be supported by proper theories they have previously learned. That is, students are offered a chance in the classroom discussion to use theories to explain business concepts and experiences. During these student-led discussions, lecturers may act as a coach instead of an evaluator of student performance (Fiet, 2001b). Through this way, lecturers facilitate students' understanding of underlying course concepts while at the same time, students could acquire more helpful feedback which allows them to better distinguish among different experience.

Because a reflection component is included in this model, we suggest that the evaluation of reflections should be conducted by lecturers in order to get a better understanding of how reflections influence students' learning. We suggest the use of the reflection scale developed by Kember et al. (2000) (please see Table A7 in the appendix section for the details of the scale). This scale has 16 items. Respondents are asked to indicate to what extent they agree or disagree with each item on a 5-point Likert scale with 1 = strongly disagree and 5 = strongly agree. A sample item is: "I like to think over what I have been doing and consider alternative ways of doing it". To enable comparison and detect the true effect of reflection on learning, this measure should be tested both before and after class (i.e. both pre- and post-course).

Component 2: Supplementary Knowledge/Skills Learning

Students should be able to apply their knowledge and skills in creating a new business. Entrepreneurs with a higher level of human capital are more likely to succeed in the business world (Coff, 2002; Davidsson & Honig, 2003). For students without any entrepreneurship experience, lecturers should help them build a basic and solid understanding of entrepreneurship by exposing the students to a variety of important knowledge topics. However, students with previous entrepreneurship experience are more likely to know where their knowledge/skill gap is because they steadily receive such feedback from their environment during the venture creation process. For example, an entrepreneur may find himself having difficulty handling financial issues due to insufficient knowledge/skills in the relevant field. Therefore, the entrepreneur may feel that there is a need for him to bridge the gap. Some thought might be given to assessing not only students, regarding their previous experience, but also lecturers as well, who may, themselves, have gaps in their own entrepreneurial knowledge.

Entrepreneurship education programs should allow these students to select courses supplementary to their current knowledge and skills. But this does not mean that students are offered a completely free choice to choose courses. Ideally, lecturers should work with students figuring out their strengths and weaknesses in their knowledge/skills base. Lecturers can prepare a list of topics of entrepreneurship knowledge/skills, and ask students to indicate their level of ability in these areas (Angelo & Cross, 1993). Through this, lecturers may be able to assess students' strengths and weaknesses. For example, a student may indicate that he/she is very strong in finance, but very weak in marketing. In addition, students' level of aspiration to growth should also be taken into consideration in this process. Some students are easily satisfied with their current status while the others are more willing to take challenges and make great efforts to achieve their own growth. For students who show a desire to learn more, lecturers could recommend extra courses that satisfy students' interests. Bird (1995) suggests that entrepreneurial competencies such as business knowledge and entrepreneurial skills are learnable with proper training and guidance. In the course-selection process, lecturers should provide enough instruction and consultation to each student, and make sure that students can receive appropriate trainings. That is, to make sure that the courses selected by the students add value to the students' current knowledge base.

Similar to component 2 in Fig. 1, the courses offered here should cover important topics related to business functions as well as entrepreneurship theory. Suggested by Kuratko (2005), several major topics have emerged and have been widely considered as the most significant subjects in entrepreneurship education, including venture financing, entrepreneurial strategies, entrepreneur cognition, entrepreneurship ethics, business strategic management, corporate entrepreneurship, social entrepreneurship, and family business management. Also, to prepare students for anticipating future and making better entrepreneurial decisions, entrepreneurship theories teaching is indispensable in the classroom (Fiet, 2001b). In addition, some students may be interested in technology start-ups. For example, a student may want to start a clean-tech startup developing solar energy products. However, he/she may not have sufficient technological knowledge. To provide learning support for students, entrepreneurship programs could work with other schools or faculties (e.g. engineering) to offer technology-related courses based on the technical needs of students.

Component 3: Entrepreneurial Projects

Students at this stage should be encouraged to pursue their own entrepreneurship projects. They have had a clear reflection on their previous experience, and have acquired important knowledge and skills previously lacking. They should apply what they have learned to real projects. Dewey (2007) suggests that one of the important sources of experience is from actual life experience of the individual. Entrepreneurship projects provide students opportunities to grow their actual experience in starting a business. Obviously, an expanding experience repertoire is important for students because they are more likely to gain useful information from it. We present three examples of entrepreneurial projects here. The first example is Chalmers School of Entrepreneurship in Chalmers University of Technology in Sweden. In this entrepreneurship program, students are required to form teams to start a new venture with a research-based idea. The ideas can come from students themselves or researchers at the university. Students take responsibility for their new venture and experience the whole start-up process, from idea identification and selection, team composition, seeking funding, and venture formation (Rasmussen & Sørheim, 2006). The second example is Jonkoping International Business School in Jonkoping University. The school offers a summer-entrepreneur program in which students are required to establish a new venture on the basis of a new idea obtained from a company in the regional industry. Students form teams and carry out the entrepreneurial activities (e.g. build products, attract customers) (Rasmussen & Sørheim, 2006). The Third example is the Monmouth University Entrepreneurial Studies program. Students are also required to start their own businesses. During the program, students select start-up ideas, build teams, develop products or services, and make contingent marketing plan to achieve their goals (DeSimone & Buzza, 2013).

The role of a lecturer in this stage is to provide guidance and assistance to students with their start-up projects. Vygotsky (1980) suggests that learning takes place in the Zone of Proximal Development. That is, students need to receive guidance from lecturers to handle tasks they cannot complete on their own. Lecturers can conduct one-to-one meetings with each student, learn about their problems, help them reflect on the new experience acquired, and detect the new gap in the student's knowledge base.

To evaluate the effectiveness of Fig. 2, there is a need to test the link between the proposed model and the educational outcomes. Here, we propose four variables that are widely used to evaluate the effectiveness of entrepreneurship education: entrepreneurial self-efficacy, entrepreneurial attitude, entrepreneurial intentions, and learning outcomes. To enable comparisons and detect the true effect of the entrepreneurship model, the four measures below should be tested before and after the entrepreneurship class (i.e. both pre- and post-course).

Entrepreneurial self-efficacy: Please see Table A3 in the appendix section for the details of the scale.

Entrepreneurial attitude: Please see Table A4 in the appendix section for the details of the scale.

Entrepreneurial intentions: Please see Table A5 in the appendix section for the details of the scale.

Learning outcomes: Please see Table A6 in the appendix section for the details of the scale.

Model 3: Students Who Are Currently Running Their Own Businesses

Students in this model are very different from the two types of people discussed before, in the sense that they are actually running their own businesses. In fact, very little literature in entrepreneurship education discusses the needs of such students because entrepreneurship courses are usually assumed to help students pursue self-employment careers and launch their new ventures (Kuratko, 2005). Although some accelerators offer a certain level of entrepreneurship education to their tenants who have fledging ventures, this education often takes the form of seminars or workshops, and the contents are usually fragmented and unstructured (Cohen, 2013). We argue that the needs of students with running businesses should also be taken care of, and a different type of education program should be designed for them based on their unique characteristics. We propose three components in Fig. 3: Problem-based learning, supplementary knowledge/skills learning, and experience sharing. This model is a dynamic cycle model.

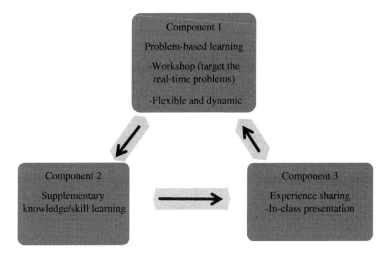

Fig. 3. Students Who are Currently Running their Own Businesses.

Component 1: Problem-Based Learning (PBL)

Entrepreneurs confront many problems in maintaining their businesses (Aldrich & Fiol, 1994). For those who are currently running their start-ups, their problems are real-time. Hence, the value of entrepreneurship courses is to provide them help with their real-time issues. Problem-based learning (PBL) enables students to embed their learning in real-life problems (Hanke, 2009; Hung, Jonassen, & Liu, 2007). During this process, students develop their problem-solving skills as well as their self-directed learning skills (San Tan & Ng, 2006). PBL also trains students to actively look for problems in their ventures and take cognitive ownership of their projects (Krueger, 2007). This problem-detecting ability is important for entrepreneurs because they are facing a world of high uncertainty, extreme time pressures and competing demands (Krueger, 2007). Hence, failing to identify problems in time may lead to business failures (Corbett, Neck, & DeTienne, 2007). The benefits of problem-based learning are widely covered in the literature. Students with PBL are more capable of integrating new information with existing knowledge structures to find solutions (Capon & Kuhn, 2004). Similarly, studies show that PBL increases students' problem solving ability, critical thinking skills, and teamwork skills (Hoffmann & Ritchie, 1997; Morales-Mann & Kaitell, 2001).

Lecturers of entrepreneurship education programs should act primarily in the role of facilitators, collect real-time problems from students and divide them into different topics based on their similarities (Hanke, Kisenwether, & Warren, 2005). The course can take the form of workshops, which we consider as brief intensive educational programs for people that focus especially on techniques and skills in a particular field. Each workshop targets different real-time needs, and students could choose to attend the ones most relevant to their problems. At the same time, students are encouraged to seek advice or mentorship from lecturers on specific problems in class, or via the internet (Hanke et al., 2005).

Component 2: Supplementary Knowledge/Skills Learning

During the problem-based learning stage, students apply and practice their skills in developing solutions. The focus of the first stage is dealing with problems that have appeared in their businesses. However, there is no guarantee that the knowledge and skills students have learned are sufficient for them to handle future potential problems, especially when the types of those problems are very different from what they are familiar with. For example, a student may be weak at dealing with finance and human resource related issues. So far he/she has only come across financial problems, and has acquired solutions from the relevant workshop. However, he/she may confront other problems not in his/her repertoire. To better prepare for future uncertainties, students should further develop their human capital in the relevant field (Skaggs & Youndt, 2004). We suggest that lecturers should help students analyze their strengths and weaknesses, and assist them in choosing supplementary courses that could bridge their knowledge/skill gap. However, it is difficult to identify all competencies possessed by a student (Morris, Webb, Fu, & Singhal, 2013). Hence, lecturers could first recommend courses for students to deal with their strengths and weaknesses that have already been identified, and later if new gaps show up, lecturers could then move on to help students tackle the new knowledge/skill gap (Sarasvathy, 2001). Further, programs that involve both team teaching (by faculty, and where possible, entrepreneurs) and team entrepreneurial experiences are more likely to provide bridges over student entrepreneurial gaps. While it would be impossible to inoculate or train students for every unanticipated entrepreneurial activity, a good training program might provide tools, resources, and experience facilitating adaptability and ingenuity.

Component 3: Experience Sharing

Social capital consists of resources that are embedded in social relationships. Individuals get access to and mobilize social capital to achieve desired outcomes (Gedajlovic, Honig, Moore, Payne, & Wright, 2013). Students participating in the same entrepreneurship education program can establish social contacts with their classmates. Davidsson and Honig (2003) suggest that these kind of social ties serve as a powerful channel through which individuals get useful information related to their businesses. Some scholars have argued that this is reflected in the organizational measurement of "Entrepreneurship orientation (EO)", although they largely avoid how, in practice, EO is facilitated (Covin, Green, & Slevin, 2006; Lumpkin & Dess, 2001; Walter, Auer, & Ritter, 2006). In Fig. 3, all students are currently running their start-ups. Different people tend to have different strengths, experience, and problems. Students enjoy many benefits by sharing their experience with each other. For example, they can share their strategies in dealing with real-life business problems. This is a good learning process for them because students are exposed to different knowledge, skills, and techniques to handle different issues. As a result, they are better prepared to deal with different kinds of situations.

However, as Dewey (2007) suggests, students need to distinguish between bad and good experience. Therefore, a lecturer in the class should serve as a facilitator who assists and guides students in the experience discussion process. For example, lecturers could use the form of in-class presentation. Students are required to present their problems, their experience in handling similar issues, and their thinking and strategy toward the generation of potential satisfactory solutions. Ideally, each student should present a different topic in each class and should provide comments for their classmates' presentations. In this process, lecturers organize the presentation and discuss sessions, and are also responsible for providing feedback for each of the students. The feedback is important for students because it can help students differentiate between good and bad experiences. Bad experiences are usually connected to business failure. It is suggested that failure provides valuable learning opportunities and is necessary for effective adaptation (Corbett et al., 2007; Sitkin, 1992). Learning from failure is a process during which individuals analyze and reflect on their unsuccessful experience, gather the right and wrong information out of it, and get adjusted (Sitkin, 1996). Hence, lecturers should guide students to carefully examine their previous failures and transfer failure into learning.

Because this component also involves reflection, we suggest that the evaluation of reflections should be conducted by lecturers in order to get a better understanding of how reflections influence student learning. We suggest the use of the reflection scale developed by Kember et al. (2000) (please see Table A7 in the appendix section for the details of the scale). To enable comparison, the reflection measure should be tested both before and after the entrepreneurship class (i.e. both pre- and post-course).

As we mentioned earlier, Fig. 3 is a dynamic cycle model. Students in the experience sharing stage (component 3) may generate new problems that may be potential topics of future workshops. That is, after component 3, the model can be moved back to component 1 again, and start a new cycle. This model is consistent with Kolb (2014)' s idea of a learning cycle, in the sense that we both consider learning as a dynamic and integrated process with each stage supporting and providing input for the next one.

To evaluate the effectiveness of Fig. 3, there is a need to test the link between the proposed model and the educational outcomes. Here, we propose five variables that can be used to evaluate the effectiveness of entrepreneurship courses. They are entrepreneurial self-efficacy, entrepreneurial attitude, entrepreneurial intentions, learning outcomes, and career satisfaction. The first four variables are widely used in entrepreneurship course evaluation, and are also recommended to be tested in Figs. 1 and 2. The fifth variable is unique in Fig. 3, because different from students in Figs. 1 and 2, students in Fig. 3 have already chosen their career as entrepreneurs, and we think it is important to know how entrepreneurship education influences their views toward their self-employment career. To enable comparisons and detect the true effect of the entrepreneurship model, the five measures below should be tested before and after the entrepreneurship class (i.e. both pre- and post-course).

Entrepreneurial self-efficacy: please see Table A3 in the appendix section for the details of the scale.

Entrepreneurial attitude: Please see Table A4 in the appendix section for the details of the scale.

Entrepreneurial intentions: Please see Table A5 in the appendix section for the details of the scale.

Learning outcomes: Please see Table A6 in the appendix section for the details of the scale.

Career satisfaction: We suggest the use of the career satisfaction scale developed by Greenhaus, Parasuraman, and Wormley (1990) (please see Table A8 in the appendix section for the details of the scale). This scale has five items. Respondents are asked to indicate to what extent they agree or disagree with each item on a 5-point Likert scale with 1 = strongly disagree and 5 = strongly agree. A sample item is: "I am satisfied with the success I have achieved in my career".

DISCUSSION

Evidence-based education has gained in prominence in recent years (Biesta, 2007). Rooted in the field of medicine and quickly promoted to other fields of professional activity (Cook, Smith, & Tankersley, 2012). It emphasizes the importance of using solid and reliable evidence to inform teaching decisions, and to challenge the traditional approach in which the teaching agenda is driven by conventional wisdom, political ideology, interest of administration, parental choice, or financial or economic requirements (Biesta, 2007; Oakley, 2002). Despite some debate on the proper implementation of evidence-based practice in entrepreneurship education (Pirrie, 2001; Simons, 2003), the belief that this model can contribute to progressive and systematic improvement of both teaching and research is widely held by some scholars in the field (Slavin, 2002). However, the lack of solid theories in entrepreneurship education research and the disconnect between teaching and research communities hinders the accumulation and utilization of good evidence to inform decisions (Hargreaves, 1996; Kuratko, 2005; Sorenson & Stuart, 2008). What is more, entrepreneurship education usually overlooks the diverse experience and diverse demands of different students (Collins et al., 2004). Using a one-size-fits-all approach, schools are rarely capable of meeting the real needs of students. In this paper, we seek to bridge the gap by proposing a set of conceptual models of entrepreneurship education for three different types of students.

The models proposed in this chapter are primarily built on John Dewey's theories of education, together with other theories including human capital theory and role theory. The merits of our models are that they explain how entrepreneurship should be taught to students in entrepreneurship courses, and provide solid theoretical evidence to support their foundation. We also propose a set of variables that can be used by lecturers to evaluate their courses based on our proposed models.

The categorization of students is based on their entrepreneurship experience. For the first group of students who have almost no experience in start-up process, the first step is to familiarize them with the role of an entrepreneur. It is also important to provide an opportunity for them to build their teamwork skills and practice their proper function in a social control process (e.g. a simulation game). Some introduction to "what is an entrepreneur" might be appropriate for this group. For students who have entrepreneurship experience, facilitating them to conduct reflective activities on previous events is the first and major responsibility of lecturers. For example, a lecturer in the class could encourage students to keep a logbook in which they provide a close examination of their past entrepreneurial experience as well as their thoughts and feelings (Honig, Karlsson, & Hägg, 2013). Because the logbook practice is post-hoc, to better facilitate students to retrieve past memories, certain techniques can be applied. Mandler (1978) suggests that students should use a story-telling strategy when they try to recall what has happened before. That is, the outline of the story (e.g. when did you first start your business? What kind of business? Where? How long did you run it? How did it go? What was the outcome?) should first be described. The outline is important because it provides basic nodes people use to connect information. In the next step, students can start to expand their outline by providing more information retrieved from memories. During this process, it is likely that some students may avoid unpleasant memories because they are usually connected to business frustrations or failures. To ameliorate this problem, Shepherd (2004) suggests that lecturers of the entrepreneurship program should guide students to manage emotions associated with failure, and he further offers several useful approaches for lecturers to use in the classroom such as emphasizing the point to students that failure represents a good opportunity to learn. For the students who are currently running their own businesses, a dynamic and flexible teaching framework enables them to bring their real-time problems to class, share experience, and receive firsthand feedback and comments. In all three models, students are required to take classes in relevant topics of entrepreneurship knowledge, which enables students to further develop their human capital in this field. Some examples are entrepreneurship theory, start-up finance, marketing strategy, and human resource management. For the first two groups of students, they are encouraged to participate in real start-up projects which could be their own or others.

CONCLUSION

This research has both theoretical and practical implications. Theoretically, we demonstrate that entrepreneurship students should not be treated as a homogeneous group, as they have different levels of startup experience and different educational needs. We take students' experience and needs into consideration, proposing three different educational models that target students without any entrepreneurial experience, students with previous entrepreneurial experience, and students currently running their businesses, respectively. The models proposed in this chapter are derived from John Dewey's theories of education, and combined with other pedagogical, human capital, and role theories, present a systematic set of conceptual models for designing entrepreneurship education. We hope that the reader agrees with us regarding the merits of our models and that they facilitate the design of more effective educational programs.

Future research will be an important aspect in improving entrepreneurship education. Scholars might examine the effectiveness of the three proposed models introduced in this chapter. The studies could adopt a pretest—post-test and control group design to explore the influences of the models on educational outcomes such as students' entrepreneurial self-efficacy, entrepreneurial attitude, and entrepreneurial intentions. By comparing students who are taught with these models and those without, we could have a better understanding of the potential strengths and weaknesses of the models in the practical use.

Research could also examine the long-term effect of these models on fostering students' entrepreneurship behavior. Studies could adopt a longitudinal design to look into the changes of students' entrepreneurial attitude, intentions, and start-up behaviors over time. For example, researchers can compare students' attitude, intentions, and entrepreneurship behavior recorded at the time they enter the entrepreneurship program (Time 1), the time they leave the program (Time 2), one year later (Time 3), and four years later (Time 4). The long-term effects of these models are important. Because there is no guarantee that students will choose to start their businesses right after they finish entrepreneurship courses, longitudinal research is necessary to examine if and how students pursue their start-ups a few years after graduation. If these models have short-term positive influences on students (e.g. students' entrepreneurial attitude and intentions are enhanced after they finish the courses), but these influences fail to last long (e.g. students' entrepreneurial attitude and intentions get back to the original level one year later), then the models may not be able to cause "real changes" in students.

Finally, future research might study the impact of entrepreneurship education on career satisfaction. For example, researchers can examine whether entrepreneurs who have received entrepreneurship education before have a higher satisfaction toward their career compared to their counterparts who have not received this education.

NOTES

1. Visit by one author with Chalmers school of entrepreneurship program, January 13, 2016
2. When this measurement is used in a pre-course survey, respondents are asked to indicate to what extent they expect the entrepreneurship program enhance their ability listed in each item on a 7-point Likert scale with 1 = Not at all and 7 = To a large extent.

REFERENCES

Acs, Z. J., & Mueller, P. (2008). Employment effects of business dynamics: Mice, gazelles and elephants. *Small Business Economics, 30*(1), 85–100.

Ajzen, I. (1991). The theory of planned behavior. *Organizational Behavior and Human Decision Processes, 50*(2), 179–211.

Aldrich, H. (1999). *Organizations evolving*. New York, NY: Sage.

Aldrich, H. E., & Fiol, C. M. (1994). Fools rush in? The institutional context of industry creation. *Academy of Management Review, 19*(4), 645–670.

Alsos, G. A., & Kolvereid, L. (1998). The business gestation process of novice, serial, and parallel business founders. *Entrepreneurship: Theory and Practice, 22*(4), 101–114.

Andrews, E. S., & Noel, J. L. (1986). Adding life to the case-study method. *Training & Development Journal, 40*(2), 28–29.

Angelo, T. A., & Cross, K. P. (1993). *Classroom assessment techniques: A handbook for college teachers*. Hoboken, NJ: Jossey-Bass.

Atkins, S., & Murphy, K. (1993). Reflection: A review of the literature. *Journal of Advanced Nursing, 18*(8), 1188–1192.

Atkinson, E. (2000). In defense of ideas, or why 'what works' is not enough. *British Journal of Sociology of Education, 21*(3), 317–330.

Baba, V. V., & HakemZadeh, F. (2012). Toward a theory of evidence based decision making. *Management Decision, 50*(5), 832–867.

Baker, A. C., Jensen, P. J., & Kolb, D. A. (2005). Conversation as experiential learning. *Management Learning, 36*(4), 411–427.

Bandura, A. (1977). Self-efficacy: Toward a unifying theory of behavioral change. *Psychological Review, 84*(2), 191–215.

Becker, G. S. (2009). *Human capital: A theoretical and empirical analysis, with special reference to education*. Chicago, IL: University of Chicago press.

Bellotti, F., Berta, R., De Gloria, A., Lavagnino, E., Dagnino, F., Ott, M., … Mayer, I. S. (2012). Designing a course for stimulating entrepreneurship in higher education through serious games. *Procedia Computer Science, 15*, 174–186.

Besterfield-Sacre, M., Ozaltin, N. O., Robinson, A., Shuman, L., Shartrand, A., & Weilerstein, P. (2013). Factors related to entrepreneurial knowledge in the engineering curriculum. *The Journal of Engineering Entrepreneurship, 4*(1), 31–38.

Biddle, B. J. (1986). Recent development in role theory. *Annual Review of Sociology, 12*(1), 67–92.

Biddle, B. J. (2013). *Role theory: Expectations, identities, and behaviors.* Waltham, MA: Academic Press.

Biesta, G. (2007). Why "what works" won't work: Evidence-based practice and the democratic deficit in educational research. *Educational Theory, 57*(1), 1–22.

Bird, B. (1995). Toward a theory of entrepreneurial competency. *Advances in Entrepreneurship, Firm Emergence and Growth, 2*(1), 51–72.

Blank, S. (2013). Why the lean start-up changes everything. *Harvard Business Review, 91*(5), 63–72.

Blank, S. (2015). *Doubling down on a good thing: The national science foundation's i-corps lite.* Retrieved from http://steveblank.com/category/nsf-national-science-foundation/

Blank, S. G., & Dorf, B. (2012). *The startup owner's manual: the step-by-step guide for building a great company.* Pescadero, CA: K&S Ranch.

Bliemel, M. J. (2014). Getting entrepreneurship education out of the classroom and into students' heads. *Entrepreneurship Research Journal, 4*(2), 237–260.

Bobbitt, L. M., Inks, S. A., Kemp, K. J., & Mayo, D. T. (2000). Integrating marketing courses to enhance team-based experiential learning. *Journal of Marketing Education, 22*(1), 15–24.

Bolton, B. K., & Thompson, J. (2004). *Entrepreneurs: Talent, temperament, technique.* London: Routledge.

Boud, D., Keogh, R., & Walker, D. (2013). *Reflection: Turning experience into learning.* London: Routledge.

Bringle, R. G., & Hatcher, J. A. (1999). Reflection in service learning: Making meaning or experience. *Educational Horizons, 77*, 179–185.

Brockbank, A., & McGill, I. (2007). *Facilitating reflective learning in higher education* (2nd ed.). New York, NY: Open University Press.

Burt, C. D. B. (1994). An analysis of a self-initiated coping behavior: Diary-keeping. *Child Study Journal, 24*(3), 171–189.

Capon, N., & Kuhn, D. (2004). What's so good about problem-based learning? *Cognition and Instruction, 22*(1), 61–79.

Cardon, M. S., Wincent, J., Singh, J., & Drnovsek, M. (2009). The nature and experience of entrepreneurial passion. *Academy of Management Review, 34*(3), 511–532.

Chandler, G. N., Honig, B., & Wiklund, J. (2005). Antecedents, moderators, and performance consequences of membership change in new venture teams. *Journal of Business Venturing, 20*(5), 705–725.

Chen, C. C., Greene, P. G., & Crick, A. (1998). Does entrepreneurial self-efficacy distinguish entrepreneurs from managers? *Journal of Business Venturing, 13*(4), 295–316.

Chin, J., Dukes, R., & Gamson, W. (2009). Assessment in simulation and gaming a review of the last 40 years. *Simulation & Gaming, 40*(4), 553–568.

Coff, R. W. (2002). Human capital, shared expertise, and the likelihood of impasse in corporate acquisitions. *Journal of Management, 28*(1), 107–128.

Cohen, S. (2013). What do accelerators do? Insights from incubators and angels. *Innovations, 8*(3–4), 19–25.

Collins, L., Hannon, P. D., & Smith, A. (2004). Enacting entrepreneurial intent: The gaps between student needs and higher education capability. *Education and Training, 46*(8/9), 454–463.

Cook, B. C., Smith, C. J., & Tankersley, M. (2012). Evidence-based practices in education. In K. R. Harris, S. Craham, & T. Urdan (Eds.), *APA educational psychology handbook* (Vol. 1, pp. 495–528). Washington, DC: American Psychological Association.

Cooper, A. C., & Bruno, A. V. (1977). Success among high-technology firms. *Business Horizons, 20*(2), 16–22.

Cooper, A. C., & Daily, C. M. (1997). Entrepreneurial teams. In D. L. Sexton & R. W. Smilor (Eds.), *Entrepreneurship 2000* (pp. 127–150). Chicago, IL: Upstart Publishing.

Cooper, S., Bottomley, C., & Gordon, J. (2004). Stepping out of the classroom and up the ladder of learning: An experiential learning approach to entrepreneurship education. *Industry and Higher Education, 18*(1), 11–22.

Cope, J. (2003). Entrepreneurial learning and critical reflection discontinuous events as triggers for 'higher-level' learning. *Management Learning, 34*(4), 429–450.

Corbett, A. C. (2005). Experiential learning within the process of opportunity identification and exploitation. *Entrepreneurship Theory and Practice, 29*(4), 473–491.

Corbett, A. C., Neck, H. M., & DeTienne, D. R. (2007). How corporate entrepreneurs learn from fledgling innovation initiatives: Cognition and the development of a termination script. *Entrepreneurship Theory and Practice, 31*(6), 829–852.

Covin, J. G., Green, K. M., & Slevin, D. P. (2006). Strategic process effects on the entrepreneurial orientation–sales growth rate relationship. *Entrepreneurship Theory and Practice, 30*(1), 57–81.

Cutcliffe, J. R. (2003). Reconsidering reflexivity: Introducing the case for intellectual entrepreneurship. *Qualitative Health Research, 13*(1), 136–148.

Davidsson, P., & Honig, B. (2003). The role of social and human capital among nascent entrepreneurs. *Journal of Business Venturing, 18*(3), 301–331.

Davies, P. (1999). What is evidence-based education? *British Journal of Educational Studies, 47*(2), 108–121.

DeSimone, F., & Buzza, J. (2013). Experiential learning: Improving the efficacy of an undergraduate business degree. *American Journal of Business Education, 6*(1), 7–24.

Dess, G. G., Lumpkin, G. T., & Eisner, A. (2006). *Strategic management: Creating competitive advantage.* Boston, MA: McGraw Hill.

Dewey, J. (2007). *Experience and education.* New York, NY: Simon and Schuster.

Drucker, P. (1970). Entrepreneurship in business enterprise. *Journal of Business Policy, 1*(1), 3–12.

Dunning, D. (2005). *Self-insight: Roadblocks and detours on the path to knowing thyself.* New York, NY: Psychology Press.

Dunning, D., Heath, C., & Suls, J. M. (2004). Flawed self-assessment implications for health, education, and the workplace. *Psychological Science in the Public Interest, 5*(3), 69–106.

Ensley, M. D., Carland, J. W., & Carland, J. C. (2000). Investigating the existence of the lead entrepreneur. *Journal of Small Business Management, 38*(4), 59–77.

Feingold, C. E., Calaluce, M., & Kallen, M. A. (2004). Computerized patient model and simulated clinical experiences: Evaluation with baccalaureate nursing students. *Journal of Nursing Education, 43*(4), 156–163.

Feldman, H. D. (1995). Computer-based simulation games: A viable educational technique for entrepreneurship classes? *Simulation & Gaming, 26*(3), 346–360.

Fiet, J. O. (2001a). The theoretical side of teaching entrepreneurship. *Journal of Business Venturing, 16*(1), 1–24.

Fiet, J. O. (2001b). The pedagogical side of entrepreneurship theory. *Journal of Business Venturing, 16*(2), 101–117.

Fontenot, G., Haarhues, M., & Hoffman, L. (2015). The benefits of the SBI program: Perceptions of former students. *Journal of Small Business Strategy, 2*(1), 56–71.

Frese, M., Bausch, A., Schmidt, P., Strauch, A., & Kabst, R. (2012). Evidence-based entrepreneurship: Cumulative science, action principles, and bridging the gap between science and practice. *Foundations and Trends in Entrepreneurship, 8*(1), 1–62.

Garavan, T. N., & O'Cinneide, B. (1994). Entrepreneurship education and training programmes: A review and evaluation – Part 1. *Journal of European Industrial Training, 18*(8), 3–12.

Gedajlovic, E., Honig, B., Moore, C. B., Payne, G. T., & Wright, M. (2013). Social capital and entrepreneurship: A schema and research agenda. *Entrepreneurship Theory and Practice, 37*(3), 455–478.

Gentry, J. W. (1990). *Guide to business gaming and experiential learning.* Dubuque, IA: Nichols Publishing Co.

Gorman, G., Hanlon, D., & King, W. (1997). Some research perspectives on entrepreneurship education, enterprise education and education for small business management: A ten-year literature review. *International Small Business Journal, 15*(3), 56–77.

Grant, A. M., Franklin, J., & Langford, P. (2002). The self-reflection and insight scale: A new measure of private self-consciousness. *Social Behavior and Personality, 30*(8), 821–835.

Greenhaus, J. H., Parasuraman, S., & Wormley, W. M. (1990). Effects of race on organizational experiences, job performance evaluations, and career outcomes. *Academy of Management Journal, 33*(1), 64–86.

Gresham, F. M., Lane, K. L., MacMillan, D. L., Bocian, K. M., & Ward, S. L. (2000). Effects of positive and negative illusory biases: Comparisons across social and academic self-concept domains. *Journal of School Psychology, 38*(2), 151–175.

Hanke, R. (2009, January). Problem-based learning entrepreneurship education: A preliminary exploration. *United States association for small business and entrepreneurship. Conference proceedings* (p. 129). United States Association for Small Business and Entrepreneurship.

Hanke, R., Kisenwether, E., & Warren, A. (2005, August). A Scalable Problem-Based Learning System for Entrepreneurship Education. In *Academy of Management Proceedings* (Vol. *2005*, No. 1, pp. E1–E6). Academy of Management.

Hargreaves, D. H. (1996). *Teaching as a research-based profession: possibilities and prospects.* London: Teacher Training Agency.

Harper, D. A. (2008). Towards a theory of entrepreneurial teams. *Journal of Business Venturing, 23*(6), 613–626.

Harrison, R. T., & Leitch, C. M. (2005). Entrepreneurial learning: Researching the interface between learning and the entrepreneurial context. *Entrepreneurship Theory and Practice, 29*(4), 351–371.

Henrekson, M., & Johansson, D. (2010). Gazelles as job creators: A survey and interpretation of the evidence. *Small Business Economics, 35*(2), 227–244.

Higgins, D., & Elliott, C. (2011). Learning to make sense: What works in entrepreneurial education? *Journal of European Industrial Training, 35*(4), 345–367.

Hillage, J., Pearson, R., Anderson, A., & Tamkin, P. (1998). *Excellence in research on schools.* London: Department for Education and Employment.

Hindle, K. (2002). A grounded theory for teaching entrepreneurship using simulation games. *Simulation & Gaming, 33*(2), 236–241.

Hisrich, R. D. (1990). Entrepreneurship/intrapreneurship. *American Psychologist*, *45*(2), 209–222.

Hisrich, R. D., Peters, M. P., & Shepherd, D. A. (2010). *Entrepreneurship* (8th ed.). New York, NY: McGraw-Hill.

Hoegl, M., & Gemuenden, H. G. (2001). Teamwork quality and the success of innovative projects: A theoretical concept and empirical evidence. *Organization Science*, *12*(4), 435–449.

Hoffmann, B. O. B., & Ritchie, D. (1997). Using multimedia to overcome the problems with problem based learning. *Instructional Science*, *25*(2), 97–115.

Honig, B. (2004). Entrepreneurship education: Toward a model of contingency-based business planning. *Academy of Management Learning and Education*, *3*(3), 258–273.

Honig, B. (2014). Salesman or scholars: A critical examination of research scholarship in the field of entrepreneurship. In F. Welter & T. Baker (Eds.), *Companion to entrepreneurship* (pp. 467–480). London: Routledge.

Honig, B. (2016). Institutionalization of the field and its impact on both the ethics and the quality of entrepreneurship research in the coming decades. In A. Fayolle & P. Riot (Eds.), *Rethinking entrepreneurship* (pp. 123–136). London: Routledge.

Honig, B., & Hopp, C. (2016). New venture planning and lean start-up activities: A longitudinal empirical study of entrepreneurial success, founder preferences and venture context. *Advances in Entrepreneurship, Firm Emergence, and Growth*, *18*, 75–108.

Honig, B., & Karlsson, T. (2004). Institutional forces and the written business plan. *Journal of Management*, *30*(1), 29–48.

Honig, B., Karlsson, T., & Hägg, G. (2013). The blessing of necessity and advantages of newness. In J. Katz & A. Corbett (Eds.), *Entrepreneurial resourcefulness: Competing with constraints*, Advances in Entrepreneurship, Firm Emergence and Growth (Vol. 15, pp. 63–94). Bingley, UK: Emerald Group Publishing Limited.

Honig, B., & Martin, B. (2014). Entrepreneurship education. In F. Alain (Ed.), *Handbook of research on entrepreneurship* (pp. 127–146). Northampton: Edward Elgar Publishing.

Honig, B., & Samuelsson, M. (2012). Planning and the entrepreneur: A longitudinal examination of nascent entrepreneurship in Sweden. *Journal of Small Business Management*, *50*(3), 365–388.

Huebscher, J., & Lendner, C. (2010). Effects of entrepreneurship simulation game seminars on entrepreneurs' and students' learning. *Journal of Small Business & Entrepreneurship*, *23*(4), 543–554.

Hung, W., Jonassen, D. H., & Liu, R. (2008). Problem-based learning. In J. M. Spector, J. G. van Merriënboer, M. D. Merrill, & M. Driscoll (Eds.), *Handbook of research on educational communications and technology* (3rd ed., pp. 1503–1581). Mahwah, NJ: Lawrence Erlbaum Associates.

Ireland, R. D., Hitt, M. A., Camp, S. M., & Sexton, D. L. (2001). Integrating entrepreneurship and strategic management actions to create firm wealth. *The Academy of Management Executive*, *15*(1), 49–63.

Jarvis, J. (1992). Using diaries for teacher reflection on in-service courses. *ELT Journal*, *46*(2), 133–143.

Jennings, C., & Wargnier, J. (2010). Experiential learning – A way to develop agile minds in the knowledge economy? *Development and Learning in Organizations: An International Journal*, *24*(3), 14–16.

Jo, H., & Lee, J. (1996). The relationship between an entrepreneur's background and performance in a new venture. *Technovation, 16*(4), 161–211.

Joinson, A. (1999). Social desirability, anonymity, and internet-based questionnaires. *Behavior Research Methods, Instruments, & Computers, 31*(3), 433–438.

Jones, C., & Penaluna, A. (2013). Moving beyond the business plan in enterprise education. *Education and Training, 55*(8/9), 804–814.

Kamm, J. B., Shuman, J. C., Seeger, J. A., & Nurick, A. J. (1990). Entrepreneurial teams in new venture creation: A research agenda. *Entrepreneurship Theory and Practice, 14*(4), 7–17.

Karlsson, T., & Honig, B. (2009). Judging a business by its cover: An institutional perspective on new ventures and the business plan. *Journal of Business Venturing, 24*(1), 27–45.

Katz, J. A. (1995). Managing practitioners in the entrepreneurship class. *Simulation & Gaming, 26*(3), 361–375.

Katz, J. A. (1999). Institutionalizing elegance: When simulation becomes a requirement. *Simulation & Gaming, 30*(3), 332–336.

Katz, J. A. (2007). Education and training in entrepreneurship. In J. R. Baum, M. Frese, & R. A. Baron (Eds.), *The psychology of entrepreneurship* (pp. 209–235). Mahwah, NJ: Lawrence Erlbaum Associates.

Katz, J. A. (2008). Fully mature but not fully legitimate: A different perspective on the state of entrepreneurship education. *Journal of Small Business Management, 46*(4), 550–566.

Katz, J. A., Gundry, L., Low, M., & Starr, J. (1994). Guest editorial: Simulation and experiential learning in entrepreneurship education. *Simulation & Gaming, 25*(3), 335–337.

Kauffman Foundation. (2008). *Entrepreneurship in American higher education.* Retrieved from http://www.kauffman.org/items.cfm?itemID=1132

Kember, D., Leung, D., Jones, A., Loke, A. Y., McKay, J., Sinclair, K., ... Yeung, E. (2000). Development of a questionnaire to measure the level of reflective thinking. *Assessment and Evaluation in Higher Education, 25*, 381–389.

Kempster, S., & Cope, J. (2010). Learning to lead in the entrepreneurial context. *International Journal of Entrepreneurial Behavior & Research, 16*(1), 5–34.

Keys, B., & Wolfe, J. (1990). The role of management games and simulations in education and research. *Journal of Management, 16*(2), 307–336.

Kolb, A. Y., & Kolb, D. A. (2005). Learning styles and learning spaces: Enhancing experiential learning in higher education. *Academy of Management Learning & Education, 4*(2), 193–212.

Kolb, D. A. (2014). *Experiential learning: Experience as the source of learning and development.* New York, NY: Pearson Education.

Kolb, D. A., Boyatzis, R., & Mainemelis, C. (2001). Experiential learning theory: Previous research and new directions. In R. Sternberg & L. Zhang (Eds.), *Perspectives on cognitive learning, and thinking styles* (pp. 228–247). Mahwah, NJ: Erlbaum.

Kolveried, L. (1996). Organizational employment versus self-employment: Reasons for career choice intentions. *Entrepreneurship Theory and Practice, 20*(3), 23–31.

Kourilsky, M. (1995). Entrepreneurship education: Opportunity in search of curriculum. *Business Education Forum, 50*(10), 11–15.

Krueger, N. F. (2007). What lies beneath? The experiential essence of entrepreneurial thinking. *Entrepreneurship Theory and Practice, 31*(1), 123–138.

Krueger, N. F., Reilly, M. D., & Carsrud, A. L. (2000). Competing models of entrepreneurial intentions. *Journal of Business Venturing, 15*(5), 411–432.

Kuratko, D. F. (2005). The emergence of entrepreneurship education: Development, trends, and challenges. *Entrepreneurship Theory and Practice*, *29*(5), 577–598.

Kwan, V. S., John, O. P., Robins, R. W., & Kuang, L. L. (2008). Conceptualizing and assessing self-enhancement bias: A componential approach. *Journal of Personality and Social Psychology*, *94*(6), 1062.

Lindström, M., Ståhl, A., Höök, K., Sundström, P., Laaksolathi, J., Combetto, M., & Bresin, R. (2006, April). Affective diary: Designing for bodily expressiveness and self-reflection. *CHI'06 extended abstracts on Human factors in computing systems* (pp. 1037–1042). ACM.

Lumpkin, G. T., & Dess, G. G. (2001). Linking two dimensions of entrepreneurial orientation to firm performance: The moderating role of environment and industry life cycle. *Journal of Business Venturing*, *16*(5), 429–451.

Main, A. (1985). Reflection and the development of learning skills. In D. Boud, R. Keogh, & D. Walker (Eds.), *Reflection, turning experience into learning* (pp. 91–99). New York, NY: Nichols Publishing Co.

Mandler, J. M. (1978). A code in the node: The use of a story schema in retrieval. *Discourse Processes*, *1*(1), 14–35.

McDade, S. A. (1995). Case study pedagogy to advance critical thinking. *Teaching of Psychology*, *22*(1), 9–10.

McEwen, B. C. (1994). Teaching critical thinking skills in business education. *Journal of Education for Business*, *70*(2), 99–103.

Moberg, K., Vestergaard, L., Fayolle, A., Redford, D., Cooney, T., Singer, S., ... Filip, D. (2014). *How to assess and evaluate the influence of entrepreneurship education: A report of the ASTEE project with a user guide to the tools*. The Danish Foundation for Entrepreneurship—Young Enterprise.

Moon, J. A. (2013). *Reflection in learning and professional development: Theory and practice*. London: Routledge.

Morales-Mann, E. T., & Kaitell, C. A. (2001). Problem-based learning in a new Canadian curriculum. *Journal of Advanced Nursing*, *33*(1), 13–19.

Morgan, M., Allen, N., Moore, T., Atkinson, D., & Snow., C. (1987). Collaborative writing in the classroom. *Bulletin of the Association for Business Communication*, *50*(3), 20–26.

Morris, M. H., Webb, J. W., Fu, J., & Singhal, S. (2013). A competency-based perspective on entrepreneurship education: Conceptual and empirical insights. *Journal of Small Business Management*, *51*(3), 352–369.

Müller, R. M., & Thoring, K. (2012). Design thinking vs. lean startup: A comparison of two user-driven innovation strategies. *Proceedings of the DMI 2012 international research conference: Leading innovation through design*, Boston.

Mullins, J. W., & Komisar, R. (2009). *Getting to plan B: Breaking through to a better business model*. Cambridge, MA: Harvard Business Press.

Nadin, S., & Cassell, C. (2006). The use of a research diary as a tool for reflexive practice: Some reflections from management research. *Qualitative Research in Accounting & Management*, *3*(3), 208–217.

National Science Foundation. (2016). *NSF innovation corps: resources*. Retrieved from http://www.nsf.gov/news/special_reports/i-corps/resources.jsp

Neck, H. M., & Greene, P. G. (2011). Entrepreneurship education: Known worlds and new frontiers. *Journal of Small Business Management*, *49*(1), 55–70.

Neck, H. M., Greene, P. G., & Brush, C. G. (2014). *Teaching entrepreneurship: A practice-based approach*. Cheltenham: Edward Elgar Publishing.

Oakley, A. (2002). Social science and evidence-based everything: The case of education. *Educational Review, 54*(3), 277–286.

O'Dwyer, M., Birdthistle, N., Hynes, B., & Costin, Y. (2011). Student knowledge acquisition and small business consulting. *Small Business Institute® Journal, 4*(1), 48–65.

Osterwalder, A. (2004). *The business model ontology: A proposition in a design science approach.* Switzerland: University of Lausanne.

Osterwalder, A., & Pigneur, Y. (2010). *Business model generation: A handbook for visionaries, game changers, and challengers.* Hoboken, NJ: Wiley.

Palich, L. E., & Bagby, D. R. (1995). Using cognitive theory to explain entrepreneurial risk-taking: Challenging conventional wisdom. *Journal of Business Venturing, 10*(6), 425–438.

Piaget, J. (1953). The origins of intelligence in children. *Journal of Consulting Psychology, 17*(6), 467.

Pirrie, A. (2001). Evidence-based practice in education: The best medicine? *British Journal of Educational Studies, 49*(2), 124–136.

Pittaway, L., & Cope, J. (2007a). Entrepreneurship education: A systematic review of the evidence. *International Small Business Journal, 25*(5), 479–510.

Pittaway, L., & Cope, J. (2007b). Simulating entrepreneurial learning integrating experiential and collaborative approaches to learning. *Management Learning, 38*(2), 211–233.

Politis, D. (2005). The process of entrepreneurial learning: A conceptual framework. *Entrepreneurship Theory and Practice, 29*(4), 399–424.

Politis, D., & Gabrielsson, J. (2009). Entrepreneurs' attitudes towards failure: An experiential learning approach. *International Journal of Entrepreneurial Behavior & Research, 15*(4), 364–383.

Rasmussen, E. A., & Sørheim, R. (2006). Action-based entrepreneurship education. *Technovation, 26*(2), 185–194.

Richardson, G., & Maltby, H. (1995). Reflection-on-practice: Enhancing student learning. *Journal of Advanced Nursing, 22*(2), 235–242.

Ries, E. (2011). *The lean startup: How today's entrepreneurs use continuous innovation to create radically successful businesses.* New York, NY: Random House.

Ronstadt, R. (1987). The educated entrepreneurs: A new era of entrepreneurial education is beginning. *American Journal of Small Business, 11*(4), 37–53.

Rousseau, D. M. (2006). Is there such a thing as "evidence-based management"? *Academy of Management Review, 31*(2), 256–269.

San Tan, S., & Ng, C. F. (2006). A problem-based learning approach to entrepreneurship education. *Education + Training, 48*(6), 416–428.

Sarasvathy, S. D. (2001). Causation and effectuation: Toward a theoretical shift from economic inevitability to entrepreneurial contingency. *Academy of Management Review, 26*(2), 243–263.

Sarbin, T. R., & Allen, V. L. (1954). Role theory. *Handbook of Social Psychology, 1*(2), 223–258.

Schön, D. A. (1983). *The reflective practitioner: How professionals think in action.* New York, NY: Basic books.

Schumpeter, J. A. (1965). Economic theory and entrepreneurial history. In H. G. Aitken (Ed.), *Explorations in enterprise* (p. 51). Cambridge, MA: Harvard University Press.

Shepherd, D. A. (2004). Educating entrepreneurship students about emotion and learning from failure. *Academy of Management Learning & Education, 3*(3), 274–287.

Simons, H. (2003). Evidence-based practice: Panacea or over promise? *Research Papers in Education, 18*(4), 303–311.

Sitkin, S. B. (1992). Learning through failure: The strategy of small losses. In B. M. Staw & L. L. Cummings (Eds.), *Research in organizational behavior* (pp. 231–266). Greenwich, CT: JAI Press Inc.

Sitkin, S. B. (1996). Learning through failure: The strategy of small losses. In M. D. Cohen & L. S. Sproull (Eds.), *Organizational learning* (pp. 541–577). Thousand Oaks, CA: Sage.

Skaggs, B. C., & Youndt, M. A. (2004). Strategic positioning, human capital, and performance in service organizations: A customer interaction approach. *Strategic Management Journal*, 25(1), 85–99.

Slavin, R. E. (1980). Cooperative learning. *Review of Educational Research*, 50(2), 315–342.

Slavin, R. E. (2002). Evidence-based education policies: Transforming educational practice and research. *Educational Researcher*, 31(7), 15–21.

Solomon, G. (2007). An examination of entrepreneurship education in the United States. *Journal of Small Business and Enterprise Development*, 14(2), 168–182.

Sorenson, O., & Stuart, T. E. (2008). 12 entrepreneurship: A field of dreams? *The Academy of Management Annals*, 2(1), 517–543.

Souitaris, V., Zerbinati, S., & Al-Laham, A. (2007). Do entrepreneurship programs raise entre-preneurial intention of science and engineering students? The effect of learning, inspiration and resources. *Journal of Business venturing*, 22(4), 566–591.

Stuart, R. W., & Abetti, P. A. (1990). Impact of entrepreneurial and management experience on early performance. *Journal of Business Venturing*, 5(3), 151–162.

Theroux, J., & Kilbane, C. (2004). The real-time case method: A new approach to an old tradi-tion. *Journal of Education for Business*, 79(3), 163–167.

Thomas, E. J., & Biddle, B. J. (1966). *Role theory: Concepts and research*. Hoboken, NJ: Wiley.

Thomas, G. (2010). *How to do your case study: A guide for students and researchers*. Thousand Oaks: Sage.

Ucbasaran, D., Shepherd, D. A., Lockett, A., & Lyon, S. J. (2013). Life after business failure the process and consequences of business failure for entrepreneurs. *Journal of Management*, 39(1), 163–202.

Van Stel, A., & de Vries, N. (2015). The economic value of different types of solo self-employed: A review. In A. Burke (Ed.), *The handbook of research on freelancing and self-employment* (pp. 77–84). Dublin, Ireland: Senate Hall.

Vygotsky, L. S. (1980). *Mind in society: The development of higher psychological processes*. Cambridge, MA: Harvard University Press.

Walter, A., Auer, M., & Ritter, T. (2006). The impact of network capabilities and entrepre-neurial orientation on university spin-off performance. *Journal of Business Venturing*, 21(4), 541–567.

Weinzimmer, L. G. (1997). Top management team correlates of organizational growth in a small business context: A comparative study. *Journal of Small Business Management*, 35(3), 1–10.

Wolverton, J. B., & Cook, R. A. (2000). Tapping the benefits of the living case methodology: A case study. *Journal of Small Business Strategy*, 11(1), 74–84.

APPENDIX

Table A1. Assessment Questions of Students' Level of Entrepreneurship Experience.

1. Have you, alone or with others, previously tried to start a new independent firm?
   Yes/No

2. If the answer is Yes, how many following start-up activities have you completed?
   (The list of start-up activities is proposed by Alsos & Kolvereid, 1998)
   - Prepared business plan
   - Organized start-up team
   - Looked for facilities/equipment
   - Acquired facilities/equipment
   - Developed product/service
   - Conducted market research
   - Devoted full time to the business
   - Saved money to invest
   - Invested own money
   - Applied for bank funding
   - Received bank funding
   - Applied for government funding
   - Received government funding
   - Applied for license, patent etc
   - Hired employee(s)
   - Conducted sales promotion activities
   - Registered business
   - Received first payment
   - Received positive net income

(Only students who answer "Yes" to the first question, and have completed at least one start-up activity listed in the second question are considered as having previous entrepreneurship experience.)

Table A2.   Measurement Instrument for Simulation Satisfaction.

Simulation Satisfaction Items (10 items adapted from Feingold et al., 2004)

Realism

    1. Scenario used with the simulation recreates real-life business situations.

    2. The simulation resembles a real entrepreneurship setting.

    3. The simulator model provides a realistic entrepreneurship simulation.

Transferability

    4. Increase my confidence about going into the real entrepreneurship setting.

    5. My interaction with the entrepreneurship simulator improved my start-up competence.

    6. Prepared me to perform in the "real-life" entrepreneurship setting.

Value

    7. Scenario adequately tests technical entrepreneurship skills.

    8. Scenario adequately tests entrepreneurship decision-making.

    9. Working with the entrepreneurship simulator was a valuable learning experience for me.

    10. Overall the simulation experience enhanced my learning.

Respondents were asked to what extent they agreed or disagreed with each item. The answer was measured by a 5-point Likert Scale with 1 = strongly disagree and 5 = strongly agree.

Table A3.   Measurement Instrument for Entrepreneurial Self-Efficacy.

Entrepreneurial Self-Efficacy Items (22 items from Chen et al., 1998)

Marketing

    1. Set and meet market share goals

    2. Set and meet sales goals

    3. Set and attain profit goals

    4. Establish position in product market

    5. Conduct market analysis

    6. Expand business

Innovation

    7. New venturing and new ideas

    8. New products and services

    9. New markets and geographic territories

    10. New methods of production, marketing and management

Management

    11. Reduce risk and uncertainty

    12. Strategic planning and develop information system

    13. Manage time by setting goals

Table A3.   (*Continued*)

Entrepreneurial Self-Efficacy Items (22 items from Chen et al., 1998)

14. Establish and achieve goals and objectives

15. Define organizational roles, responsibilities, and policies

Risk-taking

16. Taking calculated risks

17. Make decisions under uncertainty and risk

18. Take responsibility for ideas and decisions

19. Work under pressure and conflict

Financial control

20. Perform financial analysis

21. Develop financial system and internal control

22. Control cost

Respondents were asked to what extent they agreed or disagreed with each item. The answer was measured by a 5-point Likert Scale with 1 = strongly disagree and 5 = strongly agree.

Table A4.   Measurement Instrument for Entrepreneurial Attitude.

Entrepreneurial Attitude Items (33 items in 11 sub-scales from Kolveried, 1996)

A. Reasons for becoming organizationally employed

1. Security (two items): job security, job stability

2. Work load (five items): not having to work long hours, to have leisure, to have fixed working hours, not to have a stressful job, have a simple, not complicated job

3. Social environment (two items): participate in a social environment, to be a member of a social "milieu"

4. Avoid responsibility (three items): avoid responsibility, not taking too much responsibility, avoid commitment

5. Career (two items): have opportunity for career progress, promotion

B. Reasons for becoming self-employed

6. Economic opportunity (three items): economic opportunity, to receive compensation based on merit, to keep a large proportion of the result

7. Challenge (four items): to have a challenging job, to have an exciting job, to have an interesting job, to have a motivating job

8. Autonomy (four items): freedom, independence, to be your own boss, be able to choose your own work tasks

9. Authority (two items): have power to make decisions, have authority

Table A4. (*Continued*)

Entrepreneurial Attitude Items (33 items in 11 sub-scales from Kolveried, 1996)

10. Self-realization (four items): self-realization, realize one's dreams, to create something, to take advantage of your creative needs

11. Participate in the whole process (two items): to participate in the whole process, to follow work-tasks from a to z

Respondents were asked to what extent they agreed or disagreed with each item. The answer was measured by a 5-point Likert Scale with 1 = strongly disagree and 5 = strongly agree.

Table A5. Measurement Instrument for Entrepreneurial Intentions.

Entrepreneurial Intentions Items (3 items from ASTEE, proposed by Moberg et al., 2014)

1. I often think about starting a business.

2. I have many ideas for making money.

3. My goal is to become my own boss.

Respondents were asked to what extent they agreed or disagreed with each item. The answer was measured by a 7-point Likert Scale with 1 = strongly disagree and 7 = strongly agree.

Table A6. Measurement Instrument for Learning Outcomes.

Learning Outcomes Items (5 items from Souitaris et al., 2007)

To what extent did the entrepreneurship program (When this measurement is used in a pre-course survey, the wording should be changed into "To what extent do you expect the entrepreneurship program")

1. Increase your understanding of the attitudes, values and motivation of entrepreneurs.

2. Increase your understanding of the actions someone has to take in order to start (maintain) a business.

3. Enhance your practical management skills in order to start (maintain) a business.

4. Enhance your ability to develop networks.

5. Enhance your ability to identify an opportunity.

Respondents were asked to what extent they agreed or disagreed with each item. The answer was measured by a 7-point Likert Scale with 1 = Not at all and 7 = To a large extent.

Table A7. Measurement Instrument for Reflection.

Reflection Items (16 Items from Kember et al., 2000)

Habitual Action

1. When I am working on some activities, I can do them without thinking about what I am doing.

2. In this course we do things so many times that I started doing them without thinking about it.

3. As long as I can remember handout material for examinations, I do not have to think too much.

4. If I follow what the lecturer says, I do not have to think too much on this course.

Understanding

5. This course requires us to understand concepts taught by the lecturer.

6. To pass this course you need to understand the content.

7. I need to understand the material taught by the lecturer in order to perform practical tasks.

8. In this course you have to continually think about the material you are being taught.

Reflection

9. I sometimes question the way others do something and try to think of a better way.

10. I like to think over what I have been doing and consider alternative ways of doing it.

11. I often reflect on my actions to see whether I could have improved on what I did.

12. I often re-appraise my experience so I can learn from it and improve for my next performance.

Critical Reflection

13. As a result of this course I have changed the way I look at myself.

14. This course has challenged some of my firmly held ideas.

15. As a result of this course I have changed my normal way of doing things.

16. During this course I discovered faults in what I had previously believed to be right.

Respondents were asked to what extent they agreed or disagreed with each item. The answer was measured by a 5-point Likert Scale with 1 = strongly disagree and 5 = strongly agree.

Table A8.   Measurement Instrument for Career Satisfaction.

Career Satisfaction Items (5 items from Greenhaus et al., 1990)

1. I am satisfied with the success I have achieved in my career.
2. I am satisfied with the progress I have made toward meeting my overall career goals.
3. I am satisfied with the progress I have made toward meeting my goals for income.
4. I am satisfied with the progress I have made toward meeting my goals for advancement.
5. I am satisfied with the progress I have made toward meeting my goals for the development of new skills.

Respondents were asked to what extent they agreed or disagreed with each item. The answer was measured by a 5-point Likert Scale with 1 = strongly disagree and 5 = strongly agree.